'A GEORDIE BHOY'

ALAN THOMPSON

'A GEORDIE BHOY'
ALAN THOMPSON

by Jamie Boyle

www.warcrypress.co.uk

NOTE:

The views and opinions expressed in this book are those of the interviewee, in the main Alan Thompson, Wallsend they were obtained during a recorded interview and do not necessarily reflect the opinions of the author.

'A GEORDIE BHOY' ALAN THOMPSON

ISBN: 978-1-912543-43-4

Printed and bound in Great Britain by Bell & Bain Ltd, Glasgow.

Book Cover Design by Gavin Parker Art – gavinparker.uk

Editor – Georgina Kendall

Find out more at facebook.com/warcrypublishing

DEDICATION

I would like to dedicate this book to my parents Ann & Dave Thompson and my three children Scarlett Faye, Zachary Dylan & Saffron Mai.

Thank you, Mam & Dad, for supporting me from an early age to pursue my dream with nothing but encouragement. You were always there week in week out watching me play in all kinds of weather, this continued all the way through my career no matter how far away, even the midweek games. I will be forever indebted to you both… Love from your son Alan.

Also, thank you to my three beautiful children. I want you all to know just how proud I am of you and the way you've turned out. You fill me with pride daily. Love you always… Dad xx

This book proudly supports the following registered charities:-

The Sir Bobby Robson Foundation

Registered Charity number 1057213-25

The Alan Shearer Foundation

Registered Charity number 512912

The Celtic Foundation

Registered Charity number SC024648

The Watson Family Charitable Trust

Registered Charity number 1159965

CHAPTERS

FOREWORD
Martin O'Neill

March 2003, the noise cascading through every pore of Anfield makes the terraced houses in nearby Wolverton Street shudder in trepidation. A European night in Liverpool, but this is no ordinary night. It's the 2nd leg of the UEFA Cup Quarter Final, with Glasgow Celtic in fierce opposition. The tie has been dubbed, "The Battle of Britain" by the media on both sides of the border, thus ensuring a titanic struggle. Less than two minutes remain of a frenzied first half. The men of Liverpool, robed in their familiar attire, are still holding an advantage, gained by scoring a crucial away goal in Glasgow seven days earlier, but the tie still lies in the balance. A free kick is awarded to Celtic just outside the Liverpool penalty area. Jerzy Dudek, a very fine goalkeeper, lines up his defensive wall end retreats to his goal in front of a fervent Kop, confident that his man-made rampart will not be breached. Liverpool walls are seldom ruptured and never at this end of the stadium. Celtic have two players standing over the ball the briefest of conversations through cupped hands, while their teammate, the excellent Belgian centre back Joos Valgaeren pushes his unwelcome presence into that very wall with diversion and distraction his aim. One of the aforementioned players is Henrik Larsson, the mercurial Swedish international. He pretends to shoot but decoys off to his right leaving his teammate to execute the move they have practised so many times before. Valgaeren's attendance has momentarily fashioned a gap in the

Liverpool wall and immediately a powerful left-footed drive arrows the ball unerringly through that very recess and nestles in the bottom corner of the net, leaving Dudek motionless and helpless. The goal scorer, Alan Thompson, a Twenty-nine-year-old lad from Newcastle upon Tyne, wheels away in unbridled joy to be greeted by the biggest roar ever heard from visiting fans at Anfield. He has broken the deadlock and, with that goal much of Liverpool's stout spirit. Within an hour Celtic win the game and march into the semi-final of the UEFA Cup. The Geordie Bhoy, with his brilliant free-kick and masterful performance, carves for himself a niche in Celtic folklore. Tonight, he is the toast of the club's worldwide diaspora, already basking in perfect glory. An overnight sensation? Perhaps not, but in his twelve years as a professional footballer he is now an unqualified success. Tonight, he belongs on the biggest stage in football. An arena in which he should have performed throughout his whole career. On this glorious March evening I, as manager of Celtic, am witness to see these jubilant scenes. I have been in charge of the club for almost 3 years and Alan has been with me for most of that duration. I am an admirer of his play and have been for quite some considerable time.

Alan Thompson first came into my consciousness some years earlier on a bright but damp afternoon at the Reebok stadium. He was playing for Bolton Wanderers, and I was the manager of Leicester City, their opponents. He beat us almost single handedly, scoring two goals to win the match. A standout act. His control of the ball was exceptional, allowing him that extra second to survey his surroundings before decision time. Extricating himself from difficult positions on the field looked ridiculously easy for him and he could run with the ball, an endearing quality for any forward-thinking midfield player to possess. He could also score goals. Important goals. Goals that decide games, not the fourth in a five-nil victory. All this done with a swagger, reminiscent of a young Liam Brady, exuding a show of self-confidence, apparent to any casual observer. And although he later sometimes joked with me on the occasional visit to my office that defending was not written into his contract, he was courageous, never flinching a tackle.

Bolton Wanderers, with a legendary past and a new stadium, allowed Alan to develop. When it seemed likely that he would leave the club, I, still in charge of Leicester City, did my upmost to bring him to Filbert Street but he chose to join Aston Villa instead and so for the next few seasons I had to watch his progress from a distance. Six months into the new millennium and I am in Glasgow, presiding over team affairs at Celtic and Alan, while far from being a failure, is certainly not making big headlines at Villa Park, at least not to the level to which his ability should dictate. He seems to be at loggerheads with everyone and everything there, his long-term future with the club seemingly in serious doubt. Consequently, there is an opportunity to persuade him to cross the border and don the hooped jersey. This, thankfully he decides to do. Alan Thompson joins the Bhoys for £2.75 million pounds and finally becomes a real person to me.

I learn quickly that he is not all things to all men. Opinionated, somewhat stubborn, Alan finds moaning a supreme comfort. I can still recall that very afternoon at the Reebok Stadium when he delivered a shredded rebuke to one of his own teammates who had the temerity to play a hopeful lob into the channel for the onrushing striker to chase rather than pass to Alan. The move broke down, the player apologised to the mid fielder who just wouldn't let it rest. Alan continued his upbraiding of the poor unfortunate lad for a full 3 minutes after the faulty lob had run out of play.

He took a little time to settle at Parkhead, but when he got his feet under the table, he wanted to be heard in the dressing room. He had an opinion, so he wanted a voice. That is absolutely fine by me particularly if what is being said resonates soundly and makes me think about possible positive outcomes rising from such views. But the strength of that voice can be somewhat dissipated if it belongs to someone who has just been sent off the field at Ibrox for such a "minor" infringement as headbutting an opponent. And a meek apology in the dressing room afterwards doesn't meet with much approval either. Despite the fitful tantrums and the obligatory grumblings, or maybe even because of them, Alan became a major player for Celtic and, by definition, a major part of the club's success in those wonderful heady days at the beginning of this new century. He loved playing football. He loved talking about football. And, in truth, I listened to, and acted on, his opinion more often than even he thought. There is absolutely no doubt that goal scorers Hartson, Larsson and Sutton benefitted greatly from Alan's terrific range of passing and pinpoint delivery. He was simply a top-class player. Amazingly he won only one cap for England. Alan's own story in the following chapters may shed some light on why this came to pass.

Two months have elapsed since that triumphant night at Anfield. Celtic are in the UEFA Cup Final. Eighty Thousand fans descend upon a Southern Spanish City. Seville is awash with Green & White. It's the eve of one of the clubs biggest ever games. Typically, the mood is buoyant and the atmosphere is high spirited with a light breeze doing its best to cool the night air. Supporters gather inside street tapas bars fascinating antidotes about their journeys to this little historic part of Europe. A long season is nearing the end. Wonderful nights in Vigo, Stuttgart, Blackburn and Porto. Tackles won, saves made and goals scored and of course Liverpool. Who could possibly forget Liverpool? The battle of Britain fought and won. Hartson's great strike to seal the victory and naturally Alan Thompson's opening goal paving the way for the paella and drinks about to be served.

"Cheers Tommo" as glasses are raised "we're delighted you came to Celtic" I couldn't agree more with those remarks.

DAVEY THOMPSON
Alan's Father

Wor Alan's love for football began when he was straight out of nappies. He's always loved the game since as far back as I can remember.

Alan's primary, Battle Hill school was so close to our home in Wallsend that you could constantly hear the 'BOOM BOOM BOOM' of wor Alan kicking a ball against the school fence. From the minute wor Alan got up, to the minute he went to bed he just lived and breathed for bloody football. Although, he was always kicking a ball, it was only ever with one foot. He didn't seem to have a right foot and if he did it was only for standing on.

As Alan got a little bit older, he was invited to St James' Park to meet the great Jackie Milburn. All the TV cameras would be there when wor Alan met 'Wor Jackie.' I've got a tape at home of 'Wor Jackie' saying to wor Alan, "this boy will make the grade if he works on his right foot." For as good as he was, everybody noticed he had no right foot.

I'll never forget wor Alan playing for one of his school teams when a dad from the other team shouted, "GET INTO HIM HE'S ONLY GOT ONE FOOT!" Alan's teacher then shouted back, "YEAH BUT IT'S A GOODUN INIT?!"

It was all looking so well for my boy until he had his car accident, which you'll go on to read about in this book. Considering he was in the back of that car; he came off by far the worst! I'll never forget one of the surgeons saying to me, "if Alan headed a ball at the moment his head would fall off." They had to take a bone out of his hip and place it in the back of his neck. That's what has held him together for the last thirty odd years. Alan was only days away from captaining young England and that accident really put his career on hold for a year or so. The lad who did go on to skipper England sent wor Alan his strip which was a nice touch.

Wor Alan's school reports when he was growing up weren't a patch on my daughter Jane's, however I was often told, "don't worry about his poor school reports Mr Thompson because your lad's going to make the grade at football." If that car crash would have ruined his football career, I don't know what he would have done, other than sweep roads. He was a spoilt lad at school because of his football and any teacher who liked football loved him.

When he was a young professional, I once went to see him playing for Newcastle youths at the old Middlesbrough ground Ayresome Park. Before the game Alan was warming up hitting the bar from the 18-yard box. It was something he picked up from Paul Gascoigne in his prime. This day he did it twice in a row and the steward behind the goal shouted, "I bet he can't do that again" then next thing wor Alan's pinged the crossbar again and the steward just walked away in disbelief. On another occasion I went to watch him play at St James Park in a schoolboy match. That day his team won 6-0 and wor Alan had scored five of them. The one he didn't score was poached by his teammate, would-be fellow pro and lifelong friend Steve Watson. Alan would have scored all six if he hadn't of nicked it at the last second.

INTRODUCTION
Jamie Boyle

I was taken to my first Glasgow Celtic game at Celtic Park in 1982, 39 years ago, at two years of age. With Scottish parentage, having lived in Glasgow for a brief spell and coming from a long, long line of Celtic supporters, you can imagine just how huge my interest was in taking on this book.

Although this is now my twentieth published book, this is my first (hopefully of many) football related book. I've had in my mind to branch out into the footballing genre for the last year or so but wasn't sure when or where my break was going to come from. I thought perhaps it may come from a player in the lower leagues, as although they may not have hit the dizzy heights of the upper leagues, they still have some amazing stories to tell. I wondered if I would have to work my way up the leagues like football managers sometimes do and start off small. Astonishingly though, after tweeting Alan last year he got back to me (eventually) and said he'd been thinking of doing a book, it was up to me then to prove to him that I was the man for the job, and I think being an avid Celtic supporter all my life helped my case immensely.

Back around fifteen years ago there was an influx of ex-Celtic players books, especially from that Martin O'Neill era and I read them all. I often wondered, just as a Celtic fan why Alan Thompson had never done his story and at times, wondered even where the hell he'd got to. For a huge chunk of the last decade, or so it seemed, he'd simply disappeared off the face of this earth. How, where and why did he go missing from the public spotlight for all those years? I had no idea, but I knew that if he had a book, it would be a riveting read.

I got in contact with Tommo because of a friend of mine, a guy named Paul Venis whose story I also penned. Paul's a former British, European and World Champion in K1 (kickboxing) and he followed Alan on Twitter, he got a follow back pretty sharpish from Tommo whereas I'd been following Mr Thompson a while and I never had a follow, now Paul had, and he wasn't even a Celtic fanatic, to tell you the truth, well I was a bit put out (laughs). I think I must have followed then unfollowed Tommo a few times to get his attention which worked eventually because I got a follow back. In fact, it was around a year before that when I had sent Alan Thompson a tweet urging him to get his book done. At the time I wasn't even sniffing around to write it, I sent that message from a Celtic fan's point of view. He never replied that time but after he followed me, I sent him another saying, "ever thought of writing your life story!" He did get back to me this time saying it was something he'd thought about over the years and would be interested in doing if the right offer came along. Great I thought, play this extra cool Jamie lad. The secret to my end game would be to not let Alan Thompson smell my desperation. I needed for him not to pick up that I'd have jumped through blazing rings of fire to write his story and I needed to come across a bit aloof, like perhaps I could do it, if I could fit him into my hectic schedule of course. As the months went on and negotiations went well, Alan decided that I was the man to write his book and to say I was absolutely thrilled is a whopping understatement.

From a footballing sense, the first time I heard of Alan Thompson will have been the mid-90's in his Bolton

Wanderers days. Bolton, back in those days, had a team full of stars you could see wouldn't be at the club forever, plus they were partial to the odd giantkiller cup game.

I don't have any memories of Alan's Villa days really so the next time his name will have caught my attention was when he rocked up at Celtic Park just after the 6-2 drubbing over Rangers in early September 2000. Martin O'Neill proudly unveiled the signing on the same day as French flying machine Didier Agathe. Martin then went on to build his team over the next five seasons in a time which turned out to be the greatest time of my Celtic supporting life so far. Alan Thompson became a vital part of that formidable Celtic machine along with the likes of Petrov, Larsson, Sutton, Hartson, Maloney, Lennon, Balde, Agathe, McNamara and Lambert. It was a time when no matter who we come up against in European football we were always in with a chance of coming away with something from the tie.

Speaking to Martin O'Neill for the research of this book I could tell in his voice just how important a player Alan Thompson was in his development in becoming the numero uno in the city of Glasgow. Alan Thompson wasn't a player who would terrorise defences like Henrik Larsson, batter them like John Hartson, tackle a brick wall like Neil Lennon or dribble around a few like Aidan McGeady but what he brought to Celtic was unique and different to any other player in the squad. He was Celtic's version of David Beckham but on the other side, also without the millions in the bank, model looks and a Spice Girl wife but apart from that he was everything, not far off and equally as important.

When you look back at many of the deliveries which Hartson, Sutton, Larsson and Co got on the end of, then Alan was very much the unsung hero. John Robertson often referred to Tommo's left-foot as, "the wand" and it really did conjure up so much magic for Celtic over the years in the big games. Who can forget about those trademark free-kicks we also got used to seeing him put away?! Celtic fans in the stands would often think getting a free kick from around the 25 yard mark was just as good as a penalty if Tommo was on the pitch.

I think over his 7 contracted years in Glasgow the Celtic fans fell in love with Alan Thompson because essentially, he was one of us. Yes, he may have been from Tyneside but when he was on that pitch for 90 minutes he gave his all. He was prepared to tackle, cause a fight in an empty house or just take one for the team in general. A trait you very rarely see these days in football, particularly at Celtic Park anyway. Thompson has become a true Celtic great and joins only a few when it comes to club icons. He played for the jersey with raw emotion which didn't please all of the Celtic managers, particularly when he saw the odd red or two. Thompson played with that much emotion on the field that I dare say if you told him to play that part of him down, you would be nullifying a huge part of his game.

Like I said I've been a Celtic supporter my whole life, so I thought I knew all about Alan before I spent over twenty hours with him whilst writing this book. Like all of you that have seen him play football, I've seen him screaming at the ref's over next to nothing, like a toddler who has just dropped his ice cream. I've read all of the Scottish paper headlines, many were on the front rather than the back but that's what made Alan Thompson such a controversial figure during his stay in Scotland. I knew a hell of a lot about the guy before we became friends, so I already had my own ideas of what Mr Thompson was about. Having had the privilege to actually get to know the man, Alan Thompson is a far cry from the one who'd be causing havoc on a football field. The image I had of him from the front of those papers didn't add up to the guy I got to know. It may be a bit disappointing to some of you to learn that Alan Thompson really isn't the maddest man in mad land, I can only speak as I find him to be, and he is a very modest, funny and caring guy who has bouts of self-doubt and isn't as confident as you'd expect him to be given his obvious talent on the field. The one thing I quickly picked up from being around Tommo was that whatever he's endured over the last few years has, at times, broken him. I know so because at times during the writing of this book he's broken down. Physically and mentally, he's been through the mill, but thankfully now he is in a better place. I know at one point he was worried about doing this book and laying himself out bare for everyone to read or for the media to pick over. He was scared in case the issues that he's had these last few years would be used against him. So, I'm very grateful that he has been brave enough to say, "let's just do this anyway!!" It's the correct attitude to have in life but it takes guts, you'll never get anywhere if you worry too much about other people's opinions of you.

The name Alan Thompson will forever be remembered in Glasgow folklore. Half the city hates him with a passion yet the other have branded him, "the H**skelper" which is as high an accolade as you can get if you've played in those games in a green & white shirt.

It's been quite surreal getting to know Alan this year. I mean, I was once a paying supporter. I watched him so many times from the slopes of Celtic Park so to see him walking around our house in just a towel made my wife giggle. A couple of times she's even said to me, "Jamie, as if we've got Alan Thompson in our shower singing."

When Tommo first came to my home I joked to him, "it's nice to see you back with the others again after all these years". He frowned at me as if to say, 'what do you mean Jamie?' I told him our son was named after Neil Lennon (Jameson Lennon Boyle) we've got a Staffy named Georgios Samaras the 2nd and also have the ashes of our previous dog, called 'Henrik' so now we have Tommo, Lenny, Larsson and Sammy all back in one room.

On a serious note, writing this book for one of my hero's has been a real honour. Alan Thompson is a name that the Celtic family smile at hearing, even today. He put everything on the line for our club when he pulled on the hoops. It did sadden me when Alan Thompson, very much like Chris Sutton just fizzled out silently during the end of his Celtic days. Alan alongside Chris Sutton are, in my opinion, the greatest Englishmen to have ever played for the club. For what he did at Celtic he deserved better than what he got and I hope this book can fix that. I hope it shows Tommo that there's a lot of fans, just like myself, who simply adore Tommo, and that everything he has ever done for Celtic during that magical time from 2000-2006 will never be forgotten. It's been great for me writing this book and getting to know Alan Thompson the man and not the person the media portrayed him to be.

From me, my family and the millions of Celtic families across the world, thank you Tommo, we all love you and no matter how dark life gets, remember this... YOU'LL NEVER WALK ALONE!!!

Your friend & author Jamie Boyle
HAIL HAIL!

DEREK WRIGHT
Head physiotherapist at Newcastle United Football Club

When I heard about the car accident involving Alan, along with Phil Mason, Michael Young, John Watson and Michael English, I feared the worst. News was coming through of injuries sustained and I was just relieved that there were no fatalities. Alan had sustained a fracture dislocation of his cervical vertebrae. Both Doctor Beveridge and I, who were club doctor and head physio respectively, were just hoping that Alan would walk again never mind play football.

After surgery, Alan was put into a full plaster cast from his waist to his skull. When the time was right, Alan started in the gym at the Football Club and I worked on him on the static bike, mainly to keep him occupied - and quiet!

Day after day, Alan beavered away but always had a smile on his face. I was amazed at his resilience and positive attitude but the smell from the plaster cast was indescribable!

Eventually, the cast was removed, and Alan ploughed his way through all the neck exercises and rehabilitation to reach his final goal of playing again.

He never gave up, never complained. I was very proud of him to achieve what he did.

I always kept an eye out for him as he progressed through his career, full of admiration for the guts and determination he showed.

CHAPTER 1

EARLY LIFE

I grew up in Wallsend, which is in the Northeast of England, in a place called Battle Hill. The school was so close to the house I grew up in that I could kick a ball into my school grounds from my front garden, something I often did. Looking back now as a man in my late 40's I have nothing but good memories when I walk around my area, remembering playing as kids with many of my old friends who I'm still in contact with today like Geoff Stokes.

It was just a normal council estate where everybody was out playing, everyone knew everyone else and we felt safe. I didn't get up to much mischief, I think the worst thing I did was trying to get away with staying out later than I was allowed and that was only because I had a ball at my feet somewhere, I'd hear my Mam shouting, "Alan come on in now" and I'd pretend I couldn't hear her, selective hearing I think they call that!

Mam was a dinner lady at Pottery Bank first school in Walker. I remember my mam would often come home saying, "cor Alan we've got this young lad in our school who's such a good footballer" etc... It would do my head in because I was obsessed with football, and I knew I had something too. In my young mind nobody could be better than me, so I wanted to know who this charlatan was, "who is it mam, who is it?" She told me that it was some young kid called Lee Clark and that he was getting all this attention from Newcastle United blah blah blah, to be honest it would make me really annoyed. I'd heard about this Lee Clark from an early age. In fact, Lee was a year older than me, I'd have been about 6 at the time making Lee around 7 and little did I know then how our paths would cross decades later and that I would in fact become very good friends with this kid whose name alone would wind me up.

Dad worked in the shipyards in the early days, then later on he went offshore on the rigs in Aberdeen. It always made me laugh that dad could go on to do that job as you had to pass a medical along with tests that simulated going down into the sea in a helicopter because he can't swim! I never quite worked out how he wangled it but wangle it he did and he worked hard.

My only sibling Jane went on to have a great career as a police officer. As kids, Jane was a talented netball player, so I wasn't the only sporty one in the family. Me and Jane always had a good relationship, she's five years older than me so very much looked out for me. At times I must have been a hinderance but that's in the small print of what little brothers are for.

My upbringing in the fine city of Newcastle was nothing but happy and I have really fond memories of my childhood. I always found myself playing out in the streets with the much older lads. If there was ever a game of football organised on the Battle Hill school field I was there. There was many a game when the bigger lads would have been to the pub, and I'd be over there with them at 9 years old playing with these men who'd all sunk a few pints and weren't shy to put a tackle in no matter how young I was. I suppose it put me in good stead for the Old Firm derbies many years later (laughs). Just because I was only a young bairn the big lads wouldn't go easy on me so looking back it was the tough love that I needed and that would help shape the type of player I developed into.

I played with a lot of good lads and there were bags of talent around my estate. Predominantly where I lived was a council area but around 200 yards behind me was a private estate called Hadrian Park where one of my mam's sisters lived. It was all very chalk and cheese, but everybody got along. I didn't ever cause any bother because since I learnt to kick a ball, football was my only ever focus in life.

My primary school was Battle Hill First School and the Headmaster was a fella named David Scott. Mr Scott was massively into his football which was great for me. Next up for me after Primary was High Farm Middle School and we had a really good team in that school which almost reached a final in a national tournament at Wembley. Sadly, we lost in the semi-final game at Sheffield. Around that time was when I met another name who would go on to do well and who I'd also be linked with like Lee Clark and that was Steve Watson. It was the start of a great friendship with Steve, we will have been around 9 or 10 years of age then. There's no doubt that Lee Clark, Steve Watson and I inspired each other to go on and become professional footballers. We were young Geordie boys who all lived within three miles of one and another with a belief that we were going to make it. Lee was in Walker; Steve was in High Farm and I was in Battle Hill so we were in close proximity of each other. There were also other lads who went on to do well in the game in other parts of the city such as Robbie Elliott, not to mention Steve Howey from Sunderland. Although, it was me, Lee Clark, and Steve Watson that all came from within a stone's throw from Wallsend Boys Club which produced some unbelievable talent.

I first started going to Wallsend Boys Club with my next-door neighbour, he was a lad named Tony Lormor who went on to play for Newcastle too. I must have gone with Tony from the age of 6 or 7 easy. From the first day I went to the Boys Club on Station Road it was like a drug and I was addicted. I just couldn't get enough of it. Whether it was 5-a-side, pool, table tennis, or judo, the place was everything I lived for at that young age. Tragically the place has been knocked down and flattened to build houses on. The talent that place alone produced was outstanding, players such as Tony Lormor, Paul Stephenson, Alan Shearer, Peter Beardsley, Steve Bruce, Michael Carrick, Fraser Forster, Neil McDonald, Ian Bogie and of course the three stooges me, Clarkie and Watto and I could go on as the list is endless. I only stopped going to the place when I became a professional footballer so that's how much the place meant to me and just how big of a place it had in my life. For most of my youth I would spend three nights a week in there.

Just to put the football aside for a short time. I wanted to say that maybe the one thing I feel I missed out on compared to other kids was that I never knew either one of my grandfathers. Grandad Thompson and Grandad Kelly both passed away before I was born. I did have two Nana's but I would have loved to have known my Grandads, but it wasn't to be. Overall, I come from two big families with my mam being one of nine children and my old man being one of six so obviously that means I have loads of cousins. Looking back on my childhood and family life I have great memories of being at my Grandmother Kelly's with all the family.

Our main High Street in the town away from Newcastle city centre was Wallsend High Street. Although it was a great area to grow up in, there were tough times with plenty of people being unemployed. Although most of us on that council estate were hard up financially, we were all very giving. There was never a shortage of street parties if anything ever happened like Royal Weddings or England matches in World Cups, there would be flags adorning the street and everyone just pitched in. We never felt like we went without.

Newcastle is one of the biggest cities in England and up North the men are bred tough. The name everyone spoke of from our area was a fella named Viv Graham. Everybody spoke of Viv, who was known on Tyneside as the 4th emergency service really from the late 1980's. I would hear more and more about Mr. Graham in my late teens. I would often see Viv out and about in our manor with his sidekick Rob Armstrong. I got to know Viv very well over the years, obviously being from the same area. If anyone on our manor had any bother, then Viv was the man that people would go to for assistance in sorting any problems out. I found Viv to be a lovely man to be fair and he took an interest in all the local lads like myself and Lee Clark, Steve Watson, and Dave Roche who also went on to play for Newcastle. If we ever saw Viv in the pubs of Wallsend, he would never let any of us buy a drink. I never found the man to be a big drinker although he was very sociable and loved people's company. Viv did love his horse racing though and he was betting mad in general. He always looked happy, would do his best to make you feel better if you were down and if you had a problem, he wanted to help you. I know the reputation the man had but I found trouble came to him, it wasn't the other way around. One memory I have of this being true was when a couple of guys came to The Anchor pub on Wallsend High Street with crowbars. Viv was in there by himself dressed up to the nines. That was the thing I remember about Viv too was he was always immaculately dressed in designer clobber. Anyway, these two fellas came looking for bother and Viv just took them out the back, nobody followed them out. A moment or so later Viv came strutting back in the bar by himself. He'd left the two blokes asleep on the floor counting sheep. Viv didn't mess about that's for sure, but I do know for a fact on that occasion those men came looking for him and not the other way around.

It was a very sad ending for Viv when his life was brutally cut short on New Year's Eve on Wallsend High Street aged only 34. The last time I was ever with Viv was only the week before on Christmas Eve in The Queens Head on The High Street where he would be gunned down just a week later. I was playing for Bolton at the time, but I was back home for the festive period. I was having a few drinks with Steve Watson and a few of my old school pals Gary Dixon, Craig Atherton, and Mally Lant. Viv was the life and soul of the party as we were all having a bit of banter and playing pool. Fast forward one week later and I'll never forget getting a phone call from Steve Watson, who was still at Newcastle United, just before I was due to play for Bolton on New Year's Day. "Tommo you'll never guess who was shot dead last night" and when he told me I was in total shock and of course I was devastated. The news of Viv's murder sent shockwaves around Tyneside. That day when we played Notts County at home, although we won 4 - 2 and I scored, I just couldn't think of anything else. It was only one week to the day since I'd had a drink with him in our old local, The Queens Head and now the poor bloke was gone. It was so sad what happened because Viv was a proper good bloke who didn't deserve the fate he was dealt. R.I.P Viv Graham (simply the best).

Maybe the most famous of us all out of our area was Gordon Matthew Thomas Sumner aka Sting the singer. He came from Wallsend and his old school, Buddle's Primary, which is now an art gallery, was just near The Wallsend Boys Club.

Overall, in my early life, I have nothing but happy and loving memories of a typical loving Geordie home and being around good warm people.

LEE CLARK (Nash)

"I've grown up with Tommo and can't remember a time I didn't know him. Our daughters have gone on to become best friends so he's like family to me.

Me and him have worked together and it's almost like a marriage without the sex. God we've had some fallouts over the years, but we stick together and fight for each other to make sure the other one's ok in life. When we worked together in football there was a point when we even lived together, Tommo was the cook, and I was the cleaner just like a proper couple.

Alan Thompson struggles with himself overall, he doesn't realise what he's done in his career, I mean he went up to a league in Scotland which usually gets ridiculed by the media, and he was capped for England. That alone was an unbelievable achievement. Tommo was part of an amazing era at Celtic who came within inches of winning the UEFA Cup. I was proud as punch when I used to go up to those big Old Firm games to watch my mate perform. Tommo, in his time up there was classed as a king in Glasgow from the green & white side of course and he doesn't even realise that. I love the guy to bits as he's been there for me through my bad times and because we've been together for so long. Tommo's fighting spirit, desire and winning mentality was also on another level compared to most I've met in the game."

CHAPTER 2

DISCOVERING THE BEAUTIFUL GAME

I don't think anybody pushed me into the beautiful game other than myself. When I was growing up there wasn't a great deal of football on the telly like there is today so I would say I found my love for football by going out and kicking a ball against a wall every minute of the day from an early age.

F.A. Cup Day was always a massive day for me. I would watch all the build-up and I'd get really excited seeing the players getting off the bus, I'd be daydreaming that maybe one day that would be little Alan Thompson from Wallsend, that one day I'd be driving down Wembley Way and I'd be standing on that Wembley pitch in my suit with all my teammates. One memory I have from when I was 11 years old was watching Norman Whiteside (Man Utd) bend one in against Everton at Wembley with his left foot, it was 1985. After seeing that and with me being a left footer I would practice continuously in the school playground of Battle Hill primary, up against the shed where they kept all the P.E equipment. I wouldn't stop until I'd managed a shot exactly as Norman Whiteside had, and perfectly bended it in the bottom corner, then I'd run off emulating his celebration too. I would practise like that for hours on end and I would commentate like I was playing at Wembley myself. One of my mates used to pretend he was Cyril

Regis when he was heading the ball and I'd be Norman Whiteside hitting things continuously with my left foot. I can remember all of it like it was yesterday and how I so badly wanted to be Norman Whiteside.

My first team was Battle Hill First School then I started for Wallsend Boys Club under 8's. As I progressed to the under 11's I started playing for my district, my district being North Tyneside. Lee Clark by that time was playing for Newcastle schoolboys as the Newcastle schools was a different district to us so there was always a bit of a rivalry. Newcastle schoolboys had the bigger pool of players to choose from and they were really good. As time progressed and I'd proved myself for my district it wasn't long before I was picked for my county. I was around 15 years old then and I looked at it as a big honour, at that age it was, in my mind, like being capped for my country.

I was now representing Northumberland and there were some cracking players like Steve Watson and Bobby Howe who ended up at Nottingham Forest. Bobby was a hell of a player but sadly didn't quite make it. As a child I was more of an attacking player compared to how you saw me as an adult. As a lad my game was all about scoring goals and it was only as I left school that I became more of a left winger. Luckily for me I had some teachers at school who really took a shine to me because I was football mad. Teachers like Graham Netherton at High Farm Middle school and Alex Giacopazzi, those two particularly were massive influences in my early football days. Rob Kitchen was also a huge influence in Willington High school.

As a boy I was Newcastle United mad, but I do remember having Tottenham Hotspur, England and Aston Villa kits. I just loved any kind of football kit in general and as a boy that was my chosen uniform but Newcastle United was my team. If football was my religion, then St James

Park was definitely my church. My Uncle Peter took me to my first game when I was around 7 years old. From the age of about 9 I rarely missed a game until I became a pro myself for the Magpies. There was nothing I loved better than standing in the Gallowgate end and the place erupting, especially when Kevin Keegan came in the early 1980's. Newcastle crowds soared to 30,000 from 10,000 crowds. Most weekends I would play football on a Saturday morning for my school then I'd be off to St James Park to watch Kevin Keegan, Terry McDermott, Chris Waddle and Peter Beardsley. It was just an absolute joy and football was my drug. I'd have the posters up on my wall of Newcastle United but often my mam would tell me off for putting posters up as the Sellotape pulled the paint off her walls. When I saw a young Paul Gascoigne break through into the team in 1985, I knew I wanted to be like him and follow suit. It was a pretty risky plan to put everything into me being a professional footballer because if it hadn't of came off, I'm not sure what I'd have done in life. I must mention a man named Peter Kirkley who did absolute wonders for me, from the age of 10 to 16. Peter worked for Newcastle United and had a massive affiliation with Wallsend Boys Club and he was a big part of getting players from the Boys Club to Newcastle. There's no doubt that Peter played a huge part in me becoming a footballer for a living. Peter was forever taking me all over the country to matches and youth tournaments. One memory was when Scotland hosted the youth World Cup in 1989. Scotland had the likes of Paul Dickov, Brian O'Neil, Gary Bollan and James Beattie in their team. Peter took me up with Lee Clark to a game at Dundee's ground, Dens Park, when a Jaguar pulled up. Me and Clarkie were just nosey kids looking over at this posh car when suddenly, the Scotland manager Andy Roxburgh, who I recognised immediately and this black guy who also looked familiar hopped out of the car. It was only when I double checked that the penny dropped and it as the greatest player of all time Pele. Well, I was straight over and I got my match program signed which just read, 'good luck Pele'. I still have that program in a frame in my mam and dads house. It turns out Pele was some kind of guest of honour to this event, and it blew my young mind away meeting him.

My whole youth was just about football, football & more football. I played breaktime, lunch time & home time and when I was asleep, I'd be dreaming about playing. I wasn't like my pal Steve Watson (Watto) who, at that time when we were kids, could take it or leave it. Anyway, Watto was a jack of all trades, whereas I only had football on my mind 24/7, he played basketball, did gymnastics and athletics. Anything Watto wanted to do he was good at. Another thing Watto was into, and it wasn't for me, was WWF wrestling. Often Watto would get together with all his pals, they'd get the crash mats out and they would practise wrestling moves with Watto pretending he was Hulk Hogan or Andre the Giant.

I did a little bit of judo as a kid but that's as far as it goes for any extracurricular activities that weren't football. Considering there was so many boxing gyms in Newcastle that wasn't for me either, although that might surprise many considering I got into so many fights on the pitch. If ever I had to play rugby at school, I was never about getting stuck in if there was a chance I was going to get hurt. Fair play to my boy Zac who plays rugby at a good level because his old man couldn't do it. Rugby's a proper man's game and it wasn't for me (laughs).

There's never any guarantee you're going to make it as a professional footballer even if you're lucky enough to get a contract, but from maybe 11 or 12 I knew I was going to make it. At the ages of around 12/13 is when you get a lot of local scouts at games. News would travel fast if some young kid was tasty, and everyone would fight over who was going to discover the next Jackie Milburn. Scouts would promise you the world if you signed for their club and I went to many places. I went to Manchester United, Tottenham Hotspur and Chelsea but I declined, purely because I didn't want to leave Newcastle and my parents' home. I have to say it was all extremely surreal to be shown around these great clubs. At Spurs I was shown around by John Moncur Snr who really looked after us. The time I went for a trial at Spurs in 1987, it was the same day as Tony Galvin's testimonial. Tony went on to be the no.2 at Newcastle when Ossie Ardiles gave me my debut in 1993. In that testimonial Diego Maradona was playing (obviously as a favour to his fellow Argie) so I saw my hero Diego in the flesh when I was just a schoolboy. Can you imagine what that did to me at the time?! I can still remember him warming up and juggling the ball like it was on a string and thinking, 'you are simply a God'! When I went to Manchester United, I can remember seeing Ryan Giggs and Nicky Barmby. Also, a lad called Dave Gardner who's now best friends with David Beckham was there. After training at United Sir Alex Ferguson and his assistant Archie Knox took us all to an Italian restaurant near the Cliff Training Ground which is where the Red Devil's trained at. That's the sort of attention I was getting and at such a young age, it was all mind blowing. A few years later I played in a youth tournament over in Austria, I was around 15 at the time and had already signed for Newcastle. At this tournament there was some big clubs there such as PSV Eindhoven, Ajax and Bayern Munich all looking at me. We lost in the final, but I got player of the whole tournament and people were making a lot of noises about me. The year after that we won the Northern Ireland Milk Cup which was a big football competition with some of the biggest clubs in the world entering. Newcastle beat Manchester United in the final and the one player who stood out was Ryan Giggs. Giggsy was the star man even then. My buddy Lee Clark got player of the tournament over in Northern Ireland.

Looking back on it all I think it's a shame I didn't get a proper education, I just had my mind set on this one path and I would never let my kids think like that, however that's just how I was. Education is a massive part of any young person's life. If I'd never made it as a professional, I suppose I'd have had to go back to some kind of schooling because all I had was a GCSE in pottery and that wasn't going to get me very far in life. Then again, I suppose people always need plates and pottery don't they!

Luckily for me I never had any kind of injuries as a kid, as some kids do, but then again I was always falling over in the house or cutting myself. You could say I was a bit dopey and accident prone but thankfully it never effected my football. I think that's why I'm not good when it comes to seeing blood and I've been that way since I was a kid. I put it down to having so many nasty cuts as a lad which has stayed with me. One memory I have is of me falling through a window as a kid, just missing a main artery and needing stitches. If I stayed away from injuries on the pitch, believe me I more than made up for it at home in the Thompson household.

STEVE WATSON (Watto)

"I've known Tommo since we were in Primary school. Myself, Alan and Lee Clark were very close and even ex-player Robbie Elliott was in our little circle, although Robbie didn't go to school with us. The three of us were all close, but as we hit our teenage years, I would say myself and Tommo found ourselves hanging out together more because we both went out drinking whereas Lee didn't drink. Together we discovered the nightlife of Newcastle city centre as young lads do.

When we were in middle school together, we would play with rock hard casey balls and where most kids that age couldn't lift it off the floor, Tommo used to score for fun because he was the only kid in the playground capable of striking the ball cleanly and lifting it off the deck. Even at such a young age he was miles ahead of every kid in the school who played football. Not only could he strike the ball better than anyone else, but he was the only kid who could lift it and get it any kind of distance. His technique, even at such a young age was quite incredible.

When I would play in the same team as Tommo in our teenage years, he brought my game on so much because the number of goals I scored was purely down to him. It was nothing to do with great movement from me, it was down to his precise crosses. He could turn a ball on a sixpence even back then so maybe the reason I went on to become a Newcastle United player was because Tommo made me look so good. Even if there was two or three men marking me, Tommo's accuracy would always find my head, so he deserves a lot of credit for me turning out ok in my last season in the youth league before I went to Newcastle and onto signing for the club.

For the rest of my life, I'll have a great bond with Tommo, not to mention more fallouts, like the one on the millennium that I hear he's mentioned in this book.

Tommo's had a fantastic career and it's a shame he lost a lot of confidence. I myself have been through the same stuff as he has so I know exactly where he's coming from on that point. Lee Clark and I will always have his back. Tommo's took his hits but now he's coming off the back of it all and this book will be the start of great things to come from him."

CHAPTER 3

LEARNING MY TRADE

I left school at 16 in 1990 as I told you in the last chapter, with not much going for me. Looking back on my school years I wasn't a bad lad but could be a bit rowdy at times, much like I was on the pitch. One of the deputy heads at my school Kevin Vale, who was a big football fan always had a soft spot for me so if I ever got into any bother, he'd be ok with me.

I never really bothered with the opposite sex all through my school years, in fact I didn't date anyone until I was 16 and I'd left school. I had tunnel vision, I knew at 13 when I'd signed schoolboy forms with Newcastle that I was at least going to be a footballer until I was 18 and nothing else mattered. Whether I made it beyond that or not was down to me, God above and whether I could stay injury free. The YTS at Newcastle United was like a carrot dangling in front of me. I had this two-year apprenticeship in the bag pretty quickly along with Lee Clark and Robbie Elliott. Watto got it a bit later as he was going around a few different clubs before he chose. It felt like a bit of a safety net and although I was only 13, I didn't let it go to my head, like it may have done to some other kids my age. It did make me more determined to play football and I knuckled down as much as I could. My life from then on was just about trying to get a match in most nights and if I didn't have a game I would be training somewhere.

I was living the life as a pro from being 13 although, I have to admit I still had a sweet tooth and I loved a KFC. You can get away with it at that age though. I could eat what I wanted and still be as thin as a lat.

I was a YTS from 16 and I signed my pro forms at 17. I was getting £29.50p weekly and my mam was getting £50 per week from Newcastle for my board so I had everything I needed. As soon as I knew I would be earning I set up a bank account as I got some good advice from David Kelly who was a pro at the time for Newcastle. David told me that one day, if I was lucky enough, that when I was finished playing and I'd paid my mortgage, only then would I know whether or not I'd had a good career. I took Ned's (David) advice and I started paying into a pension very early. I think it was something like £5 a week and everything I did from then on was building for my future. Now you may be reading this thinking well Tommo was a switched-on kid at such a young age but I'd be lying if I said that was the case. The real picture at Newcastle Utd at the time was that we had some good old pro's around like Mickey Quinn, Mark McGee and Roy Aitken who were only too happy to help the young lads coming through.

When I think about Mickey Quinn back then he was horse racing mad, it's a trait he still has today. I would look at the likes of Roy Aitken and I'd be thinking, 'wow he's been the captain of Glasgow Celtic him'! When Roy was at Newcastle in the early 90's it wasn't a great time in Newcastle's history, but he always put a shift in. In training the lads used to shout to Roy, "FEED THE BEAR" which was what they used to say to him at Celtic as it was his nickname. Mark McGee was another ex-Celt and equally just as hardened a pro as Roy was and it was great for the likes of myself and the other young lads to learn from them.

Watching what they did in training day in, day out gave me really good grounding.
At that time one of the chores which any young player had to undertake was cleaning the older lads' boots. I used to clean Roy's boots weekly so, all of that gives you good grounding because if it wasn't done properly, you were getting told about it! On the plus side, usually if you cleaned them to the required standard then the older players would treat us to a new pair of boots that Christmas. Coming through as a young player I was given other jobs like cleaning the players bath, sweeping and mopping floors and we were never allowed to leave until all our jobs were done. If anything, it was incredibly military like, and the discipline was instilled into you from day one. Most days I wasn't allowed to leave Newcastle until 4pm even though we'd finished training at around dinner time. The days began at 9am and it was like that Monday to Friday, and you'd have a game on a Saturday morning. If we had to travel far for games, we'd have to set off at 7am to places like Scunthorpe and we'd be playing on boggy rainy pitches, some weeks it was like playing on a battlefield. We'd travel all over England in a little minibus and if you were last on then you'd have to sit on the floor at the back. I'd always make sure that I was on time because I didn't fancy a dead arse before playing a game.

All this discipline at the beginning of my football career, I've always firmly believed, put me in good stead for whatever was shot at me in the football world throughout my career. I had the years at the Boys Club in Wallsend from an early age before that too so, I quickly learnt that things like time keeping, and presentation were really important and there were expectations that must be met. Getting that right would serve me well in later life just like the tough love I received playing against the older lads, after they'd come out of the pub and the 50/50 tackles they put in on my old estate Battle Hill.

ALAN SHEARER

"I first heard the name Alan Thompson when he was just a kid coming through at Newcastle. Although I was away down in Southampton, people would always be making noises about Alan Thompson, Lee Clark and Steve Watson because these lads were going to be special. I didn't really get to know Alan until I came back to Newcastle in 1996 but I played against him many times over the years.

Tommo had a great cultured left-foot and, as he would tell everyone, he could open a can of beans with it (laughs). As a forward myself I know just how important it was for the playmakers to find you and that was something Alan could do time and time again. Nobody has to tell me what a brilliant footballer Alan Thompson was, and he went on and played football at the highest level. He's one in the minority who's achieved every schoolboy's dream.

When you look at some of the names who came through that famous Wallsend Boys Club, which me and Tommo were a part of, that iconic place which produced not only top-class footballers but helped them become top class people for life."

CHAPTER 4

THE NIGHT I ALMOST LOST MY LIFE

September 5th, 1990 is a day I'll never forget because it's a day that changed my life. I trained in the morning with Newcastle youth side and on that very same day in the evening the Newcastle reserves were playing Leeds United at Elland Road and I was asked if I wanted to go as one of the lads had space in his motor. I was told that there was going to be some decent names playing for Leeds that evening, such as Chris Kamara and Vinny Jones, so it was something I really wanted to see. At the time I was only 16 and in the youth team, the next step up being the reserves. One of our youth players, Micky English had just passed his driving test and he was going through to Leeds so a few of us got together and went through to watch the game. John Watson and I were first year YTS' and Micky was a second year YTS. Phil Mason was also in the car, who at the time was a first-year pro, and Micky Young who was also a second year YTS was also with us, so there were five of us in total in this old Mini. We finished training quite early around 2pm and made our way through to Leeds excited at the prospect of being able to see some real quality pro's. The five of us go down and watch the game, I can't remember what the score was but it was a pleasant evening.

On the way back, we're driving home on the A58 from Leeds to Wetherby and decided we would stop off for fish & chips. After our meal we head onto the A1, and by the time we get Peterlee/Bowburn way it was pitch black. I was sitting behind the passenger seat and wearing seat belts wasn't mandatory then, which is scary thought looking back. Anyway, as we were driving along the vehicle began to steer to the right towards the crash barrier, just before we hit it the driver pulled the car violently away from it but with the weight of us five lads in this tiny Mini it caused the car to flip and roll. It's true what they say, everything slowed down, a million thoughts went through my mind all at once and the noise! My God, the noise, it's something I'll never forget, the sound of metal distorting was deafening then there was deathly silence. The car had come to rest on its roof. I was trying hard to process what had just happened.

The two lads in the front, Micky English driving and Micky Young the front passenger were absolutely fine, apart from a few cuts on their faces that is. John Watson, who was in the middle, was ok too but the lad who was sat behind the driver Phil Mason wasn't there. I was confused and numb, nothing made sense, why was the car upside down and where was Phil? I didn't feel any pain, although my mouth felt gritty and I could smell petrol. Everywhere was too dark and too quiet now. I regained my senses enough to know that I needed to get out of the car sharpish, smelling petrol wasn't a good sign. I pulled myself from the wreckage and I stood up, as quickly as I had stood up I collapsed. A woman appeared from nowhere and grabbed me saying, "It's ok Son I'm a nurse, I'm off duty but it's ok because I've got you" she was reassuring me that she was going to look after me and of all the thoughts I could have had at the time, I just remember thinking she smelt funny.

Now that might sound odd and not very grateful at all as she had probably just finished a very long shift at work, but my mind wasn't processing anything properly. I had no idea at that point how severely injured I was.

It wasn't until the emergency services got there that Phil was found, he had gone out of the side window and was found 100 yards up the road under the central reservation. He had a fractured spleen and a broken pelvis. I can only think that I was pain free because of the shock and trauma of it all, there was that much adrenaline pumping around my body, I honestly thought I had escaped, by some miracle, unscathed!

Not long after the good Samaritan appeared to reassure me then the ambulance came and whisked me off to the hospital. On the journey to the hospital I realised that the gold chain I wore around my neck that had a gold football on it had been crushed completely flat, obviously I was upset at that as it was a gift from my Mam, but not half as upset as I was when the paramedics started cutting my Umbro shell suit up, "woah, you can't cut my tracksuit off man" but of course I had no idea then how bad I was and quite rightly the paramedics don't give a shit when they're trying to save someone's life, they were there to do a job and they got on with it. I was gutted. It was a Wednesday evening and I had turned to the ambulance crew and asked if I'd be fit for a game on Saturday as in my head, I was still meeting up with the England under 17's. I'd only just been told that I would be captaining England away in Reykjavik on the coast of Iceland.

When I got to the Dryburn Hospital, Durham, appearance wise I had a few cuts in my mouth, that grittiness I had experienced turned out to be glass from the windscreen. I also had cuts to an ear and my swanky Swatch watch had stopped at 10:56pm, which had been the exact time of impact. My mam made her way to the hospital immediately with my aunt Cathy by taxi as neither of them drove. Dad was not home as he was working away on the rigs.

I ended up staying in that hospital for around three weeks at first, so me playing in Iceland was well out of the window. My fellow passenger Phil Mason ended up in the bed next to me on my ward. As I was laid there in my bed looking like a Transformer with my neck brace, I was beyond devastated. This whole episode was a true living nightmare for me, there were no promises that could be made at that time that I'd walk again let alone play football for a living. I felt like all my hopes and dreams were on the scrap heap along with the car we'd been in. What the hell was I going to do now?!

The staff at that hospital were amazing and all of the Newcastle first team at the time came in to see me. Lads like Mickey Quinn, Kevin Scott, Kevin Brock, Bjorn Kristenson and the manager at the time Jim Smith (God rest him) all visited. As a joke the lads brought some porno mags in for me and Phil. Well as we both couldn't get out of bed, we had to shoot these mucky magazines to each other through the air. One time Phil chucked a mag over to me, but regrettably it didn't reach my bed and it landed on the floor. Well, the only thing I could do was shout at the nurse to ask her to pick it up. It was so embarrassing. I was practically in tears trying to convince the nurse that the players had brought them in for a joke and that I really wasn't a pervert!

What was incredible was that there was a young lad opposite mine and Phil's beds who was unresponsive and had been for a while. This young kid had all Newcastle stuff around his bed, and he'd been in for several months by then. When the nurses started telling him that these two young footballers were in from Newcastle and that the first team players were visiting, this kid started responding and moving. I don't know what happened to that poor brave lad but for that period when all the players, who were his hero's, were in he was moving his hands, feet and was blinking which he hadn't been doing before.

Many years later after my accident, when I was back playing, I was asked to go to a spinal hospital in Hexham to visit this young lad to try and perk him up. I went there full of good intentions but as soon as I got there it brought so many bad memories flooding back that it made me ill, I couldn't do it, it didn't matter how much I tried to talk myself around to going in, I just couldn't do it. The thought was making me want to be physically sick, whether that's PTSD or a phobia I'd developed because of the trauma I don't know but I had to make my apologies to the boy's parents and leave. I felt like I was going to pass out, I hadn't realised until then the impact it had on me mentally as well as physically. The boy wasn't as lucky as me as he was paralysed, I felt so bad that I couldn't make it in to see him that day.

Derek Wright has spoken about my injuries at the start of this book, I'd dislocated C4 and C5. The two were squashed together and for over a week, when I first got there I didn't have any feeling in my legs. I thought I was going to be in a wheelchair for the rest of my life. My injury was exactly the same as the Superman actor Christopher Reeve's, who never recovered and spent the rest of his days in a wheelchair being fed with a tube until he sadly passed away at 52. At first it felt like my world was coming to an end just because I wasn't going to make Iceland, but as the weeks went on my focus shifted to where I honestly thought I may not walk again. At such a tender age it already felt like my life's dream, like my shell suit, was in tatters!

The first surgeon from Dryburn Hospital told my parents and Newcastle United that they couldn't do anything with me and that my injuries needed attention from more specialist doctors. That was a massive shock to the system. I started to feel myself slipping into a dark depression, I didn't know what to do with myself anymore.

Thankfully the Newcastle Physio Derek Wright told me that him and the club were going to take me wherever I needed to go to get fixed and the recovery wheels were put into motion. The next step was to go and see Derek Stainsby at Newcastle who was one of the top surgeons in the Northeast. Derek told me that he wanted to do a certain type of operation and although he couldn't give me any guarantees it would work, it was the best available option for me. The plan was to take some bone from my hip and pin it in my neck. This operation came with risks, and I may struggle later on in life with arthritis, but I didn't give a monkeys what might happen in my later life, that seemed a million miles away then, my aim back then was just to play.

The operation was finally done at the Freeman Hospital in January 1991, Derek wanted to do it before then but the skin on my neck was not in great condition as it had been under my neck brace obviously and so hadn't been getting any fresh air. Although I was in a right mess, the hospital got me up a day or two after the operation to take me in the shower. The staff put a mirror behind me and one in front of me to show me the scar. When I first saw it, I was horrified, it was huge and I just didn't want to look at it. The scar on my hip where they'd taken the bone from didn't bother me. I know it sounds silly, but I've always been a bit embarrassed by the scar on my neck.

I knew if I was going to have any chance of recovery it meant working hard in the gym with Derek Wright so that's what I did. Around this time Jim Smith left Newcastle and Ossie Ardiles took over. I didn't allow that to distract me because to get in the first team I was going to have to get back to where I had been fitness wise before I could worry about impressing whoever was in charge. Things are so different when you're young and although what happened to me was bad, I was more positive than I would have been if it had happened later in my life.

My first match back after the operation was in August 1991. I'll never forget going up for an aerial challenge and thinking, 'I don't really want to do this; however, it was something I had to do if I was going to be a professional footballer. I think in the end I just jumped up, shut my eyes and got on with it hoping for the best. After the first few times of doing that, I started to get my confidence back. I had to start tackling again too and although I was never the bravest, being a footballer was my everything, so it was something I had no choice in.

In my time at Celtic, Martin O'Neill always knew that I was a bit reluctant about sticking my head in places and I really appreciated that he fully understood why and never held it against me. Martin never expected me to go up for any set pieces where I was going to be in a position to head it. Martin let me take corners and leave that side to the big monsters in our team like Bobo, Sutty, Johan, Joos, Pearo, Stan Varga, Stubbsy and big John Hartson etc…

Thankfully I managed to get through it and have a great career, but I can't pretend there wasn't dark times. The main thing was that I came back after Mr Stainsby's operation to play for my boyhood team Newcastle at St James Park and went on to live the dream.

One of the most amazing memories not long after my injury involved Paul Gascoigne. Now at this time, which was just after Italia 90, Gazza was one of the most famous people in the world and at the height of his fame, or what the papers called, 'Gazza mania!' The boys were getting their hair cut like his and the girls were covering their pencil cases with stickers of him. He was everywhere you looked.

After I had my surgery in January Gazza was at Spurs, but he got in touch with me. He had got my number from somebody and rang me up to tell me he was taking me on a night out. Gazza took me to a place called Berlin's next to Central Station in Newcastle. At the time I was on £29.50p a week and Gazza knew this. At the start off the night, I went out with £30 and at the end of the night went home with £80. Gazza kept giving me £20 notes to go to the bar and saying, "keep tha change wor kid." It was most bizarre because I wasn't long out of school and now, I was out on the Toon with Gazza and his footballing pals Chris Waddle and the big French defender Basil Boli, who would also follow Gazza to Rangers. I spent the evening drinking bottles of Sol then Gazza was pushing these shots of Bailey's into the mix. Needless to say, it became a bit of a messy night. Here I was getting drunk with one of the best footballers in the world in my neck brace looking like Optimus Prime. At the end of the night me and Gazza got a taxi to my mam and dad's in Walker, Newcastle. Gazza came in and we finished the night there with my parents and my sister Jane and we watched an Erasure concert on the telly. Gazza ended up sleeping in my sister's bed whilst Jane slept on the couch. it was crazy looking back because it was at the height of the Paul Gascoigne story when if he wasn't on the telly playing football then he was on it with Terry Wogan, he was that big. It seemed so surreal, and my sister Jane kept a few hairs of his off her pillow to mark the time one of the most famous footballers in the world came to stay at the Thompson's. I think Jane still has them hairs from Gazza's napper in a little money bag, seriously!

The next morning it was a Saturday and Newcastle were at home at St James and there was a young lad on loan from Spurs at Newcastle who Gazza knew so Gazza got us some free tickets. Before the game me and Gazza nicked into the Strawberry pub at the back of the Gallowgate end. "Gazza are you sure you wanna go in there?" I said, he just shrugged his shoulders and said, "of course wor kid" not fully realising he would be getting mobbed. Well, we went in and we did get mobbed, I say we but in reality, nobody knew who I was, I was just a young kid in a neck brace but he had to fight his way in and the same on the way out. That was typical Paul though, always had time for other people.

PETER JOYSON
Best Mate

"I've been with Alan through his up's and his down's, so I know how much character he's had to show, particularly in the last few years when there's been some dark times. I've been there with him through the thick and the thin, so I know what kind of a great & loyal guy he is. The man's devoted to his family and everyone that meets him will take to him as he has this great ability to get on with people.

I've had a lot of daft times with Alan going on holiday together when he's just spent the week playing pranks on people. For instance, one time he drew a moustache on a lad's passport picture and that lad just to say got out of the country when it was time to go home. He's set me up on so many pranks over the years there's far too many to mention. I was his best man on his wedding day back in the 90's and I was very proud to be by his side.

I'm so pleased that he's now turned a corner in life, and he's found the courage to tell his story in this book. I don't think Alan realises just how many people out there love him. It means a lot to myself to see him now, out there, back on his feet because I know just how low he'd fallen. At times he's rang me in the early hours, and I've had to speak with him until the birds were cheeping just to reassure him everything's going to be fine.

Tommo is my son Henry's godson and Henry idolises him. Henry's like his second son but I'd just like to say to

Tommo that he's got people in his life and around him who think the world of him like me and Henry will always do.

GEOFF STOKES
Childhood Friend

"I've been friends with Tommo since the 1970's as we lived in the same street. As kids we played knocky-knocky hido, leavo and kick the can. If I played heads & volleys with him and he was losing, he'd have a tantrum and go home with his ball. Tommo always had the best of footballs to play with and us other kids had nothing.

Today, 45 years later we are still in regular contact. We've had many great times together during his football career, at sporting events and watching live bands. As for the hard times, Alan broke his neck, and I snapped my tibia and fibula. I used to call Alan a Teenage Mutant Ninja Turtle or Robocop when he had his cage over his neck.

When Alan got his driving ban, I helped him out when I could by trying to base myself in Glasgow so I could drive him places. People often ask me what Alan Thompson's like, and I say he's from good stock. His parents Annie and Davey are great as is his sister Jane. It runs in the family with Nessy (David Longstaff) and now his sons Matty and Sean who both play for Newcastle.

I always knew Alan was going to make it as a pro years before he did as he was golden bollocks with a great left foot. Alan is a guy who's great to be around with brilliant craic. Yes, he does get emotional from time to time but that's what makes him who he is. He's a proper Geordie."

CHAPTER 5

I'D MADE IT!

I made my debut in 1991. Everything I had been through, the rollercoaster of emotions because of the accident and the long road to recovery had all been building up to this moment. I remember getting told on the Friday before the game that I would be in the squad. When you were in the squad of the first team it meant it was a jacket & tie number for the match day. At that time, I didn't even own a jacket & tie, so I had to walk from the Gallowgate after training on the Friday to Topman in the town centre of Newcastle to get rigged out. As it happened, I wasn't going to be starting I was going to be a sub, but right before the kick-off I was told I would be starting. I was like 'EH?' As it turned poor Lee Clark had got injured in the warm up at St James Park.
Obviously, apart from Lee's injury, this was an ideal way to be making my first team debut as I didn't have any time to get nervous about it. I mean this was the moment I'd dreamt about since I was around 6 or 7, I was finally going to be pulling on the Black & White stripes of my beloved Magpie's at St James Park, I can't begin to say how proud I was that day. I was finally about to live the dream that tens of thousands of young Geordies dreamt about, I could hardly believe it. Lee Clark's nightmare became my wish coming true and I had only minutes to think about it as I ran out against Grimsby Town on Saturday November 9th, 1991. We won 2-0 and I assisted a goal for Steve Howey. The sad part was that because I wasn't due to start my mam

and dad weren't there to witness me making my debut. I played the full 90 minutes, although I can't really remember much of it, I was caught up in the game but remembering every second didn't really matter to me at the time though because I knew I'd finally made it. I was now a proper professional footballer and everything, my vision had at last become a reality.

My debut overall was an emotional day for me, not only because I was living out my boyhood dream but also because of everything I'd been through in that car crash a little over one year previously and the months of anguish that had followed it. All of the worry and turmoil we'd all been through, wondering if I'd walk and here I was playing football for Newcastle United. It meant the world to me to be stepping out onto the pitch wearing those stripes, especially as I was just a local boy from Wallsend.

If I'm going to be honest, then my only regret about that time was that I didn't get to pull that strip on enough. I went on to make only twenty appearances for Newcastle Utd. I really wish I'd have had more to do for the Toon like Watto and Clarkie did, because they were local lads just like me. As much as it hurt leaving Newcastle United, I knew it was something I was going to have to do if I wanted to play regular first team football.

I left Newcastle in 1993. I was offered a new contract, but what really made me unhappy about it was that the manager at the time Kevin Keegan, sent me the new contract in the post, rather than sit down with me. It really lacked that personal touch and I didn't think it was a professional way of going about business, I know my dad was pretty disgusted at the time too. Basically, I was sent this legal document, which was obviously of importance, through the mail offering me £500 a week, and basically it was a take it or leave it deal! As much as I bled black &

white, I didn't want to take the new contract, it gave me the impression that I perhaps wouldn't figure much in the managers plans going forward and it's the only time my auld fella was pretty vocal in telling me of his disapproval. Dad advised me that I should look elsewhere for a new club as he thought I should have been spoken to face to face about my new contract like the others got, it was only common courtesy, and I have to say I agreed with my Dad on that one so I decided to see what other opportunities there was out there for me.

It broke my heart to leave United, especially as it looked like exciting things were now happening under Kevin Keegan. Although I would have loved to have stayed and played with the likes of Andy Cole, Peter Beardsley and Robert Lee. I knew really that whatever Keegan's future plans were, they didn't really include me, other than having me warming the bench. At this time the attendances at St James Park were quite poor, although plans were in place to build a new stadium.

My best mates Watto & Clarkie went on to become familiar faces during the most exciting time of Newcastle's history, a team which were branded 'the entertainers'. People may be reading this now thinking, 'well why didn't you stay and fight for your place Alan?' But I'd spent the best part of a year out injured, in a neck brace watching my mates, who I'd come through the youth system with playing, I couldn't bring myself to do that again, it was going to be too bloody hard to do, especially as I knew Scott Sellars was well ahead of me in Keegan's mind. Kevin had signed Scott in '93 when I was in Australia with England in the youth world cup to fill my position and a lad named Mark Robinson from Barnsley, who was a right back, was brought in for Watto's position as he was over in Oz with me too. Me and Watto thought, 'well what chance have we got when we get back to Newcastle when they've signed two new signings in our positions?!' Really the writing was on the wall from then on.

It hurt that I felt I had to leave my boyhood heroes Newcastle United but if I didn't do it then I wouldn't have gone on to do the things I did with my other clubs. I firmly believe in the saying, 'what's meant for you won't go by you' and in my case it was certainly true. Everything happens for a reason, doesn't it?!

Funny enough my very first away fixture for Newcastle was at the old Roker Park against Sunderland. We drew 1-1, with Liam O'Brien scoring ours but the whole experience was rather intimidating, which was what I expected really, being a Geordie. That's just the nature of a Newcastle/Sunderland derby. I played in 26 Old Firm derbies and although that's the biggest derby in the world in my opinion I'd be lying if I said coming onto the pitch at the old Roker Park to the Queen song 'We will rock you' as a Geordie wasn't a little unnerving. That day playing in the Tyne & Wear derby, Sunderland had a veteran player older than me called John Kay who blatantly tried to bully me. He was saying things like, "you do this, and I'll snap ya legs" and "I'll wire ya jaw up" etc you know the drill. John constantly tried to put it on me all the time I was on the pitch, but it never worked. As a player you've got to just get on with it!

It was Ossie Ardiles who brought me into the team and Kevin Keegan was the one who saw me out. One of my last appearances was versus Cambridge United away in an evening kick off. I'd been rooming with Watto, and Keegan had not named his team yet, so I wasn't even sure I'd be playing. I told Watto I was still hungry, so I ordered room service and told them to send some double chocolate gateaux along. It didn't matter because I wasn't in the starting eleven, or so I thought! Soon after I'd finished the cake Kevin Keegan calls a meeting not long before we leave for the game and it turns out that I'm in the starting eleven. Well before games I had a problem with throwing up so I thought I'd just chuck this chocolate gateaux up and everything would be ok. Nobody, including Kevin Keegan, would be any the wiser that I'd been a bit of a pig and done a full cake in. As soon as everybody was out of the way I sneaked into the changing room toilets, then began looking for Huey over the sink to get rid of the cake. I thought that was the end of it until Kevin Keegan starts getting his coat on and does his last-minute rehearsals before the game and he notices something different. Then Kevin shouts to his right-hand man Terry McDermott, "Terry, what's going on in here? There's spew all over the sink, it looks like chocolate cake to me". I thought there's no way it could come back onto me, that was until I heard Kevin shouting, "GET ON TO THE HOTEL AND FIND OUT WHICH OF OUR LADS HAD ORDERED CHOCOLATE CAKE, THE SNEAKY BASTARDS." To cut a long story short the boss found out through excellent detective work that Sherlock himself would have been impressed with that it was me who made a mess of the changing rooms. Kevin put that story in his biography and named me as the No.1 suspect so if you're reading this Kevin then I'm truly sorry but, in my defence, I didn't know I would be playing, and also, I had a problem with vomiting before games.

The throwing up issue lasted from those early Newcastle United games right the way through to me finishing up at Hartlepool United. It was something which was always there, it just depended on where and who I was playing against. As I got older, and the games and stages got bigger I learnt to control it that little bit more, but every boss I played under was aware of it. Most of the time it would be just before a game, sometimes it would be at half time. In my time at Bolton when Bruce Ricoh was the manager, he sent me to a sports psychologist about it. I was then put to sleep using relaxation methods and they tried to fix my problems and get to the bottom of it once and for all. The sports doc who examined me at Bolton went on to tell me that in his expert opinion I was doing this because I was scared of sustaining a serious injury. The doctor told me he thought my body was worried after the trauma I'd suffered with my neck injury, and the fear of getting a serious injury whilst playing made by body react that way. That was his conclusion from the sessions I'd had with him anyway, and it makes the most sense I suppose. I remember talking to Sammy Lee about it and he told me he did the same all the way through his career for Liverpool. Players throwing up before games is more common than you think, although the groundsman at Celtic Park weren't too happy at my antics. Often the fans would see me doing it at half time and even the opposition players sometimes. Many times, the other team would take the piss out of what I did but I couldn't help it. Other times nothing would even come out, but it was just this reaction I had and it became part and parcel of my makeup at each club I was at. It wasn't only the big games that would cause it either, once I remember playing at Stranraer in the Scottish Cup and chucking up behind the goal. No disrespect to Stranraer but it was just how my body reacted to nerves, stress and adrenaline. Sometimes I was chucking up on the pitch, other times I'd be doing it in the dressing room but when the game started there was none of that at all, it was business as usual.

DAVID LEE
Bolton Teammate

"I'd not heard of Alan Thompson before Bruce Rioch brought him to the club. My first thoughts on him were that he was loud and very outspoken, however once you cracked the nut of him you realised he wasn't just that. First meeting him he did give that loud, brash and cocky young Geordie lad persona off in abundance. The footballer, Alan Thompson is very different to the man Alan Thompson though, the one I found out about with him becoming a family member as Alan would go on to marry my sister-in-law.

On the pitch I would say he had a bit of a spoilt brat syndrome, away from the pitch and with his family he was extremely grounded.

When he arrived at Bolton, I have to say he came in and hit the ground running. His hunger and appetite for the game really was quite something. He seemed to just have this natural ability and he definitely made an impact at the club.

It was during one of my first training sessions with Alan that we had a bit of a spat. Tommo was one of them that when he got the ball, he just seemed to keep it. I must have nicked the ball off him, much to his displeasure, Alan then went in for me and we've grabbed onto each other, then it was broken up by teammates. From that day on, I think Alan gave me the respect I deserved being his teammate. Today we always laugh about it because that's how we kind of met each other, him wanting to put it on me. It's funny because further down the line he became my brother-in-law.

CHAPTER 6

THEY CALL THEM THE WANDERERS

I knew of Colin Todd at Bolton Wanderers through his son Andy from the Newcastle Centre of Excellence which we both attended in our youth. I would say he was the one who first told Bruce Rioch about me at Bolton Wanderers. Colin was assistant manager at Bolton, and they'd also been together at Middlesbrough. It turns out that's exactly what happened when Colin explained to Bruce that there was this young Geordie lad at Newcastle who wasn't happy with the way his contract talks had been going. I can't really remember much about how I ended up at Bolton, other than I drove down to have talks with them and then signed. I believe Newcastle received a fee of around £250,000 as compensation.

At the time at Newcastle, I think my weekly wage was around £150 a week and after signing for Bolton it jumped up to £500 a week, which at the time was a huge amount to a young lad like myself. It was hard leaving Tyneside and moving away from home, I didn't really want to go, especially as I was still a teenager, but I knew if I was to have a fighting chance of playing regular first team football then this move was imperative. What really appealed to me about moving to Burnden Park was Bolton was a club on the up big time! Bruce Rioch was the boss, and he was a guy with ambitions in the game who wouldn't take any shit from anyone.

Looking back now at it now, almost thirty years on, the move to the Trotters was a fabulous decision and everything turned out great for me. When I got to the club they had players of a high calibre, such as Alan Stubbs, Jason MacAteer, David Lee, John McGinley, Scott Green, Andy Walker, Mixu Paatelainen, Simon Coleman, Neil MacDonald, Simon Patterson then the likes of Owen Coyle and John Sheridan came along not long after. Nathan Blake came along also, and he was very good along with the big burly Northern Irishman Gerry Taggart. Another player the club signed when I was there was the Serbian midfielder Sasa Curcic. Nobody knew anything about him when he arrived in 1995 and he made his debut against Arsenal. Honestly, he was a scruffy little thing who wore the same clothes daily until he got his first wage packet. After he was paid then he came in everyday in every designer label you could think of. He bought a nice house in Bolton, and he did that well in his career that he then got a big money move to Aston Villa the year after. Funny enough I ended up buying his house off him in Woodsleigh Coppice, Bolton. When I moved into the home, there was a yellow BMW M3 Convertible in the garage. When I rang Sasa to tell him he'd left this plush car in the garage he just said, "aaah I don't want it Tommo, just keep it." This was amazing considering the year before he didn't even own any clothes. I told Sasa I couldn't keep it and he needed to pick it up, it was picked up eventually. I loved cars at the time, but I had my own and didn't want this bright yellow BMW. I could have accepted his offer and sold it for a fortune, but I was too busy. Not only that but he had already left the most amazing furniture such as settee's and the fully fitted out kitchen. Once he was so poor, then he became that wealthy that he didn't care about money, it didn't mean a great deal to him, and obviously as his gesture to keep the car shows, he was generous with it. That just goes to show you what the life of a professional footballer can do for you doesn't it? I saw him only a few years ago at Bolton, he's a great lad and it was nice to catch up.

Now I had some incredibly good times at Bolton with a few promotions, relegations and a few cup finals for good measure. The very last game at Burnden in April 1997 against Charlton Athletic where we won 4-1 was overwhelming for the fans, after all over 102 years of football had been played on that ground and not only was it the very last game at Burnden but we also got promoted and completely romped The Championship. So, in the new season in August of that year, we not only started in the Premiership but also in a brand-new stadium, The Reebok Stadium.

The season before we were in the new stadium, we all used to drive past it as it was going up, right from the foundations being laid to the finished article, it was interesting to see it coming on and when we were able to start playing there it was just, WOW!

Over the years since I've retired, I get so much attention from the Celtic fans across the world but also from the Bolton fans too which totally blows me away. The fans always want to talk to me about the great cup runs we had where we slayed a few giants. I not only scored 45 goals for the club in a total of 180 starts but I contributed to a lot of assists. I was involved in a successful Bolton Wanderers team that played good positive football.

The Trotters following were always extremely loyal and knowledgeable about the game. I scored some cracking goals for the club and that's where I first started to become noticed for my freekicks, however I was doing it a lot for the Newcastle United youth team. The freekicks were something that became a huge part of my game and something I enjoyed doing. I would make sure I practiced them with military precision in training daily. It was nice to score in the very last game at Burnden and then I scored the very first ever goal at the Reebok, so it's also an absolute honour to be in the club's history books for that and it's a great pub quiz question to boot! In that first game at the new stadium, it was a penalty that I scored against Ian Walker's Spurs in what ended up in a 1-1 draw and it got us off to a good start.

Jason McAteer and Alan Stubbs did start to attract a lot of interest from clubs in the mid-90's and it was always going to be impossible for a club like Bolton Wanderers to keep their stars when the big guns came calling. Jason and Alan were a couple of years older than me, but I'd noticed for a few years before Jason left for Liverpool (1995) and Alan for Celtic (1996) there were always scouts at the games. At that time Blackburn were linked to any player half decent and paying big money for them not to mention Manchester United, Liverpool and Arsenal. In the end Jason went to Liverpool but I know the both of them were banded about, very much like Scott Brown and Kevin Thompson in 2007 when they were about to leave Hibs. At one point Jason's move nearly broke down to Liverpool with Stubbsy pulling out also because he was a lifelong Evertonian. He eventually left the year after to Celtic, but he did end up at his boyhood club in 2001. At the time it was a shock that Celtic landed Stubbsy instead of the big teams in England, but it was no surprise to me. I played against Stubbsy in training daily and the guy was a quality player. Left foot, right foot he had it all, although he may well have been the biggest moaner I ever played with and I played with some face aches and that's coming from me! I was a real pain in the arse to every referee I ever came across, but Stubbsy put me in a tin hat.

The number of arguments Stubbsy was involved with in training, dressing rooms or on the pitch was frightening, all forgotten afterwards mind. He was one incredibly passionate yet talented guy who could look after himself. Jason had this unbelievable engine for our Bolton side, he'd fly up and down the pitch, a bit like Didier Agathe at Celtic. Jason went to play in the World cup in the USA for Jack Charlton's Republic of Ireland and he did well.

Going back to our team under Bruce Rioch, I must say we had a good blend of everything under a very good manager in Mr Rioch. Where do I start with Bruce apart from saying the guy was the strictest of strict disciplinarians. He wouldn't suffer fools gladly and everything had to be how he wanted it. Although Colin Todd took a lot of the coaching tasks, Bruce knew the game as good as anyone I've ever met in the game.

Now I've finished my playing days, I've been involved in coaching and no doubt will be going back into it at some stage and I'll openly admit to picking things up from Bruce that I've taken into my approach on coaching. Bruce himself was a top Scottish international as was Colin although for England, so they were proper footballing men. Both were hard men too, so as a young footballer it was a great opportunity for them both to educate me in the beautiful game.

In the mid-90's I knew eventually Jason and Stubbsy were going to go long before they did and then I knew that it would be up to me to do my bit and step up to the plate for Bolton Wanderers. I myself left the Trotters in 1998 but had we stayed in the Premier League I might have stayed there. No disrespect to The Championship but I needed to be at the topflight at that stage of my career as by then I was in my mid-20's. For all the love in the world I had for Bolton and the great time I had for over five years there I knew it was the right time to leave at 24 years old in 1998.

Bolton Wanderers getting to the Coca-Cola League Cup Final at Wembley in 1995 was an incredible achievement and pushed an extremely talented Liverpool side so close I think we more than punched our weight. The man of the match was Steve McManaman that day and as well as scoring the winning goal he was pretty much unplayable. It wasn't any surprise that he would end up at a club like Real Madrid winning Champions League medals. I scored our goal that day in the Cup Final. What I remember clearly from that game was that it was still 0-0 and I hit a volley with my right foot (Thompson's right foot, perish the thought) and big David James in goal tipping it onto the bar. Most keepers wouldn't have got it but because of how big Jamo is then he got just enough onto it. That would have put us in the lead, and it may have been a different game but it just wasn't to be! I was about to run off and celebrate and he scuppered my chance.

The day itself, although not the result we wanted, was truly an unforgettable day and just how I imagined it to be when I was a little boy kicking balls against a wall over and over in Wallsend. My full family came down to the Twin Towers of Wembley for the day to mark the special occasion and they all made a weekend of it. Yes, we lost the game, but it set us in good stead to come back to Wembley for the play-off final against Reading only two months later to get promoted. We won 4-3 after extra time in that game and that's the only game throughout my full career that I ever got cramp in. Whether it was the occasion or just the size of the Wembley pitch I don't know but I ended up ravaged with it. In that Play-Off Final we were almost down and out for the count at half-time being 2-0 down. Those two occasions were the only times I ever graced that Wembley pitch in my seventeen-year career.

Talking about playing at Wembley, I remember driving to the historic stadium to face Liverpool for the first League Cup final and we'd taken the legendary Peter Shilton on loan. As we were travelling on the team bus, I asked Shilts for a bit of advice. At the time Peter was well into his 40's and the reason we took him was because Bolton had a bit of a goalkeeping crisis. It was quite ironic because here's me travelling to the Twin Towers down Wembley Way for the very first time and here's me sat with England's all-time record holder, so I asked Peter what it was really like! Shilt's told me that although he knew the place and had the whole experience of playing there, it was a truly unique experience. Shilt's told me that when you're in the dressing room you can't hear your own teammates sitting next to you because of the noise from the 92,000 in attendance. Shilt's told me to expect a wall of noise when I walked out of the tunnel besides the opposing side. As he's telling me this on the bus, I'm getting more and more nervous/excited in equal measures, I mean, this was what I'd wanted since I was that little boy at the Boys Club of Wallsend. When the time came big Shilts was not wrong because in all of those years that I'd watched the major Cup Final's, this new experience took my breath away. To be able to live this dream, standing there listening to the national anthem and to wave up to my loved one's was magical. To be able to do that, twice in two months was magical and slightly surreal.

My last season at Bolton in 1997/98 was a difficult one. Although we would eventually go down, it was the manner in which it happened which hurts, and I'll give you an example. In that season we played Everton on a Monday night game on Sky. During the game we had a perfectly good goal disallowed when Gerry Taggart scored with a header which was around three clear balls over the line, however it was chopped off. Fast forward to the end of that season, Everton stayed up by one point which meant that if that one goal would have been given then we would have stayed in the Premiership. That shocking decision literally cost Bolton Wanderers millions of pounds. It was so hard knowing this when we eventually went down on the very last game of the season to Chelsea at Stamford Bridge. Going down a division is truly a living nightmare. Anybody who knows it knows it's the worst feeling in football. Obviously at the other end of the scale, going up is the best feeling in the game. In my last season at Bolton, although we went down my own personal statistics were very good. I'd scored into double figures from midfield and with that came a lot of interest, much in the same way that it had for Stubbsy & Jason a few years previously.

As I'm talking about this now in 2021 what comes into my head was Colin Todd pulling me aside and saying, "look Tommo we don't want you to go anywhere, however the big boys have started sniffing around you talking of big money!" One day I remember going to my agent's office in Wilmslow and he wrote the number of teams that had already enquired, and it was a phenomenal list. Arsenal, Manchester United, Leicester City (good auld uncle Martin again), Leeds United, Blackburn Rovers, Aston villa and PSV Eindhoven. Where the latter came from, I don't know! As I sat down with my agent, and he proceeded to tell me just how much interest there was in me now it was staggering.

In the end we narrowed it down and I'll tell you how. For some reason at that time, I didn't fancy the big smoke of London so that was Arsenal ruled out. I did speak with Sir Alex Ferguson on the phone. Sir Alex called me whilst on holiday in the South of France. I'll never forget it. I have to give him credit because although I didn't really want to hear it at the time, he was brutally honest with me. He told me he was rather impressed with me, but I wouldn't be coming in as a regular first team player because he already had Ryan Giggs. However, I would be given opportunities when Giggsy needed a rest due to hamstring issues, which I totally got. You've got to remember this was just before United's treble winning season in 1998 but I'd already had a taste of playing regularly and I didn't fancy losing this, even if the big money softened the downside of it all. Sir Alex went ahead and signed the Swedish winger Jesper Blomqvist instead of me. After deciding against Manchester United I would go to Birmingham first to speak with Aston Villa in the Belfry Hotel which is near their training ground. I would spend a few hours with Villa then on the same day we drove up the M6 to speak with Blackburn, Roy Hodgson was in charge at the time. Again, after a little while speaking with Rovers I would pop over to a place just outside of Leeds and while my agent spoke with Leeds United Chairman Peter Ridsdale, I spoke with the Leeds boss at the time George Graham. I was taken into a private room to talk football with George and although he impressed me, I found him to be Bruce Rioch but x10. He was saying things to me like, "I don't care if we've won the previous game 3-0, if I want to change things then I will. end of." I was sitting there thinking, if I've just played in a team that's won 3-0, I certainly want to be in the next starting eleven for sure mate! After the meeting with Leeds, I was driving back to Bolton thinking it was all too much to take in. Then my agent enlightened me that Leeds hadn't even put a bid in yet, they were holding off to see how much Villa, Blackburn and United were putting their bids in for first. All very understandable from a business sense on their part but that ruled Leeds out in my head. My agent dropped me off and I went home to think about things. Then my agent called me around one hour later to give me the news that not only had Villa been back in touch, but now their bid was higher than any of the chasing pack. At the time the venerable John Gregory was the manager, so I was picked up again the very next morning to be taken back to Villa to pick the talks back up. As I was in Villa Park in the chairman Doug Ellis' office, I could see he was quite the eccentric character. Doug even took me out in his Rolls Royce with his reg plate of AV1 around the city of Birmingham. Doug did give me a lot of great advice on where I was going to live in the West Midlands even though at that point I hadn't even agreed to sign yet.

Looking back 20 odd years on, I just feel that maybe I was cajoled a little bit into going to Aston Villa. I hadn't even discussed it with my wife, yet Jo had already seen it on Sky Sports News that I'd already agreed terms and conditions. I was just a young lad of 24 at the time and it probably suited my agent far better than it did me and my situation at the time. In my own opinion perhaps, the agent may have been getting a better personal fee from Villa than he was at the other clubs that were in the running. Certainly, the events after I'd signed would suggest this was the case. I did feel that when dealing with Aston Villa in the second part of negotiations, it was 75% already a done deal in that summer and I signed a 5-year contract with the club that day in 1998.

Looking back at my five years in Bolton I must say it's littered with great memories. The club were brilliant, and the fans were even better. I just found the place a wonderful football workingmen's town and I have nothing but good to say about Bolton Wanderers.

One story I'll tell you on my time in Bolton was when our striker John McGinlay had won an award. John had won the Boddingtons Sports Personality a few times over the season so at the end of the season there was this awards ceremony. John, at that time, was our main man always scoring goals for fun, so he won this award at this plush swanky hotel in the middle of Manchester. I was at this award ceremony in my dicky-bow and suit. The main award that year was won by Eric Cantona of Manchester United, but John McGinlay did quite well that evening I remember that much. I went along in my little Fiesta XR2i, so I wasn't drinking but that meant I would be on taxi duties for a few of my teammates such as goalkeeper Aidan Davison, club captain Phil Brown and John McGinlay. Eric won his award that evening and was wearing Timberland boots, jeans, lumberjack shirt and still being as cool as a carrot when everybody else in the building was dressed like James Bond. Eric stood on the stage receiving his award and coming out with something incredibly cultured like only Eric Cantona could, probably something about the seagulls following a boat, I can't remember. My teammates are all boozing away and getting pretty tanked up. I don't know how this even came about but I was roped into going into the city centre of Manchester, no doubt I was the free chauffeur for evening, which I didn't mind so I agreed to go along. We headed off into the city and after I parked my car in the area of Deansgate we went off into a few bars. I'm on orange juice and the lads are on alcohol in the trebles. It began to get a little bit rowdy, but everybody was in fine spirits, literally. Aidan and Browny then, for some bizarre reason, started to have a little bit of a dig at each other. Something to do with goalkeepers should be on as much wages as the outfield players etc blah blah blah... It was all drink infused and it started to get a bit heated. Now I don't know if God above was pulling some strings but John McGinlay then went outside to make a phone call because he was eager to find out if he'd been called up by Craig Brown for Scotland. With John now outside it left me, Aidan and Browny in the bar when all of a sudden, Aidan picks a bar stool up and just throws it through the bar window. I'm talking about a trendy bar bang in the middle of a busy town centre full of people. Well, I was stood thinking this wasn't in the script at the beginning of the evening for me, I'm not even drinking. As soon as the window went through, I, at least, had the sense to get out of the bar as fast as I could back into Deansgate taking those two with me, and into a bar called 'Mulligans'. I try to tell them to behave, and I order three more drinks, I'm still on alcohol-free. I'm trying to take in what had just happened and was reflecting on the madness of it all when I see McGinlay outside still on his phone and still probably trying to find out if he'd got his Scotland cap, he was totally oblivious to what had happened. I look past McGinlay and I see flashing blue lights. Of course, it's the boys in blue and I'm not talking about Manchester City. I'm not sure if McGinlay had some kind of sixth sense but he must have twigged what had gone on, and that it was also his teammates at the centre of it all. John had the sense to think, fuck that! I'm not getting put in the old bill vans because whatever had happened, although he was out with us, it wasn't anything to do with him. John stays outside which is what saves him a nicking. The next thing I see is the manager of the bar with the broken window coming into Mulligans with a very large police officer. it didn't take a rocket scientist to know what was going to happen. Well, my world fell apart when I could lip-read what the bar manager was telling the police constable while pointing over to us, "IT WAS THEM THREE LADS THERE,

THEY'RE THE TROUBLE CAUSERS ALRIGHT!" Well, oh my God you know what's about to happen next don't you? Yes, that's right the three of us were put in the back of their plod wagons and we were taken to Bootle Street police station in Manchester. Well, I'd never been inside a police station in my life up until that point so I wasn't happy, especially as I hadn't done anything other than allow myself to be talked into being a taxi service for the evening. Anyway, there wasn't a great deal I could do about it by this point other than realise that in the plods eyes I was now an active criminal. Then the realisation came that they were the last of my worries, what was going to happen when big bad Bruce Rioch found out what had happened. The thought of Brucie flipping his lid over this scared me more than the police ever could. By the time we get into the custody cells it's around 10pm so then I realise that we're probably in there for the night. "Alan do ya wanna cup of tea" the sergeant said as he looked in my boudoir for the evening. Could I hell get to sleep that night, but obviously my buddies could because they were well oiled by that point, so it worked out well for them. Well to cut a long story short the manager of the bar whose window Aidan broke had already told the police he'd done it, the thing was Aidan was now asleep and we couldn't be let out of custody until he was awake, interviewed and sober enough to function properly. Well, I didn't sleep at all but I was relieved when the sergeant looked through the flap and said, "Alan ya mate's up (Aidan) and now he's doing sit-ups, press-ups and burpee jumps in his cell trying to work the ale off." I thought the nightmare was getting worse by the minute. I was relieved to be told not to worry and I would be getting out ASAP as Aidan was planning on putting his hands up which would put me and Browny in the clear. Eventually we get out, but by now it's a full twelve hours later around 10am and not far off reporting to training with Bolton, plus we were dressed up still like penguins. If only we had followed Eric's dress code that evening eh! Well, we didn't even have time to go home and get changed when he got out of the slammer because we'd have been late for training. Driving there I'm saying to Browny in the car, 'we need to tell the boss first', but he told me he'd go ballistic. I think we concluded that the three of us would train first then break the bad news when we'd trained well. In the training session I couldn't concentrate, and I had a shocker! Every time someone passed to me, I had flashes of me going to the guillotine/Bruce's managers office and I'd scuff it. I suppose my one saving grace when it came to getting the death penalty was that I wasn't drinking the night before, whereas Aidan and Browny were well hungover! After the training session had finished, I couldn't wait any longer and I didn't even wait for the other two, I wanted to be put out of my misery, so I bit the bullet by myself. 'KNOCK KNOCK' I knock on the boss's door and as I do I see my life flash before my eyes, I'm like a soon-to-be dead rabbit in the headlights but this rabbit needed necking so it would be quick and painless. 'Boss can I see you?' I said, as I walked into his office. "Yes son you can and close the door behind you" Bruce told me, then he said, in an almost sinister tone, "everything alright lad?" You know that tone you hear from your parents when you're not sure if they're trying to call your bluff or not, do they know what I've done or don't they? That kind of tone. I just gave him it straight and said, 'not really boss' but before I could murmur another word Bruce opened his draw and brought out a fresh copy of the Bolton Evening News with the headline of, 'BOLTON THUG PLAYERS' he already knew the full story and not only that but there were pictures of me and the other two in there for good measure. Luckily for John McGinlay there wasn't anything in about him but of course he wasn't involved in the crime because of his Scotland call-up phone call.

At this time, I was renting a small cottage in Redbridge just on the outskirts of Bolton on my own, but Bruce told me that I couldn't be left to my own devices any longer and I had to ring my dad because he wanted to meet him. At the time I wasn't even sure why he wanted to speak with my father but as you all know Bruce was a strict disciplinarian, he was making sure that this type of behaviour wasn't going to happen again. It did make me feel uncomfortable that Bruce demanded to see my old man, a bit like I'd done wrong at school, but I wasn't going to tell him that. At the time I was still only in my first season for Bolton, so I'll have been around 21, and sometimes young lads, however sensible they are, still needed guidance of some sort. Bruce spoke to my dad and it was decided that I had to move out of the cottage and be put into what he called, more suitable digs. Bruce made me live with a landlady named Carol and her daughter which was far more suitable for a young footballer on his own who had endless money in his pocket it was decided. Living with Carol and her family was like living back at my parents as I was getting fed every day and my clothes washed. That's what Bruce was like and although he was hard, it showed that he also had a heart.

Scott Green was another Bolton player who once had to do what Bruce told him. His crime was turning up for training in this Astra Convertible which may be deemed as a bit of a boy racers motor. Bruce made him sell it and use the money to get himself on the property ladder. "Never mind driving around in cars like that" were the words I remember Bruce telling him and that's the way the man was. He was as hard as they come but also fair.

Going back to me, Phil brown and Aidan Davison, Bruce fined us all one week's wages. Although I was the less guilty of the trio, he simply did not give a monkeys that I hadn't been drinking and that I was only guilty by association. My name was on the front page of that newspaper, and I'd brought great embarrassment to Bolton Wanderers Football Club.

I'll also never forget Bruce sent me away from the training ground one day when I'd been playing a 5 a side game on the astro turf. I had pulled out of a 50/50 block tackle with him, so he stopped the game, then told me off in front of the full squad then told me to do one for the day. "DON'T YOU DARE PULL OUT OF A 50/50 TACKLE WITH ANYBODY LAD, NOW IN YOU GO" and that was me off to shower. Looking back, I think I just pulled out with him because I was a young lad and he was an old bloke to me at that time, he'll have been then around the age that I am now I imagine but it didn't matter to Bruce. Bruce Rioch was a man's man like your Graeme Souness type of players, no nonsense. If it was anyone's birthday at Bolton, then he would make them buy all the pies and cakes for the day. I'm talking about being expected to buy around thirty of each for all the staff, even the cleaning ladies. I'll never forget one day it must have been someone's birthday, so Bruce was about to sit down with a cake, only unknown to him John McGinlay had put a bar of soap in this cake, then stuck the cover back on. Anyway, the gaffer sits down with a cup of tea and this cake and bites into the cake with the bar of soap in it. Back in that day the full team used to use bars of soap for their front, backs and God knows what else, these days it's all shower gel. Well Bruce takes a bite, and everybody scarpers from around him as he's shouting, "WHAT THE FUCKING HELL IS THAT"! Instantly the gaffer knew it was McGinlay as before Bolton they'd been together at Millwall, so he knew his craic and what he was all about. John could be a very funny man, always taking the piss doing some prank or another.

Whilst we're talking about Bolton craic, I must tell you all about painted toenail gate. I was in the house the night before a game when I decided to paint my toenails blue with ladies varnish. Well, the funny thing is the next day I scored an absolute 'worldie'. Now I don't know why but I'm really superstitious and always have been, I had routines like putting my left shin pad, sock and boot on first, always. Well because I scored with painted blue toenails, I kept doing it. Then as the weeks went by things were getting better, like I was getting assists and we were winning constantly. I think we ended up on a run of seven games unbeaten, something like that. It got to the point where the full Bolton Wanderers team started wearing nail polish too. The physios at Bolton were thinking, 'what the hell is going on here as we've got a full team of men wearing blue nail varnish'. You can just picture big 6ft 2 man mountain, tough as anything Gerry Taggart walking about with these painted toenails can't you! You could understand poncey wingers like me wearing it but on Gerry, it was rather comical I must say.

The Bolton dressing room was a proper good one for non-stop banter 24/7 which Bruce Rioch allowed because it built good team spirit and morale, it was only if you crossed the line, you would be dealt with, no matter if you were the best player in the world. Bruce's old man was a regimental sergeant-major in the Scots Guards and you could tell by being in Bruce's company just that tiny little bit.

JOHN McGINLAY

Bolton Teammate

"Alan Thompson was brought into Bolton around a year after I arrived. The story I heard was this young kid had recently had this horrific car crash and he was rebuilding his confidence. As soon as I saw Tommo in training, I could see right away the kid had quality. Not only did he have this special left peg, but he had a real appetite for the game. The young Thompson had the energy to be a box-to-box player who not only scored goals, but who created them also. The lad had the whole package.

In the Bolton dressing room, we gave Tommo the nickname, "Hooch" from the film Turner & Hooch. If you put a photo of that dog which was a Dogue De Bordeaux and a photo of Alan Thompson side by side you'd not know the difference."

CHAPTER 7

THE BIG MONEY MOVE ARRIVES

My Aston Villa career got off to a start playing at Goodison Park on August 15th, 1998. I didn't play particularly well and was brought off for Mark Draper late in the second half. It ended in a 0-0 draw against Everton.

My home debut at Villa Park was against Middlesbrough the following week which was more eventful. To be honest I couldn't have got a better opportunity when we won a penalty and I stepped up to the plate to face the Boro goalkeeper Mark Schwarzer. I was eager to impress in front of the Villa fans, so I was confidently thinking 'I'm going to bury this, show off and I'll run to the fans' but there was to be no celebrating, not yet anyway. I missed the penalty and I thought 'SHIT' this is looking really bad for my here. I'm Villa's new signing for the big fee of £4.8 million and I've missed a penalty at home, this definitely wasn't in the script, and I was dreading the fans shouting, "WHAT A WASTE OF MONEY".

Paul Gascoigne was playing for Boro at the time and even though he was on the opposite team, he was talking to me throughout the match because he could see the nightmare my home debut was turning into. "Just don't let it affect ya man keep ya head up" Gazza was telling me. That just shows the class of the man because even though I was part of the rival team he was genuinely worried for me. I'm glad to say that things improved in the second half when we got a freekick on the left side of the pitch, this meant it wasn't really made for a "lefty" like myself, but I thought what the heck. I managed to salvage my pride by running up and sticking it in the top right-hand corner at the Holt End to the delight of the Villa faithful. I felt I'd redeemed myself a little after missing the earlier penalty and we went on to be 3-1 winners.

We got off to a decent start that season and I was beginning to feel really positive about the move now. That was until, early on in that season, our best player Dwight Yorke went to Manchester United in a £12 million pound record move. Having Yorkie there alongside the likes of Stan Collymore, Darius Vassell, Dion Dublin and Paul Merson in attack was one of the main reasons I signed for the club and if I had known he was about to be off I don't think I'd have signed. I played golf with Yorkie a few times at the Belfry and although he told me that United were in for him, he never told me that he wanted to go. Dwight was the type of striker I wanted to be providing the ammo for on the pitch, much like I would for Larsson a little later in my career and Yorkie leaving was a bit of a sledgehammer when it happened. I know we had some cracking young lads coming through at Villa such as Lee Hendrie, Gareth Barry and Jlloyd Samuel (God rest him) but it was still a blow to be losing Dwight.

I was the gaffer John Gregory's first signing when he came to Villa that year in 1998. I found John to be a little bit odd. Don't get me wrong he was very approachable but sometimes if you needed a chat with him, he'd be sitting in his managers office strumming his guitar as we talked football tactics which was quite off putting. We had some other issues further down the line in my Villa career, but I'll go into that later. I've seen him since I packed in football, it was in Marbella around 2013 and he came over for a chat. I was with my ex-wife at the time and as John came over, I said, 'hiya gaffer', then she went on one saying, "you're calling him gaffer after the way he treat you?" etc… Well, you can imagine the atmosphere was a bit frosty, but I tried to defuse the situation. Truth be told it was good of John to approach us after all these years but to be honest I don't think he treat me well towards the end of my time at Villa.

In this period for Aston Villa, we had some top-quality players in like your Benito Carbone, David Ginola and of course Paul Merson, who has since apparently been a bit vocal about me in one of his biographies. I was told Merse spoke on his time at Villa and mentioned me, it was along the lines of Villa being too big a club for Alan Thompson. Well Paul if you're reading this then I wouldn't mind having that discussion now because the reality of it was, I moved from Aston Villa to an even bigger club in Glasgow Celtic so I don't get your theory. Aston Villa is a huge club but Glasgow Celtic are far bigger and much more demanding in every aspect. Although Merse said that I don't think he actually thought that remark through. Something I will say about Paul Merson is that he was a top-quality player and a magician with a ball. Paul went on to have a highly successful career at some big clubs but in my opinion, as good as he was, he was very insecure in my opinion. I'm not talking about his well-publicised personal issues either, I'm talking from a football aspect. If anyone at Aston Villa couldn't find Merse in the dressing room, then the one other place you were likely to find him was in the manager's office looking for reassurance. Even though Paul was a top-class player, he needed telling he was. He was possibly in John Gregory's office more than the boss was.

One of the other strikers at Villa who I really did get on with was Stan Collymore. I rented a flat not far from Stan and he would show me around Birmingham, and where all the nice restaurants are, one being an Italian place called San Carlo on Temple Street. In actual fact Stan really went out of his way to make me feel welcome. I could never quite believe just how much food Stan could put away but he was a big, strapping, bright lad at 6ft 4, so he needed it. Stan was a giant of a man and an unbelievable talent on a football pitch. He was just one of those players who could turn it on and off when his mood chose. On Stan Collymore's day he was totally unplayable, then when he wasn't playing you may as well have been playing with ten men from the start.

Gareth Southgate, the club captain, was another really nice lad who went above and beyond to welcome me to the club. Whilst playing on the pitch with Gareth I found him to be a real leader and a superb talker on and off the field. I wouldn't have said Gareth was a great centre half in the Rio Ferdinand, Sol Campbell or John Terry bracket but what Gareth did well was he'd put himself in places bravely and happily take one for the team so to speak. Whether that was a red card to stop a goal opportunity or sticking his head in somewhere it would hurt.

One man I mentioned earlier was the very glamourous French man David Ginola and whilst I'm talking about my old Lions teammates then he just has to have a mention. John Gregory signed David at the age of 33 and even though he may have been a little older than what was considered as being in your prime, I had heard just how good he was from Watto and Clarkie at Newcastle. David most certainly had a presence about him when he walked in the dressing room. It wasn't only how handsome he was, but he was incredibly well dressed at all times. Sometimes I would stare at his hair in hope he would give me some free L'Oréal shampoo. Wherever he was David would always make a point of coming over and shaking everyone's hand, he was just so friendly. He was also one big, incredibly powerful lad and ripped like a Greek god. I ended up rooming with him and I used to watch in amazement just how well he did everything, from folding his bedcovers to placing his clothes down when he stripped off. I would just throw my clothes on a peg Geordie style, but everything Ginola done was done with class, flair and precision. Even silly little things like putting his socks inside his trainers meticulously. The fella was just a great guy and Watto and I often socialised with him. David often enjoyed a cigarette, which you wouldn't imagine to look at him. I would see David walking around full of muscles in his designer underwear, no hair on his body, he obviously waxed, and his massive quads. The first time I saw him in the Villa dressing room in all his perfection I thought, if he takes his boxer shorts off and he's got a great big tadger then there's not a God. Thankfully when he took them off, my faith was restored and I jumped up in the middle of the dressing room like, 'YEEESSSSS' and all the lads are laughing their heads off. Every single Aston Villa player there knew why I'd celebrated without even explaining why because they were all thinking the same as me. It was great football dressing room banter, but also a nod that the rest of the male species had a chance after all!

One of my memories of being at Villa was at the turn of the millennium, New Year's Eve. Myself, Jo, Watto and his ex-wife Victoria all decide to go to a restaurant in Bolton to see the New Year in. At this time Watto is playing at Villa with me. This eatery back in Bolton was called Yu and U and it was the most amazing place you could find; Peter Reid and big Sam Allardyce would eat in there often. The place was ran by a lovely family, who are sadly no longer there now but I loved it. It was just a really popular place and worth going to, so that was why me and Watto wanted to drive the one hour and forty minutes' there to see the new year in and we'd then planned to stop in The Moat House in Bolton town centre. Me and Watto had decided to drive back early in the morning back to train with the Villa team and leave the girls to have a lie in. Watto and I probably had a bit more to drink than we should have done but it was the only time in this lifetime we were ever going to see a millennium in. So that's what we did, we saw the New Year in at Yu and U and got back to the hotel just after 1am. Around this time I'm thinking, if I go to bed now I'm not getting up in the morning and I'll miss training so what I do is ring a taxi which really pisses off Watto. Now, Steve Watson has been my best mate all my life, we've grown up together and now we're Aston Villa teammates. Not only are we Villa players but he even lives next door to me in a lovely new development in the area Alrewas, which was just outside Lichfield. When Steve Watson signed for Aston Villa just after me, he moved next door to myself which in hindsight maybe wasn't a good move. You could say we led each other astray to say the least. Not long after Watto signing, Steve Stone also signed for Villa another Geordie, so Birmingham had its own version of Geordie Shore for social gatherings. Anyway, the taxi turns up and Watto decided he wasn't going to let me get in it. It ended in a bit of a fracas to say the least and Watto then gives me a clip which pops my eye. I'm annoyed now so I'm definitely getting in this taxi by myself for the 90-mile drive to Alrewas. When I get home, I find my parents in the house sitting up as they were babysitting. My Dad asks, "What you doing home Alan and what have you done to your eye?" I give him some story to take the heat out of the situation and get my head down for training in the morning. The next morning, I make it to training on time but I'm sporting a black eye, there's no sign of Watto though. Training starts and it must have been around twenty minutes later that Watto turns up looking very rough indeed. John Gregory knows me and Steve Watson have been out together the night before and with my black eye and Watto's punctuality the boss thinks 'aye aye' (pardon the pun) what's going on with these two?' He knew something had happened, but he couldn't work out what. Anyway, as the training gets underway, I receive a pass, try to control it with one foot but the other goes over and I snap my ankle ligaments in my right foot on New Year's Day. Happy New Year Tommo or what! It was a 6-to-8-week injury which was horrific to sit out. It was so stupid to have even gone out the night before because essentially, I had brought this on myself. It was no way for a professional sportsman to live and it was a bad decision. More misery followed for my mate Watto as he was fined for being late to training. Not only that but me and Watto had to explain our childish schoolboy pugilistic behaviour to John Gregory who, as you can imagine, wasn't best impressed. I think the writing was on the wall for my Aston Villa playing career from then on as I would leave exactly eight months later. That was the beginning of the end.

That year we reached the F.A Cup final but I didn't even make the bench, we lost to Chelsea 1-0. We played my old club Bolton in the semi-finals which was also a tough one as I didn't even make the bench for Villa that day either. Although Sam Allardyce was now the manager of Bolton and Bruce Rioch was gone, most of my old teammates were still playing for Bolton that day which totally guttered me.

Talking about the F.A Cup final against Chelsea in the May of 2000, we trained and planned the team shape on the

Thursday, and I was in the team then. On the Friday I was still in the team, but John Gregory had me swap bibs with Ian Taylor which kind of let me know that it was now between me and "Tayls" for this one position. I actually didn't know I wasn't playing when the full squad went down to London and stayed in the team hotel. I had absolutely no clue until Jo, my wife at the time, rang me up on the Friday evening saying, "Alan you're not playing tomorrow, and Tayl's Mrs has just told me he's playing." All the WAG'S (wives and girlfriends) had got together, and Ian's wife had told mine that he was playing instead of me. Well as you can imagine it wasn't a nice way to find out and it probably explains a bit more about Jo's hostility for John Gregory when we saw him in Marbella all those years later. John Gregory named his team on that Saturday morning of the cup final after the team had a walk together after breakfast. I've got to be honest I was absolutely raging not to have even made the starting eleven at this point, so I go back to my hotel and smash the room up, which I'm not proud of, but emotions were running high. The physio Jim Walker and club captain Gareth Southgate then rush to my room to try and calm me down. Another thing I remember from John Gregory's team talk when he was giving out the starting eleven was him saying that he wouldn't be naming the substitutes until we arrived at Wembley Stadium. The reason the gaffer did that, in my opinion, was because he knew I was going to lose it when I found out that I didn't even make the substitutes bench. Well low and behold, when we arrive at the national ground he names the subs and me and Watto are not in. I was just like 'WOOOW', so I just went up to the Mezzanine Bar at Wembley with Watto and the families to sit and sulk like a kid who's not been picked for his school team. The funny thing is that when I was in there sulking and telling anyone who'd listen about my harsh treatment, I would see a guy in the same boat as me but for the opposing team. I didn't know it as yet but I was talking to Chris Sutton, who by now was so frozen out at Chelsea that he might as well have been in the North Pole, we would go on to become extremely familiar with each other over the next five years and cause havoc within the Celtic squad for years to come. At that time, I didn't really know "Sutty" but I got talking to him in the bar and we were trading each other's sad stories, anyone who overheard would have thought they were listening to an episode of Steve Wrights 'Our Tune'. I suppose we were giving each other a shoulder to cry on. At the time, in my opinion Gianluca Vialli just didn't fancy big "Sutty" and I'm not talking about it being because of his sense of humour or his dress sense which are both shocking, as I would go on to find out. Life, fate or God above in general has a funny way of moving the goal posts because from that day in May 2000 I didn't really know Chris Sutton, but we virtually became best pals/neighbours and were doing great things for Celtic only four months on from that conversation.

Another famous face I remember being there that day in the mezzanine Bar was Prince William, he was a big Villa fan. Some of the players kids who were there were running about high on E numbers and orange juice asking the Prince's bodyguards if he'd sign their match program. Of course, the Royal's aren't allowed to sign anything, but he was good enough to pose for photos with his Villa scarf on.

It's fair to say it wasn't a great day for me, and the big after party which was planned in the plush hotel was all very depressing. I thought about giving the gaffer both barrels true Geordie style, but I thought I was in enough trouble for smashing my room up, plus Villa didn't win the F.A Cup so I kept my mouth shut this time, for once!

At that point I had three years left of a five-year contract and it wasn't IF I was going it was when and where! I came for big money, and I knew that Aston Villa weren't going to let me go for free, it was a matter of who was willing to take a chance on me, as temperamental as I was. I knew by now that my big money move to Aston Villa wouldn't be all it was cracked up to be. As I said the writing was on the wall and I was out of the club from that day and on my way, only months later, to the no mean city of Glasgow. My Knight in shining armour was a bespectacled eccentric Northern Irishman who spoke at speed, had funny ways and mannerisms about him and whom I would get to know very well over the next five years.

STAN COLLYMORE

Ex-Aston Villa Teammate

"The first time I came across Alan Thompson was when he was at Bolton Wanderers. I played against him for Nottingham Forest in the Championship at Burnden Park. Back then Bolton had an excellent team and I remember watching Tommo and thinking, 'fucking hell what a left foot he's got', although he was a pain in the arse with his mouth on the pitch. That was the day I became aware of this wonderful midfielder by the name of Alan Thompson.

When Tommo came to Aston Villa, which is the club I've supported from being a boy, we used to mix a lot off the pitch and would go for food. Him and I would often go to San Carlo in Birmingham which is a really posh place for food. Myself, Tommo and Mark Bosnich started this kind of takeout food dash at the place which was bizarre because it was like the poshest restaurant in the city and wasn't really for pulling in like you'd pick a McDonald's up. Me and Tommo kinda started this posh delivery service at the place like today has 'Just Eat'. I suppose it's the equivalent of driving past Gordon Ramsey's top place in London and asking for a quick takeaway because we couldn't be arsed sitting in (laughs).

Tommo was always very gracious and funny to be around. Him and Steve Watson, who was another Geordie at the club, used to seem to bounce off each other. On the pitch his set pieces were amazing, and people know I have a big soft spot for Celtic so watching Tommo going up there when he left Villa to join my old teammate Neil Lennon and my former gaffer Martin O'Neill was great to see. In terms of Alan Thompson's left foot in open play he didn't have to beat a man to whip a ball round and get it into the box. Tommo could strike the ball as good as anyone I've played with and that includes Stuart Pearce, Robbie Fowler, John Barnes and Bryan Roy."

BRUCE RIOCH

Bolton Wanders Manager 1992–1995

"I first heard of Alan Thompson from my first team assistant Colin Todd. Toddy was my scout in the Northeast because he lived in Chester-Le-Street so it was part of his job to look for the North's up and coming talent. I can remember one day Toddy came in and told me he'd been at a game the day before and seen this young lad Alan Thompson, and he liked him. I asked Toddy to tell me more. Toddy said Thompson was a left sider with a great left foot. He also said he was 6ft tall with good stance and he was only young. I asked when this lad was due to play next and he said next week so I told Toddy to go and have another look at him. After the next game Toddy came back and said to me that we needed to move sharpish as this lad was going to be a player with a bright future. I always knew to put my trust in Toddy because he had a good eye for talent when he saw it. The next thing I did was get on the phone to the Newcastle boss Kevin Keegan to try and get a deal sorted, for as cheap as possible. In the end we paid £250,000, we did try to get him cheaper with a sell-on, but Kevin said it was that price without a sell-on and the deal was done.

During the first week that we had Alan Thompson in training at Bolton I was blown away by him. In fact, I told my chairman Gordon Hargreaves that this young lad Thompson who we'd just signed for £250,000, we'd eventually get £2.5 million for when the time came to sell him on. He said, 'really'? I said, "of course, this kids that good." It turns out I was actually wrong because Bolton sold him for £4.75 million!!! He came into the Bolton team not only at the right time for us, but also for him.

Looking back on the transfer the one thing Kevin Keegan did warn me of beforehand was about Alan's throwing up before games. Kevin told me he felt he needed to make me aware of this situation. Kevin told me that before every single game Alan would go into the toilet and vomit. Kevin said it must be due to nerves before games which I took on board. Then I told him I'd read about Stanley Matthews doing exactly the same, and he wasn't bad was he?! I pulled Tommo to one side one day when he was finished chucking up, to reassure him that his vomiting didn't worry me because the great Stanley Matthews used to do it so he would be fine.

Alan Thompson went on to become one of the main figures in my Bolton Wanderers side. My midfield consisted of David Lee, Jason MacAteer, Tony Kelly and Alan Thompson. I had John McGinlay up front with usually Andy Walker or Owen Coyle alongside him and trust me, my whole team could run. They could all play football but they could also run any team into the ground on fitness. For me, my players needed two ingredients, one being work rate and two, enthusiasm. I'm going to quote the great Bill Shankly on something he said when I was speaking to him one day. At the time I was at Everton as a player, but Bill would often come into our dressing room and I was forever picking his brains with questions. One day in 1976 I asked Bill what else he looked for in a player apart from talent? Bill looked at me and replied, "Bruce son, they have to be fit, not just fit so they can run and cover the ground, but fit and clear from injuries." He then said, "I don't sign players who constantly get calf, groin and hamstring injuries because it disrupts my team's continuity." When I had David Lee, Jason MacAteer and

Alan Thompson they were always free from players niggling injuries. Sometimes players get serious injuries, and you can't help that but it's the constant niggles that ruin a player, Tommo was never one of them.

Alan's personality was very loud. I'd often hear him before I'd see him, in fact I had to have a word with him once. Our captain Phil Brown came to me one day and said, "gaffer you've got to tell Tommo to stop coming around my house. He keeps coming around my house." I had to pull Alan to one side and say, Tommo, you've got to leave our captain alone." Tommo didn't mean any harm but he just had so much energy and he was on his own, so he needed someone to talk to and poor Phil was his target. Most days I could hear Tommo coming before he got to my office, the guy was just total noise on legs, but his enthusiasm and buoyancy was infectious.

The first move as a footballer is always the hardest for any player so moving from Newcastle, which was his home, to Bolton was big. You've got to integrate into a whole new environment which he did so well. At the time we had some pretty big characters in the Bolton dressing room, it was always full of banter/fun which meant you needed good humour to be part of the team. In my team I feel we had the right balance between a time for banter and a time for work and Alan quickly picked that up.

I was just looking at Alan Thompson's career stats recently and what he did overall for Bolton Wanderers was fantastic. Absolutely fantastic! When I signed him, he was only 19 but he went on to have such a bloody fabulous career and I'm so proud to have been a part of it. When you start out at the very beginning of your football career, you'd hope to have the career Alan Thompson had."

CHAPTER 8

WELCOME TO GLASGOW

The first time I would hear of Glasgow Celtic's interest in signing me was at the back end of August 2000. In fact, it was the day before the famous 6-2 victory for Celtic over Rangers. Celtic had got in touch with my agent to say that Martin O'Neill had enquired about my availability. The day that Celtic beat Rangers in that 6-2 game Villa played Chelsea at Villa Park and I wasn't even in the squad. I remember watching that Old Firm Derby with great interest now I knew that Celtic could be interested in signing me. The problem was Aston Villa v Chelsea and Celtic v Rangers were both early kick offs so they were on at the same time. I don't mind saying at that point I had no interest in watching the Villa game, so I decided to sit and watch the Sky Sports coverage of the Old Firm Derby because I was all but out the door at Villa, even if I didn't end up at Celtic it was sure to be a good game. As I sat watching the Celtic game, it added a touch more excitement to it all knowing that I could possibly be going up to Glasgow quite soon.

In the days after that game, I remember being at Gareth Southgate's house for his 30th birthday but I couldn't drink because I was making plans to go up to Glasgow with my agent. It turns out myself and my agent flew up to Glasgow from Manchester Airport in a little three-seater plane. Me, my agent, the pilot of course and a little flask of coffee, with biscuits and crisps, like a proper little outing. I thought it wouldn't take long to get up to Glasgow, but it turns out it would have been quicker driving by the time we got there.

When we got to the city that was when I first met Martin O'Neill and the then Contracts Director Jim Hone. To be honest there wasn't much negotiating done, it was more about the main man himself Martin filling me about the club. He didn't need to sell the club to me, and he certainly didn't need to sell himself because I was already sold. Martin sat and told me about the previous season under John Barnes and now what visions he had for the club with his trusty sidekicks Steve Walford and John Robertson. Talking about the previous season, Martin was referring to just how many points Celtic finished behind a very good Rangers side. He told me his plan was to just stay within reach and get as close to their oldest rivals as they could.

Talking to Martin in that September of 2000, I don't think he himself even envisaged just how spectacularly Celtic would romp home in the league and that they would go on to complete the treble in his very first year in Glasgow.

Martin took me around the ground and showed me places like the director's box. Just seeing the whole of Celtic Park in the dark with the emergency lights on just blew me away. As I was looking around the ground in its stark silence, I started to think of watching the 6-2 game and how the whole stadium was bouncing. I knew from that moment that I wanted to be part of whatever Martin had in his plans. I told Martin to show me where to sign and my fee was agreed with Aston Villa for £2.75million. Celtic were good and just took me on the same wages that I was on at Villa on a five year deal. After signing for the club Martin took me into Glasgow City Centre to a Chinese restaurant called Amber Regent. As I sat there with my agent, Jim Hone and Martin, I noticed how the gaffer holds court and has this aura about him. As he was speaking, I was just sat there thinking, 'I can't wait to start working for this fella', particularly after what I'd just come from with John Gregory at Villa. Listening to Martin that day, he was a breath of fresh air to me. When we'd finished up, I stopped in a Glasgow hotel thinking about how I couldn't wait to turn up at training tomorrow for Glasgow Celtic and meet all the players. Of course, I already knew Stubbsy from my time at Bolton and fellow Geordie Tommy Johnson. In fact, I'd spoken to both quite recently to get advice when I heard that a possible move to Celtic was on the cards. I believe Martin had made the biggest statement to prove just how bold his plans were in becoming the number one team in Glasgow by taking big Chris Sutton from Chelsea to Celtic for £6 million. Martin, by that point, hadn't signed his old comrade Neil Lennon who he was with at Leicester, but he did tell me that was on the cards, although it would take a few months from then. Lenny came in early December for a fee of £5.75million. Martin told me he would also be going for big John Hartson at some point and that he would be letting a lot of players go, he wanted to freshen it up at Celtic, which is exactly what he did.

One of the players that was already there who I didn't know a great deal about was a certain Henrik Larsson. Henrik was just coming back from injury around this time and Martin was telling me just how good this Swede with magnificent dreadlocks was. He also told me about this young kid from Bulgaria named Stiliyan Petrov who I'd never heard off at that point. Of course, he would go on to become an absolute star in the Martin O'Neill teams for many years. At the time Paul Lambert was also there so I knew there was a great mix of youth and experience in this potentially great Celtic side. I knew with Martin's plans we were only going to go from strength to strength which is exactly what happened.

I was unveiled to the press at Celtic Park with fellow new boy the Frenchman Didier Agathe, in early September. I have to admit, although I knew that Glasgow Celtic was a massive club, I was taken aback at just how huge the passion for football is in the city of Glasgow. I'd seen Celtic in Testimonials like Jimmy Phillips' at The Reebok Stadium in 1998 so I knew their following was big but I didn't consider that it's literally some people's lives up there. To be fair it isn't just Celtic it's Rangers also. The good people of Glasgow are fanatical about their clubs. Martin spoke about the demands when I arrived and at the time, I thought I understood because I'd played at big clubs such as Newcastle United and Aston Villa but at Celtic it's another level. In Glasgow if you don't win then you're nothing. The demand on the players to not only win but to play well is huge and I learnt this very quickly after arriving at Parkhead. At times in football, you can win and you might not play particularly well and get away with it at other clubs, in Glasgow you're not allowed this. Sometimes the big clubs in England such as Arsenal, Manchester United or Liverpool scrape by with a scruffy 1-0 win and as long as they get the win it's ok. That will never be the case in Glasgow for either club. There were times we didn't play well and even though Henrik, Sutty or big John would bail us out, we would have to face the flack.

Coming into the Celtic side for Martin, I knew he liked me as a player because he'd tried to sign me for Leicester City a few years earlier. I knew it wasn't going to be like when Sir Alex Ferguson rang me with a mind to me just being a backup player if Ryan Giggs wasn't playing for whatever reason. I knew it wasn't going to be easy at Celtic but if I was playing well, I had a good shout at being in the team. Saying that, when I watched that 6-2 game Bobby Petta tore Fernando Rickson to shreds and he had to be substituted at half-time because of the mauling he received. Bobby Petta, although he played in my position, was a different player altogether. Bobby was electric, skilful and got to the by-line whereas I was more of a pass-move get the ball out from my feet and put quality into the box. I liked to manoeuvre the ball around, like players such as David Beckham, he was so good at that. Beckham never really dropped his shoulder, beat three players then did a fancy stepover like Ronaldo, and I was the same but on the left.

The one thing I must say, from that very first season of 2000/01 I developed a great understanding with Chris Sutton and Henrik Larsson. It wasn't even something we even worked on at Barrowfield training sessions. In training we rarely ever played on full size pitches. Martin O'Neill would make us play 8 v 8 on small pitches which makes you learn quicker about which of your teammates can do what. Myself, Sutty and Henrik created this bond on the pitch which lasted for the next four years until Henrik left for Barcelona. Often Henrik would make a run in one direction, but I knew he'd make a turn, then end up going in a totally different direction so I'd spin it quickly for him with accuracy. I just instinctively knew where Henrik wanted it down the side, above or far over. I was the same with Sutty and them two, Sutton and Larsson, had a great understanding between them, although I'd like to think my vision contributed to their games. I have to say that supplying those two made my job easier also.

My first Old Firm game was November 2000 which wasn't so memorable. In fact, we got completely mullered 5-1 at Ibrox, however it was only 2-1 when I was shown the red card in the 64th minute for a tackle on Barry Ferguson.

Credit to Dick Advocaat's team, who were well up for this, because they were still hurting from the mauling they'd received three months earlier at Parkhead in the 6-2 game. Facing Rangers that day in my first Old Firm game I was playing against some top-quality players such as Konterman, Ferguson, de Boer, Albertz, Numan, Mols and Amoruso. Rangers had spent big money on this team because they knew with Martin O'Neill, they were going to face a serious test, more so than the one John Barnes put up the year before. Before the game I was really looking forward to my time playing at Ibrox because I'd heard so much about it from the other boys. I'd researched the great history and tradition in this world famous fixture. As soon as I arrived in Govan and got off the team bus, I knew all eyes would be on me and my every move would be watched. The thing is when the opposing team arrive at Ibrox the home fans are on top of you all crowding around you and the hatred is real let me tell you. The Rangers fans might have thought they were intimidating me by shouting the things they did at me, but it used to do the opposite. It actually spurred me on more to go out there and make my mark in the game which I usually did, whether it was scoring goals against them or getting the early bath. Often players put their Sony headphones on when getting off at a rival ground, but I used to like taking it all in, whatever the response was. I embraced it because when there was a few hundred outside the front gates at Ibrox I knew once inside, there was going to be 50,000 of them all in red, white and blue baying for my blood and anyone else's who was in a green & white shirt. Playing on the pitch at Ibrox didn't have any negative effect on me, although many of you may be reading this thinking, 'well, how can you say that Tommo when you received three reds there through lack of discipline?!'

Any away player at Ibrox taking corners learns very quickly just how hostile the crowd is let me tell you. Getting sent off there, which I was three times, I had 50,000 Gers fans laughing at me whilst shouting, "CHEERIO CHEERIO" and much more industrial Glaswegian language than that, you won't be surprised to hear. Getting sent off there and Martin O'Neill looking at the ground as I walked past because he was far too disgusted to even look at me wasn't at all nice. Afterwards in the dressing room I was sitting there by myself in my very first Old Firm Derby thinking, 'god Tommo what have you done!' I thought my Celtic career was over before it had even started. I knew I'd let everyone down from the fans, players, club and Martin, who, by the way, was not shy of giving me his opinion when he clapped eyes on me after the game. Martin came in, he was very quiet however, his eyes were taking me to bits and only in his own good time did he unleash his disapproval on me. "WHAT WERE YOU THINKING TOMMO YOU COWARD?" along with "DIDN'T YOU EVEN WANT TO BE OUT THERE?" I specifically remember those two but there were some other hurtful remarks he lashed out at me with. I retaliated back verbally and as I was standing my ground it was making Martin angrier. He accused me of being a bottle job and I was screaming that I just mis-timed a tackle. John Robertson, Martin's assistant was telling me to shut up and take my grilling like a man. Martin then came really close into my personal space with clenched fists and I was starting to think he was actually going to put one on me as he was blowing fire! Looking back now John was right, I should have just shut my mouth and took my medicine. At the end of the day, it was me who was in the wrong but when he called me a coward it stung and I felt like I had to fight my corner.

If walking into Ibrox didn't bother me then walking back out after being sent off in the game certainly did! Of course, the crowd were laughing at me in their hundreds and it was humiliating. I'll never forget being sat in my rented house in Newton Mearns after my first Old Firm match having a takeaway. Sat there that depressing evening I said to the wife, 'I don't think we should buy a house in Glasgow because I may be done here already! Low and behold I got my head down, cracked on and got on with it. I served my suspension and Martin pulled me into his office with two options. He could either fine me one week's wages or I could nip out to a cashpoint and I could get him some cash. I was told if I chose the latter the money would then be given to the captain of the club and then he'd dish it out among ground staff, tea ladies, cleaners and other Celtic FC workers. I did exactly that and I went to the bank to draw out £5000 to give to Tom Boyd. Boydie then walked around Celtic Park like Santa Claus giving away all this money to anyone who deserved it for working for the club. My loss was their gain and rightfully so. That's the kind of thing Martin O'Neill did, he looked after everyone, no matter who they were or what their job within the club. That's why, when he would eventually leave in 2005 to look after his sick wife Geraldine, everyone at the club was heartbroken.

The next time we faced Rangers was at Celtic Park in February 2001. I'm on my best behaviour considering the last time and we came out 1-0 winners, and I scored the winning goal, a tap in with my left foot but it didn't matter. I knew I needed to make it up to a lot of people including Martin. The pressure was on me, and it was a huge relief winning that game and putting a proper shift in like I did.

I won my first trophy for Celtic the month after at Hampden in a 3-0 victory over Kilmarnock. Henrik scored all three goals. Winning that first trophy gave everyone a lift, especially after the dreadful season the year before when they were getting put out of cups by Inverness Caley Thistle which eventually then cost John Barnes his job. Who can forget those iconic headlines in the Scottish Sun which read, 'SUPER CALEY GO BALLISTIC CELTIC ARE ATROCIOUS'. When we got our first cup win we were top of the league and still in the Scottish Cup and the treble was in sight. I mean, to go on and win the league by 15 points when only the season before Celtic lost it by 21 is some ground made up in a phenomenally speedy turnaround. Celtic FC is about winning trophies and making the fans happy and I understood this fully after my first season.

When I went into the trophy room at Celtic Park for the first time the club's great history screams out at you. Since the year 1888 this club's been built on success. The first Celtic living legend I met when I arrived at Celtic was Tommy Burns, God rest him. Martin kept him around the first team, and I took a real shining to Tommy and his crazy antics. I'd heard a lot of fabulous things about Tommy from his spell at Newcastle, so I knew he knew the game inside out. Tommy Burns was a super guy with a wacky aura about him and if you'd have cut him in half he'd have bled green & white. Tommy, in his playing days was my type of player and a lefty as well. Tommy was intelligent and would often stop to tell me he was better looking than me. Not only was he such a fit man for his age but he was also incredibly witty, with the most amazing sense of humour you could ever come across. I'll never forget once we were drawing at half-time in a pretty dismal performance when Tommy gave an out of this world speech for Martin. As Tommy was talking, I was thinking, 'wow what a great thing to say to a bunch of players'. He asked us all who was going to be the brave one out of all of us to step up and make a difference in front of 60,000 fans? Tommy kept it simple, never ranted or raved but it was to the point. Some of Tommy's footballing knowledge has stayed with me and I was able to use it in my coaching career. He'd love to cheer players up and say things which would really make you think like, 'don't let the game pass you by' which was powerful and thought provoking when you were on that pitch.

As my time went on as a Celtic player Lisbon Lion Bertie Auld would often pop over to me to give me positive words of encouragement. I used to love going to have a cup of tea with another Lisbon Lion and kitman John Clark. Being at Celtic was like being at one big happy family and I used to love nothing more than sitting there listening to the players from yesteryear telling their stories. Meeting Jimmy Johnstone, Billy McNeill, Jim Craig and Bobby Lennox was surreal. I got to become friends with Bobby because I used to go down the coast to play golf at Western Gales, Irvine and him and Stevie Chalmers would often be there. Sometimes I would have to pinch myself and think, 'I'm playing golf with guys who've won the European Cup in 1967'. Bobby and Stevie, I played with often and I found them to be very humble considering these were living legends to millions of supporters around the world. Danny McGrain was another who I spent a bit of time around as we shared a desk and he's one hell of a nice man too.

By beating Hibernian at Hampden Park 3-0 we completed the treble in that first season. Jackie McNamara opened the scoring then Henrik got a brace which completed the treble in truly a dream come true first season for me. Martin O'Neill's plan back at the start was to just try and win the title so to do a clean sweep of the domestic cups, it couldn't have got any better. Don't forget there were a lot of new players coming in that season like myself,

Chris Sutton, Neil Lennon, Joos Valgaeren, Didier Agathe and big Rab Douglas and many going out such as Mark Viduka, Marc Rieper, Eyal Berkovic, Regi Blinker and Vidar Riseth it was a big task. We just all seemed to bond so quickly when we were on the training ground with Martin, Wally and Robbo. What you've got to remember is in that first season we weren't up against a Micky Mouse Rangers team; it was a team full of international quality who were on big money. Today in 2021 I would have to say that that first season and the way it went was the greatest achievement of my whole career.

JACKIE McNAMARA (The Toy)

Celtic Teammate

"I knew of Alan Thompson before he came to Celtic from him playing down in England. I got to know him as a person when he came in from Aston Villa and he was a different class from day one.

In the dressing room he was definitely close to Sutty, he was always on Chris Sutton's coattails getting up to things. One memory I have of Tommo was when we were over in America for the winter break. Martin O'Neill took a few of us to play golf. This was the day before we had a bounce game against Tampa Bay. To cut a long story short, after we played golf a few of us had a few beers but Tommo was well oiled shall we say. The next day everyone in the squad was due to play a wee bit of the game but because Martin found out that Tommo had been a bit too naughty on the beers, he made him play the full 90 minutes. We were all on the side laughing at Tommo playing hungover and watching him struggle. It was amazing that even thought he was a bit worse for wear, Tommo then scored an absolute "worldie" with his right foot which was unbelievable for him. After he scored, he ran to the dugout were we were all standing and shouted, "GET US A BUD LIGHT"! The next day in training Martin made him do even more rigorous workouts for good measure.

CHAPTER 9

HAIL HAIL

My second year in Glasgow was the season 2001/02 and we would be defending our SPL title. Our main focus was to retain that title because by now Alex McLeish was having his first full season and had brought in some real quality players such as Claudio Caniggia, Michael Ball, Shota Arveladze, Sebastian Rozental and Russell Latapy. We knew by their activity in the transfer market that they meant business and would be coming after us. We set out to win the league that year back to back and that is exactly what we did but by an even bigger margin than the year before with 18 points, so it was mission accomplished. Rangers, that season were a good side, and they went on to win the League Cup beating Ayr United in the final and of course us 3-2 in the Scottish Cup Final.

Losing to Rangers in early May at the end of that season was a horrible way to end the season. Especially painful was the way we lost, a last minute winner by my old mate Peter Lovenkrands, it was heart breaking. Despite our unsuccessful attempts in the cups, we'd well and truly put down our marker to say that we were the number one force in Scottish football and Rangers were now well and truly in our shadow.

There was a great bond and spirit in our team that season. We weren't only teammates; we were the best of friends off the field also. My best mate at the club at the time was Chris Sutton but we were all a close-knit bunch.

Me and Sutty being neighbours travelled to training together. The night before games we'd all sit together playing cards and have a coffee together. Usually someone was getting the mick taken out of them and we'd all be laughing. Lads such as Lenny, Henrik, Sutty, Jackie Mac, Lambo, big John, Stan, John Robertson and Steve Walford. Wally liked a brandy or two sitting with us enjoying our banter.

I did score a high number of goals every season at Celtic for Martin, and I was happy with my game. Me and Didier Agathe would play on the wings or as we would call it, 'the graveyard shift". You had to be fit to do the graveyard shift and that's one area that my game improved in when I went to play for Martin O'Neill. I was on the left and we had 'Roadrunner' aka Didier on the other channel. Didier would all but literally 'MEEP MEEP' when he was running because he was absolutely lightening quick. The guy was just a phenomenal specimen he really was. He was built like a middleweight boxer; he was lean and had powerful legs so me and him worked the channel well with each other. As good as Didier was, he did get a lot of injuries because of the style of his game. Martin knew at times Didier would be out for spells, so he had other players such as Momo Sylla to fill the gap. Often if Agathe was out he would go to the medical team at Celtic and say, "can you pull a few strings because I want him for such and such game" then after the game he'd rest him again. Didier, as much as he was injured, he was like Henrik Larsson. What I mean was if I'd been out for four weeks then I'd need a game or two to get up to speed, Agathe could come back into a big game and be like he was before he was injured. Larsson and Agathe were naturally remarkable athletes.

The one thing about that Celtic side was that we were all super fit. At times we'd all stay back and train after training. Me, Sutty, Stan, Lenny would often go to Jim Henry or Kenny McMillan the sports science man and we'd ask them for extra work. That normally doesn't happen in football so that just shows you the desire we all had. The difference between me and Didier Agathe was Didier was naturally fit, whereas I had to work at it. I did love playing left on the wing for Celtic and usually big Joos Valgaeren was playing behind me and that guy could cover ground for fun. The man was just an absolute gazelle, and he didn't get enough credit at the club in my opinion. Joos was a great lad and, although very quiet around the dressing room, you knew on the pitch he had your back.

One player I've got to talk about from that time is Lubomir Moravcik. That season was Lubo's last at the club, as at the end of that season he would be 37. Lubo was probably one of the worst trainers I ever played with in my whole career, he liked the odd cigarette also. You'd be surprised at how many football players like the odd ciggie whilst playing. When we used to play 8 v 8 Lubo would go and play at the back because it was easier but as time went on you realised that this guy didn't have a weak foot! The fella was so talented even though he looked so nonchalant. He was the same as Eric Cantona in the aspect that they never looked in a hurry. You find that with all class players that they're never in a hurry. Matt Le Tissier was the same and so was Lubo. The good thing about having a player like that in your team was that it rubbed off on everyone around you. When we all saw just how relaxed Lubo was at Celtic Park playing Rangers in front of 60,000 fans it made us relaxed. If Zinedine Zidane said Lubomir Moravcik was the best player he'd ever played with then that tells you something doesn't it! To be quite honest, I knew nothing of Lubo when I arrived. At that time Lubo was 35, but I used to look at him and think, Jesus Christ you can only imagine the price tag on him if he was ten years younger! That guy had talent that was out of this world and to think he only cost £300,000 when his fellow Slovak Dr Jozef Venglos (R.I.P) brought him over here at the back end of 1998. He scored a brace in his Old Firm debut and the Celtic faithful just fell in love with him from that moment on. He was another like Martin O'Neill who had this aura about him, and he was quality on and off the pitch. Although the guy was only at Celtic for four years, he's cemented himself as a true legend of the club at the very top.

One of the most staggering things from that 2001/02 season was going out of the Champions League on nine points. We had Porto, Juventus and Rosenberg in our group, and we beat them all at home but still failed to even get second place which I don't think will happen again, Porto and Juve went through. At the start of the season, we had to beat a good Ajax team to even make it to the group stages despite many not giving us a chance. Didier scored a blinder over there when he just ran forever and slotted it in the far corner to make us qualify for the first time ever in the group stages. The standout game in that group was on Halloween night at Celtic Park and was against the Italians Juve. We'd been so unlucky to have been cheated out of a point in the last minute when Amaruso dived for a penalty in the first game over in Italy. Of course, Martin's iconic interview happens after the game which he describes as, "extraordinary… extraordinary". I actually never played in the 4-3 game at Parkhead when big Sutty scored a total "worldie" against the Italians. To go out of the Champions League with nine points sent a really negative vibe around the dressing room and at that time there was no drop down into the UEFA Cup.

One of the biggest talking points of 2002 was the infamous Christmas party in my home city of Newcastle.

On the way down on the Parks of Hamilton team bus on the M74 we could see the Rangers bus in front of us. Rangers use the same bus company and the blues were also heading to Newcastle. Anyway, as we were both driving down the motorway for some time their bus goes past the A69 to get to Newcastle. I remember it like it was yesterday so well. The reason that Rangers did a U-turn when they were supposed to be going to the same city as us, well nobody knew, that was until Jackie McNamara rings up Neil McCann on their bus and asks what the craic is. Jackie and Terry (Neil's nickname from the old series Minder) are good pals. He's a good lad is Neil McCann I got to know him quite well when I did my UEFA pro licence with him, Lenny and Sutty as our careers were winding down. "We've changed our minds and we're going to Liverpool" Terry McCann tells Jackie Mac. It came out that the reason for this change of heart was because the Gers team had been tipped off that there was going to be hordes of Scottish press in Newcastle so they have very sensibly changed their minds at the last minute. At least this gave us the heads up that there was going to be lots of reporters sniffing around the Toon. "Lads I know it's a Christmas party, but we've now got to be on our best behaviour" was the word from the club captain Paul Lambert to us all before we got off the bus. So, we got off the bus, put our gear into the hotel and every single member of Celtic Football Club ventured into the city of Newcastle on the lash. Martin let us stay over for one night and he probably wishes he hadn't let us go at all after how it all unravelled. With me knowing the city like the back of my hand I sorted out the route. We get a nice bite to eat and then head off around the hectic bars of the West End of Newcastle. My dad comes along for the evening with my cousin David Longstaff, a lot of people know the name Longstaff because his sons Matty and

Shaun are now playing for Newcastle. My cousin David actually didn't do too badly either as he played for the Great Britain ice hockey team over one hundred times. I would often be at Whitley Bay ice rink growing up watching him play. My dad and David knew all of the lads at Celtic anyway, so nobody minded that the two tagged along for the evening.

I'd had a few beers on the bus on the way down and this caught up with me as the evening went on. My old man ended up putting me to bed in the Copthorne Hotel on the Quayside which turned out to be a stroke of luck, or I'd have gone down on the ship with the rest of them. I had an early night and woke up rough as Tarzan's feet, and only then did I discover what had occurred in Celtic's own version of Bhoys behaving badly. Chris Sutton knocks on my hotel room door and says, "ere Tommo ya not gonna believe what went on last night!" I asked him what happened, and he said, "four of the lads got locked up last night and it's all kicked off." I was told then big Rab Douglas had thrown this cameraman's recorder into the River Tyne among some other wild incidents. There was hell on in several bars on the Quayside and one of the bar managers of the premises had come and pointed the finger at four of our lads then they'd been locked up. I don't want to sound like a grass almost twenty years on, but the player who started all the trouble got away scot free. I won't name him, but he was a Bulgarian. Anyway, it wasn't even a major incident, but the doorman wanted our lads out of some of the premises and fingers were pointed. The four players who had their collars felt were Johan Mjallby, Bobby Petta, Joos Valgaeren and Neil Lennon. Now this gets even more crazier because my sister Jane is a police constable at the very same station they got pulled into in Gateshead at that time. When the Celtic lads were brought in the sergeant of the station has rung our Jane to tell her she had some of the Celtic team in and he thought her Alan might be one of them. Jane told me when she heard the news her heart sunk with embarrassment. Can you imagine our Jane working at this police station and her own brother comes in, so she has to look after him in custody! As soon as Jane looks in one of the cells expecting to see me, she was relieved to see it wasn't me at all but Neil Lennon. "Neil is everything alright I'm Alan Thompson's sister?!" she asked him. Lenny was sat there with his head in his hands despairing. Lenny told her he just wanted to get out but this whole episode caused absolute carnage for the club. Me knowing the full picture by now, I didn't hang around and wait for the team bus, Sutty and I got the train straight back up the road to Glasgow as neither of us fancied the gloomy ride back up to Celtic Park on the bus whilst hungover and waiting to be gotten hold of by the gaffer Martin. When I arrived in Glasgow, I saw all the news billboards which said, 'CELTIC FC THUGS & THIEVES' and also 'CELTIC PLAYERS LOCKED UP' well you could imagine what Martin O'Neill was going to do when he got wind of this can't you! Martin had to get people down to the Gateshead police station as the lads were still in custody and he wasn't a happy bunny. Like I said the real culprit who started all the mayhem escaped justice. The lads who got hauled in; well, I can understand Lenny because he could be a pain in the arse when he'd had a drink and Lenny also had previous from when he was at Leicester City and Martin O'Neill had to bail him out then also. Regarding Joos, Johan and Bobby well they'd be the last three of our squad you'd think could be capable of causing mischief, so I think those three were incredibly unfortunate, in fact Bobby Petta told this same story in The Scottish Sun paper quite recently.

Martin O'Neill hit the roof like the cartoon character Yosemite Sam when he's chasing Bugs Bunny with his two guns. Martin would be calm then all of a sudden, he'd just lose it like The Ultimate Warrior from the WWF. Martin could lose it, but he didn't lose it very often, unless it was for a very good reason. He picked and chose his times well, just like old gaffer Brian Clough did. Being a football coach is like being a parent, if you lose your rag all the time your players are going to get used to it. The fear of something is psychologically greater than the action itself and that was Martin O'Neill. He could be very scary just stood there in his glasses on his own with his sidekicks Wally and Robbo just glaring at you and not saying a word. At half-time and after the game Martin spoke, and I do mean only he spoke. His presence demanded respect in abundance. As big a part as Wally and Robbo played in the Martin O'Neill success, Martin was the boss of all. After he finished speaking only then Wally and Robbo would walk around the dressing room speaking to us all individually.

As much as it was a pig's ear that Christmas night out for the club, I believe it was kept in house. In actual fact the lads who got locked up hadn't done anything wrong, so I don't think they were hammered with a fine or anything like that. I think even in the end the Bulgarian came forward and said he'd dodged a bullet behind closed doors. There's no doubt about it though the good name of Glasgow Celtic Football Club was dragged through the mud. From what I got told on good authority the whole episode was a stich up. It's alleged that certain photographers asked some doormen, 'can you throw some of these Celtic players out so we can get some snapshots for the front cover' type of thing. The fact that Glasgow Rangers went straight down the M6 to avoid what lay ahead says everything. I think they were tipped off to keep away from the city centre of Tyneside and no doubt they'll have found the whole thing very comical that we were the ones who got tangled in the net of chaos and drama.

PAUL LAMBERT

Celtic Teammate

"Alan Thompson was part of a really good Celtic side. The guy gave us balance on the left side and was lively, in a good way, off the pitch. The guy seems to be always on the go winding people up. He never seemed really down and would be constantly laughing and joking. What a moaner he was by the way, I'll give him that! Me and him had a right argument away at Dunfermline which got quite heated but straight away off the park it was forgotten about.

Tommo was a player who never needed any nudges in the motivation department and wore his heart on his sleeve. Off the pitch he lived for the banter and could hold his own when anyone was getting a verbal battering in a jokey manner. Thompson and Sutton were a sort of tag team like Giant Haystacks and Bid Daddy, I don't know which was which. The two of them came up at the same time and Celtic certainly had two flamboyant and loud Englishmen in the dressing room then that were at the centre of everything."

CHAPTER 10

THE ROAD TO SEVILLE

The 2002/03 season in Celtic's illustrious history will be forever remembered for the Seville UEFA Cup run. That run started in the July against FC Suduva, we went through 10-1 on aggregate and I managed to get on the score sheet over in Lithuania.

At the start of it all, although we had a special group of players, none of us in our wildest dreams thought we could get to the final at the end of the season. It was only when we started beating some very good teams and we were progressing that the serious thought that we could do something arose. When we'd beaten FC Suduva, Blackburn Rovers, Celta Vigo, FC Stuttgart and Liverpool we then knew it could be within our grasp. Blackburn, at the time, were a really strong side, as was expected for a club that Graeme Souness was managing. They had the likes of Andy Cole, Dwight Yorke, Damian Duff, Lucas Neill, David Thompson and Garry Flitcroft in the team. It was a Blackburn team that was holding its own in the Premiership, hence the reason they were playing in Europe. We knew we had to be going into the tie at our best. In the first game on Halloween 2002 which was at Celtic Park, well there was no doubt that Blackburn battered us in that first game. Luckily Henrik bailed us out and scored from close range with five minutes to go.

The second leg was at Ewood Park a fortnight later and that was when Graeme Souness was quoted as saying that the first game was like men v boys, and we were very lucky to have come away with the advantage in the tie. Garry Flitcroft, the Blackburn club captain, also said that if the first leg was a boxing match the contest would have been stopped, and I can see his point. At the end of the day though the fixture of the round is over two legs and so really it was only half-time. All of our lads knew we couldn't play any worse than we had in the game at Parkhead and even then, we came out victorious, so we fancied ourselves to go to Blackburn and progress in the competition. I didn't start but I came on late in the game at Ewood Park, all the lads were seething about some of the comments that had been made by the Blackburn lot that were being circulated by the media. Before the game Martin delivered his team talk which totally centred around those statements that were in the press. In fact, Martin had the quotes from the newspapers blown up and put on the walls in the away dressing room we were in, so it would rile his team up and that's exactly what happened. Martin, Wally and Robbo plastered these 'MEN AGAINST BOYS' pages from the papers and used it as reverse psychology. Although the second leg was a fortnight after the comments by Souness, Flitcroft & co, it was still fresh in the minds of our lot, and we wanted to go out and ram their words down their throats which is what happened. Goals by Larsson and Sutton finished the tie to make it 3-0. It was ironic that Sutty would go back to Ewood Park and grab a goal against his old club because he did a lot of great things for Blackburn with his co-frontman Alan Shearer when they were known as the SAS. That victory was so sweet because of the comments they'd all been throwing around for the last fortnight. When we'd finished with Blackburn we were on a cup run and the Spaniards Celta Vigo were up next. They had some proper players such as Benni McCarthy and

Sylvinho. The first leg at Celtic Park wasn't pretty but again we managed to get the victory with a goal from who else but Henrik Larsson.

We went over to Spain for the second leg early in the December of 2002 and scraped by with a 2-1 defeat, however the goal big John Hartson scored over there took us through and that meant European football after Christmas for the club for the first time in 23 years. Big John showed real technique to score considering his back was to goal but that was what big John was about. Most people, when you mention John's name just think of him as this big rough and ready centre half, but he also had great skill in his locker and it showed that evening in Spain. Hartson wasn't all about being that big bull in a China shop boshing people around. The thing about big John was he never gave any central defenders a minutes' peace and when you've got world class defenders such as Rio Ferdinand saying he was always one of his hardest opponents, you know he was doing something right. Sometimes if these top defenders got too tight against Hartson then the power and intelligence he had meant that he could roll them like a crocodile with his strength and power. That was something I saw big John doing often.

In the second leg over in Vigo we really rode our luck because Celta Viga had several chances to go through having free kicks around our box but we kept our nerve. I'd actually played in Vigo prior to this tie with Aston Villa so I knew just how hostile the little compact 26,000 crowd at the Estaio de Balaidos would be. Although it was kinda small compared to some grounds I've played in, it didn't lack intimidation.

On leaving Vigo, it was a magical trip home with all the boys. Martin, Wally and Robbo were all in high spirits and the odd sneaky brandy may have been consumed with some good music playing. Beating Celta Vigo meant we would play a very good German side, FC Stuttgart in the February of 2003. The first game we battered them at home 3-1 with goals from Paul Lambert, Shaun Maloney and Stiliyan Petrov. Although at first, we battled to come from one down to beat a ten-man Stuttgart side. That set us up to go over to Germany and match advantage is ours. Welsh star Bonnie Tyler entertained the fans by singing before the game.

Playing against them at Gottlieb-Daimler-Stadion we lost 3-2 but managed to go through. In the Stuttgart team was a certain Andreas Hinkel who would go on to sign for Celtic five years later. Over in Stuttgart we had a ridiculously huge following. I mean Celtic always bring a huge crowd, but this particular night was something else. Before the game we knew that Stuttgart were a good team and this was the stage in the competition where you don't play any mugs. Their manager at the time, Felix Magath, was a renowned football genius and great tactician who was highly thought of in world football.

The Belarusian Alexander Hleb was playing for them that night too, he would go on to do very well at Arsenal for big money. Another two tasty players for them were Krasimir Balakov and Kevin Kuranyi, I swapped strips at the end with the Bulgarian Balakov. I managed to get on the score sheet after only 12 minutes with a diving header which was unusual for me, then I did this silly celebration where I ran off, arms out like an aeroplane in reference to the war then jumped up in the air proper Martin O'Neill touchline style. Looking back that goal celebration was a bit risky but thankfully nobody asked me the meaning behind it.

Only three minutes after my goal Chris Sutton scores to put us 2-0 up and we think this is it, game over, only for them to come back with three goals, but we hold on for a great night for the club. Again, like Celta Vigo in the previous leg, Stuttgart had us with our backs to the wall fighting for our lives. In the last third of the game, they have the momentum of the game and we're tired and almost out on our feet. As a team we really had to dig deep in Stuttgart but that's one thing that group of players could do. When your lungs are burning, and you can't get the ball because there is wave after wave of attack you've got to be strong. We managed to hang on and we beat Stuttgart 5-4 on aggregate which set us up for the battle of Britain against Gerard Houllier who had won the competition two years previously. The first leg was at Celtic Park and Gerry Marsden led 60,000 fans in a rousing version of 'You'll Never Walk Alone'. Michael Owen later went on record as saying that game, out of all the games he'd played in during his career, had the best atmosphere. Henrik who was just coming back from a broken cheekbone scored his 25th European goal for Celtic in that game in the first 2 mins.

It was a 1-1 draw and Henrik scored with his knee from my cross, but the talking point of that game was when El Hadji Diouf spat at a Celtic fan. Within minutes he had to be subbed for his own safety but rather astonishingly his manager Gerard Houllier backed his player, no one else did thankfully. It wouldn't be until twelve years later that Houllier said, "And, of course, what happened at Celtic, when he spat at a fan, was totally out of line. He was fined and banned for that." When you see what Diouf went on to do in his future career it wasn't surprising. Shambolic really. Middlesbrough manager Neil Warnock once was quoted as saying, "He's a disgrace, I'd call him a sewer rat but that would be insulting sewer rats" and I think that was a fair comment by Neil. There's another story with 'Spit the

Dog' and a touchline spat which involves Neil Lennon and Ally McCoist but we'll talk about that a little later in the book.

Going to Anfield for the 2nd leg Liverpool had the advantage due to Emile Heskey's 17th minute equalizer and all the press had pretty much written us off. We travelled down to Liverpool knowing we had to score otherwise we would be out, but with Liverpool being odds on to go through, I would have said all the pressure was on them. What sticks out in my mind about that eventful evening at Anfield was the gaffer's team talk before kick-off. Although, I've spoken to many of the lads such as big John, big Rab and Stiliyan at various events over the years and not one of us can remember what was said, only that it was sublime and made us all feel ten feet tall when we ran out onto the Anfield grass. I think we forgot because of the adrenalin, I've even asked Martin what he said that night and he couldn't recall it either. Martin did say that when he was playing for Nottingham Forest under the great Brian Clough, 'Cloughie' was forever giving him and his fellow Forest teammate John Robertson these outstanding almost Winston Churchill like speeches before the big games. Don't forget that Martin & Robbo played for that outstanding Forest side when they won the two European Cups and took over a rampant Liverpool side that was full of Keegan, Dalglish and Souness so he already knew a thing about putting a great Liverpool team in their places. As a player for Forrest, Martin O'Neill's record had been outstanding, and I think that's what Martin based his team talk on. Martin also had a great record for Leicester City as a manager, so he knew how to get a result against Liverpool. It was a magnificent night for us with me opening the scoring under the Liverpool wall just before half time.

Before the game in the build-up, I was asked by a guy called Chris Tovell who worked for Reebok if I could I do him a favour. He went on to say that he would be at the game and because I was sponsored by Reebok at the time, who also sponsored the Liverpool kits, he asked me if I scored tonight, would I run off, smack my left boot whilst pointing to it so it gets Reebok a bit of attention and if I did then he'd sneak an extra few quid in with my next Reebok bonus. When Celtic get the free kick in the 45th minute I thought, 'I'm going to have a go and see if I can bag that lucrative Reebok bonus here!' As I sized it up, I knew it was within my distance, meaning not too far and not too close to the 18 yard penalty box mark. It's an art to whip a ball up and over with the preciseness, power and weight on it to score. People just assumed I was going to put the ball over the wall and go for goal but I had studied Liverpool's defending on set pieces in the build up to the game. Maybe you noticed, as I did, at the Euro's 2021 that during the oppositions free kick they will lay a player on the ground behind the wall to stop the ball going under the wall when they jump. I bet Liverpool wish they'd have done that. One of the things I got from watching Liverpool was that their wall always jumped, this meant I was always going for the low and hard approach rather than my usual up, over and bend. I hit the ball so hard that when you watch it, the ball is not even spinning, it's only travelling to its destination. Of course, that time I'd spent watching them paid off and just as I thought, the wall jumped and the keeper stood still because he hasn't seen a thing. It was right off the laces, and nothing was stopping that and that's when I ran off to do my silly celebration slapping my left boot. It was a great feeling scoring in front of the Kop End, I had the pleasure of doing it once before for Bolton a few years earlier and I hit that one so hard it got the goal of the month on Match of the Day, in fact I hit it that hard that the pace of the ball caused the cameraman to miss some of its flight. Although I hit this one hard it was a different goal. This one had been low, hard and under a wall, so it was meticulously executed to a tee. My good man Chris Tovell held his word and not only did I get a Brucey bonus but the next day in the papers was a snap of me scoring and smacking my left boot pointing at the Reebok sign.

The tie was put to bed when my pal big John Hartson dropped his shoulder, played the simple one-two and blasted one on his right foot into the net. It was no surprise to see big John do that, as I've already told you he was a great technician, but John never really spoke about himself like that. That goal also meant the world to big John as he'd grown up supporting Liverpool wanting to be like Kenny Dalglish or Ian Rush. I would say that was our best performance out of that full 2003 UEFA Cup run. I would have tackled a brick wall on that unforgettable evening for Celtic when we ran out worthy winners against one of the best teams in England. Playing in front of that crowd at Anfield, I would put that up there as one of the top three greatest ever atmospheres I ever played amongst.

Maybe the first stain on Martin O'Neill was when we lost to Inverness Caley Thistle in the March 1-0 away to put us out of the Scottish Cup. Only three years previously that exact same result put John Barnes out of a job but that was never going to happen to Martin, especially as we'd only beaten Liverpool that very same week. I would put that down to the comedown after our high at Anfield which I'll get to in a bit.

In the semi-final of our European run, we come up against a relatively unheard-of team from Portugal called Boavista. The opening tie was at Celtic Park in an absolutely dismal 1-1 draw. Henrik was the saint and the sinner in the first leg, and he scored but also missed a penalty which would have given us the edge going over to Portugal. Big Joos Valaeren scored an own goal so this gives them the away goal, so we needed to score over there like we had to in the previous round against Liverpool. Boavista weren't anywhere near the level of the team we'd just beat in Liverpool, so we had to roll our sleeves up and get on with it. I just remember those two legs against Boavista as being two shit games if I'm honest. They were both scrappy games and there wasn't any quality from either side. We'd beaten much better teams than Boavista on the run but for some reason they just caused us problems until Henrik saved us in the second leg with his 78th minute goal. Until Henrik scored, we were twelve minutes from going out and I just remember thinking, we'll take any type of goal here and we got that when Henrik scuffed his shot, but it still went in. The goal was a bit of a fluke really which goes to show that sometimes you just need a bit of luck on your side. As the time was ticking down against Boavista I just remember Robbo stood in the dugout having a fag. Normally, John Robertson would never have a smoke on the touchline when the game was on, but this was obviously getting to him. Martin was nervous too and I'm surprised he wasn't asking Robbo for a drag. Thank God we managed to keep our focus and I think the overcoming sense of relief was evident in the pictures of our players when the whistle went. Also, that was the first time that Celtic had reached a European final since 1970, 33 years earlier by that point. Martin O'Neill then did what Martin O'Neill does and he started leaping about like a salmon trying to get upstream. You can see what it meant to Bobo, Lenny, Stan and Henrik when they're walking around the pitch and celebrating with the supporters who had travelled such a long way for this game and now, we'd repaid them for their efforts. That moment of sheer ecstasy will live with me and the other players for years. It's astonishing to think a great club like Glasgow Celtic has been absent from European finals and now it was back for our supporters. Some of the scenes were just breath-taking and the buzz in our dressing room was sky high. We had to come back down to earth though because although this was a Thursday night, and we've just qualified for a major European final, we had the little matter of an Old Firm game to prepare for on the Sunday. Which will be forever remembered as beachball Sunday because the fans threw holiday themed inflatables on the pitch to mock Rangers that we were now in a European cup final. We flew back with Sunday's game in our foremost thought.

I couldn't possibly do my experiences of playing against Rangers justice by putting the odd line here and there so that's the reason why I'm leaving it for a full chapter in itself further on in the book.

When we went to the final on Wednesday 21st May 2003 at Esadio La Cartuja de Sevilla against Portuguese outfit FC Porto, the locals had never seen anything like it. I mean, it was reported that Seville was taken over by 80,000 Celtic supporters that day. Fair play to UEFA and FIFA who awarded the Fair Play Award to Celtic for "extraordinarily loyal and sporting behaviour." The Spaniards had never seen an invasion like it and there were no arrests or any trouble during the whole build up. We went out together as a squad three full days before the final to give ourselves time to adjust. We stayed just outside Seville in a place called Jerez which had great facilities. There is a Formula 1 circuit there and it is deep within the sherry producing south of Spain. The families of the squad came over and stayed nearby, not too far from us. At that time of year in Spain the weather was something else, so Martin didn't want us laying in the sun too much. There was no drinking of beer for anyone despite the scorching weather. Martin, Wally, and Robbo had made sure every minute of our time was filled up preparing for the biggest game in Celtic's history for several decades. We had to follow Martin's lead and the most we could get away with was taking a walk into town for a coffee, but we all knew we had a job to do.

Our training had been excellent, and we were all really in high spirits. With the WAG'S all being over with our families, many of our kids would play with our teammate's kids. My Zac would be out playing with Jordan Larsson (now playing for Spartak Moscow) and Chris Sutton also had a few boys Zac's age so they all kind of grew up together. For as good as everything was over in Seville for the preparation, I'll never understand the suits the club provided for us! Black suits which were 100% wool. We were all sat sweltering going to the game, all of us shouting to the driver to put the air-con on. When the time came for us to walk around the pitch in our black suits the Porto players must have thought we were all mental. I mean the Porto squad were walking about in shirts and t-shirts and here is us walking around in the boiling hot sun dressed in black wool.

We trained on the pitch the night before the game, and it had only just been laid. It wasn't any good at all and you could still see where all the joins were. My teammate John Hartson never started the final and he's said over the years he's glad that he never because he wouldn't have coped with the heat. I can really understand John's comments on this because, honest to God the heat was ridiculous! Nothing, throughout the rest of my career had ever come close to having to play in those temperatures. I've played in scorching pre-season games in America, but this was another level. It was that hot I remember talking to my dad after the game and he said he couldn't drink. Now that is seriously unusual because my old man likes a pint of Newcastle Brown Ale so for the weather to do that, I've never known anything like it. FC Porto were a good team and their boss at the time, was an arrogant big mouth, which everyone in Britain would find out about for themselves given time, as their boss was the self-proclaimed Special One Jose Mourinho. When you look at some of these players in their team such as Deco, Tiago, Carvalho and Maniche it was no surprise that only a year later, in 2004, the same squad won the Champion's League. Jose's men knocked Manchester United out that year so that shows the calibre of Mourinho's team and why he was making a big name for himself as a top coach in European football.

During the match against Porto, I don't think any of us played particularly badly, however I've never been able to watch it on tape since. I don't think we deserved to go in at halftime a goal down so there was a bit of a fracas in the tunnel. Well, you may have noticed that Jose Mourinho was a bit of an arrogant so-so and I can't remember who's started this big scuffle, but I had a full bottle of Lucozade and when Jose was going off on one, I've stood back aimed for his face and squirted this drink right at him, it got just him full on in the canister which cooled him down. I wasn't sticking about to see the aftermath though and I did a runner into our dressing room. I was in there on my own wondering what the hell it was that I'd just done! I'm sure Jose must remember me blasting him even today, but what it did was cause more havoc among the players. If there was a problem before I came along then I only made it worse. I pretty much just lobbed a grenade in amongst it in the heat of the moment. Talking about lobbing a grenade I imagine you all remember just how much cheating was going on from the Porto team that evening so most of our players were becoming seriously fucked off by now and emotions were bubbling over. In my opinion, it was obvious just how much of a top-quality side that FC Porto team were so they didn't need to act the way they were, there was just no need.

Only recently I watched a documentary on Jose Mourinho for Spurs and when you hear some of his team talks before the games then it's clear he doesn't care how he wins as long as it's a win, which was exactly what he was like in the 2003 UEFA Cup Final against us. Jose shows no shame about winning a 1-0 victory even if his players were perfecting their diving skills or practicing a bit of skulduggery. The man is clearly all about winning at any costs when you watch him on the 'All or Nothing' 2020 series on Amazon. He is even quoted as saying, "good guys never win." By hook or by crook you win the game, and that was his antics that evening in Seville.

Although 1-0 down at halftime, we knew, going back out we could get back in the game which is exactly what we did. Two minutes into the second half we get back level with who else but Henrik. He latched onto a Didier Agathe cross, and we were back in the game and a sea of green, white and gold went wild. Again, they take the lead in the 54th minute when Alenichev converted a Deco cross, only for Henrik to pull us out of the shit again. In the 57th minute I swung a corner into Larsson who's jumped up Martin O'Neill style to beat everyone in the air and get us back level. With Deco remaining a threat for the match the gaffer brought on Jackie McNamara to nullify Deco which he did brilliantly. It finished 2-2 at full time and so into extra time we go. We get back in the game but what really kills us is when Bobo Balde picked up his second yellow in the 96th minute. Martin shifted Jackie Mac into covering for

Bobo in the centre of defence. In the second half of extra time, we were unable to hold out for penalties, as Derlei reacted quickest to a Rab Douglas block in the 115th minute and rounded Jackie Mac to make it 3-2. With a few minutes to go we did manage to win a freekick in what would typically be my territory but by now I was too fucked to take it. Luckily, young Shaun Maloney had just come on as a sub and he took it. I just wish I was fit enough to have had a crack at that because it was perfect for me being an in-swinger. Little Shaun was marvellous at free kicks but that last freekick favoured my left foot better but by then I was ravaged and hardly on my feet. Shaun tried to pass the ball to me, but I shook my head and told him he was going to have to hit it and that's what he did. Porto did have Nunu Valente sent off in the last minute of extra time, but it was too late. Whichever negative approach they came into this game with had worked and they were now victorious.

We did well but when Bobo was sent off with five minutes left in that heat, well you're asking a lot for any team. At the end I just remember thinking we'd given it our all and now it was over we had nothing left. We lost the game five minutes from going to a penalty shoot-out and I would have been one of the takers. Over 80,000 Celtic supporters from all corners of the world had come to witness our efforts and now it was over. One of my lasting images was just seeing the gaffer on his knees looking up to the skies on the pitch very much a broken man. Many of the Celtic supporters travelled to Seville to just watch the match then sleep rough after the game which is exactly what we felt like doing after the Slovakia ref Lubo Michel blew his final whistle. Although we felt like crawling into a corner to have a good cry and disappear, we couldn't. We had to stay on the pitch to thank our wonderful supporters. We also had to walk up and receive our runners-up medals which was humiliating especially listening to all the Porto players joyous screams. It just annoyed me the way they cheated to get the win and many who watched that share the same view that I do all these years on. When we got back in the dressing room, I don't think any of us said anything to anyone. Deafening silence, even when people were in the shower.

There was a function on afterwards, put on by the club for all of the players to spend time with their families but nobody was interested. I think a few went for one or two but to be honest we just wanted to get behind our hotel door so we could have a good cry. Martin, Wally and Robbo basically told us we could now do what we wanted to but to be honest, we all stayed in the same hotel and didn't move.

The next day we were flying home back to Glasgow because we had the small matter of a third SPL trophy in a row title to win at Rugby Park only a few days later. May 25th, 2003 was the Sunday of a Bank Holiday weekend when our season would be finishing. We took on Kilmarnock away and Rangers faced Dunfermline at home. That title race, like the one two years after, went right down to the wire, that's why they were both called 'Helicopter Sundays,' because the chopper changed its direction of flight at the very last minute. On the pitch in our game against Kilmarnock we're aware of just who's in front by the vibes we were getting from the fans. I scored a penalty yet was also guilty of missing one, so it was very back and forth like the Wacky Races with us and Rangers that day. Rangers would seal the SPL title in the very last minute via Mikel Arteta to make the final score Rangers 6 – 1 Dunfermline and we would win 4-0. We lost our title in the last minute of the season on goal difference. This was on top of losing a European final only four days earlier. If

Carling made disappointments, then this was probably the hardest disappointment in football, two in a row. Afterwards Chris Sutton got into really hot water by giving an interview saying that Dunfermline had laid down to Rangers to give them the SPL title. Sutty would receive a ban plus a hefty fine by the SPL for letting his mouth run off, but to be honest Chris was just saying what we were all feeling.

I think, looking back in 2021, all retired and middle-aged, what the rest of the team should have done was stand by Sutty and said the same and stood as a team, because everyone of us thought exactly like Chris Sutton did, only he was brave/stupid enough to open his mouth. If you're reading this Sutty then me and a few other of the senior players should have stood with you and backed you with what you said. Sutty had the balls to say what he did and that sums up Chris Sutton. Today, he's still got it and that's why he makes such a colourful and controversial football pundit.

Looking over the 2002/03 season, we didn't win a thing. The disappointment pained us to the core but there was also a sense of pride in what we'd achieved as a team for the supporters. We lost but we held our heads high going into the next season which would also be an incredibly emotional one being Henrik Larsson's last season with the club. If you ask the fans at Celtic which they would have preferred, another Celtic SPL title or the Seville run and the good times it produced, I think I know what they'd have picked! At times we did well just to take the league to the last game that season because at times we played some big teams across Europe on the Thursday, then had to be back for the game on a Sunday afternoon. For me, I took great pride in what we achieved that season, and the memories will forever live with me.

It's crazy the amount of people that I meet at functions that just want to talk about the Seville run. These fans are in their element when they can still tell me about all the great things they got up and countries they visited to watch our cup run. Yes, we didn't win a thing, but I wonder just how many people out there came out of it with great experiences and memories to last them a lifetime, and we did that! If I do a function with big John, Sutty, Jackie Mac or Stiliyan it always gets brought up, even though it was nearly two decades ago. At times, these functions can be for four hundred and as soon as someone mentions the Seville memories everyone just stands up and adds their bit. It had such a huge profound effect on people's lives, and I'm not talking about the players and staff I'm talking about your average everyday person. I was proud to have been a part of it, let alone get player of the tournament jointly with Henrik from a Celtic fans poll vote.

JOHN HARTSON
Celtic Teammate

"I'd played against Alan Thompson in the Premiership when he was at Bolton and Aston Villa. We crossed each other's paths taking each other on as rivals. I didn't really know him until I arrived in Glasgow. We used to call him the wand at Celtic because his left foot was extraordinary, and the lad had a goal in him also. Alan used to score some spectacular goals and was a real mainstay player in our team. Alan Thompson was one of the big game players in that Martin O'Neill era who has gone on to become a really good friend still to this day.

I know he's been through his troubles but haven't we all?! It can be hard for the likes of us because all our lives we've only played football and it's through those tough times that God casts trying times on you which you have to deal with. Tommo, like myself, was thrown off a little bit in life but now he's really happy. I'm delighted my old friend Tommo is doing this biography and not only putting his demons to bed but putting his great career on paper because he played with some fantastic players. I like Alan and I think the Geordies are pretty much like the Welsh who call it as it is. They're very humble people with no airs or graces about them.

Tommo absolutely stitched me up once in a prank when I shared the 2005 player of the year award with Fernando Rickson. Tommo rang me and put this dodgy Dutch accent on, he had it down to a tee and wound me up to the point that I was blowing fire. I ended up screaming all sorts of obscenities when all of a sudden, I heard Thompson and

Sutton crying with laughter down the phone. The pair had me on loudspeaker and were pretending to be Fernando who was saying I was a crap player, and he was keeping the trophy all year round etc etc… The pair had me raging as I was driving, and they thought it was hilarious."

CHAPTER 11

A TITLE TO WIN BACK

At the start of 2003/04 we had to block out the heartbreak from the season gone. Our plan that season was to go out and get our SPL title back at all costs. Also, we wanted to get back in the Champions League mixing it with the big boys, that was our aim at the start.

We started the European campaign in the July of 2003 away in Lithuania. We beat FC Kaunas 0-4 then 1-0 at Celtic Park the week later. There was one more obstacle that we faced in getting to the Champions' League Group Stages and that was a tie against MTK Hungaria. Again, we win over there 4-0 and at home 1-0 which sees us get to the group stage with Bayern Munich, Lyon and Anderlecht.

We had a real sense that we belonged on this stage now considering how well we'd done at this level against the top teams, and we wanted to prove it. I think the group we were in was definitely the scariest and was the group of death in my opinion. The first game we played was Bayern in Germany and I opened the scoring in the 57th minute with a diving header from a Didier Agathe cross, very much like the one I scored in Germany against Stuttgart. Bayern's ground then was the Olympic Stadium. Any football buffs out there will know it was the very ground where Holland won the Euros in 1988 and where Marco Van Basten scored that unbelievable volley. It was also the very stadium where John Robertson crossed the ball for then record signing Trevor Francis to score the winning goal against Malmo to win their first ever European Cup, so Robbo and the gaffer had a lot of memories there.

It was really looking like it was going to be a memorable night for Martin and Robbo but like typical Celtic away we don't hold the lead and lost 2-1. Two goals from Roy MaKaay in the 72nd and 86th minute means we go away pointless. We get a 0-0 draw with Bayern in the return leg at Celtic Park and with Lyon and Anderlecht we beat them both at home but of course lose over at theirs which only takes us to seven points. Bayern and Lyon go through, but we finish above Anderlecht which means we have the parachute to the UEFA Cup, which was a great consolation, it meant more European football after Christmas for the second season in a row.

The first team we met was Teplice from the Czech Republic. At home we win comfortably 3-0 with a double from Henrik and one from Sutty which means we've won the tie in the first leg because we lose 1-0 over there. Great, now we've got a cup run and apart from getting someone ridiculous like Barcelona we really fancy ourselves to get to another final. Well, you could not have made it up because who did we get in the last 16 of the competition? Yes, Frank Rijkaard's Barcelona, which was jam-packed full of superstars such as Ronaldinho, Luis Garcia, Iniesta, Xavi, Marc Overmars and Carles Puyol. If, and it was a big if, we got through this team we deserved to win it, but nobody was giving us a chance, even with the likes of Larsson, Sutton, Petrov & co, the media gave us no hope. We now had the mighty Barca coming to Celtic Park, and this was as big as it gets in world football. In the first leg in early March 2004, I just remember being on the pitch against them in the first twenty minutes thinking, 'I've never played against a team who could move the ball so quick as these fine footballing specimens.' It just didn't seem real that all of us fit lads in that Celtic team were just gasping for breath after twenty minutes. We just could not get the ball to be even in the game. I remember looking around the pitch to the likes of Lenny, Jackie Mac and Stiliyan thinking how the hell are we going to get out of this one? Honestly, this team was frightening and like something I'd not seen before. Ever!

Thankfully after twenty minutes we got our second wind and they started looking slightly more human. We did well to get to halftime at 0-0 but then something magical happened and it swung in our favour.

There was an incident in the tunnel and before you lot think I was responsible for the chaos which unfolded, I wasn't. Now for some reason unbeknown to man, one of their players Thiago Motto, decided that with a crazed look in his eyes it would be a good idea to attack our man mountain defender who's built like a heavyweight boxer Bobo Balde. For someone to try and pick a fight with Bobo they've got to not be wired up right in the first place. You just do not go near the big fella, yet Motto wanted a "square go" with arguably the biggest, strongest and toughest man mountain in European football. Bobo didn't need anyone to fight his battles and I think Rab Douglas getting involved stemmed from him trying to be the peacekeeper but then he's got roped into a battle. When the match officials have seen this, they've thought that big Rab was looking to cause bother which wasn't the case. The next thing is the officials have gone to their dressing room and sent Motto off and rightfully so, then came into our room and asked to speak to the captain which was Jackie Mac (Jackie's nickname at the club was The Toy, maybe down to his small stature I never did ask. If you're reading this Jackie, you're in my phone as The Toy) and they've told him that big Rab is off also. Big Rab got a straight red for sticking up for the weak, vulnerable and defenceless 6ft 5inch tank Bobo Balde (HA!

HA!). By now in the dressing room all you could hear was this really fast Northern Irish accent shouting, "WHAT... WHAT... WHAT'S GOING ON?" Well, it was Martin in his high pitched voice and he wasn't happy. The one thing about the gaffer you quickly learnt was that you could tell when he was stressed as he always put his hand up to his mouth, like he did to me when I was sent off first at Ibrox back in November 2000. That's when you know Martin is angry and irate with the charm of a spitting King Cobra. Well now the gaffer's really on one but there's nothing we can do about it. Rab was off and crazy Motto's off, so it was ten v ten, as if it wasn't hard enough, I mean, ten v ten against this lot on a full-size pitch was only going to make it harder for us.

I think God above knew this as well and that's why he may have helped us shake the game up. Just after half time I had the ball near our dugout and as I've passed it back to one of our defenders, Saviola's taken a swipe at me in the 49th minute, proper Wallsend style. It didn't really hurt me to be fair, but it was well late, so I've jumped up, gone down, been shot and the rest of it. I knew with what was going on here we needed anything we could get to give us a chance. I was never one for play acting in my career but this night I wasn't stupid, and I used my head. Let's just say I took a leaf out of Jose Mourinho's Porto's book and played the game. Whether by hook or by crook Saviola saw the colour red and now its ten v nine and we're well in the game. The crowd now are sensing we can "do these", as they'd say in Glasgow, and we get extra wind in our sails as we're going up to attack.

Our very own Roadrunner Didier was running up his flank like he did so well and looped a long ball over, Henrik had done remarkably well to win the header and lay the ball off to me perfectly. That was one thing about

Larsson, although he was 5ft 10 he was phenomenal in the air, not just from a running jump but also a standing jump which he executed perfectly in this case.

I've then adjusted my feet and did some sort of scissor kick aimed at the floor. If he saved it, it would have been a world class save but thankfully Valdes didn't get anywhere near it, and it hits the back of the net. Great scenes in the Celtic stands and of course the gaffers jumping like a fish out of water on the side-lines as Parkhead erupted. Little old Alan Thompson from Wallsend has only gone and scored the winner against the mighty Barcelona, wow what a feeling! Life doesn't get any higher than this as a professional footballer let me tell you that! We see the game out and that puts us in a position to go over to the Nou Camp a fortnight later with a fighting chance. Whether it was 10 v 9 or not, it really didn't matter because Celtic beat Barca at Celtic Park.

When we went over for the 2nd leg, we knew we were going to be under the cosh, we thought we would have conceded at some point in the game which was never the case, largely down to young Marshy. The teenage David Marshall came on for us in the 1st leg which was like a story straight out Roy of the Rovers by making his debut against the world's best team. In that 2nd leg young Marshy really became known to the world with his display that night. Honestly, the kid was like Spiderman between the sticks, and I dread to think how much we'd have been beat by if it wasn't for him. I don't think the Barca players could believe him also. Marshy had a phenomenal night and it was the making of him!

In the second game we had Chris Sutton back, he missed the first game, but I've got to give a special mention to the Celtic defence which was a young John Kennedy, Stan Varga, Jackie Mac and Didier. Also, Liam Miller (God rest him) when he came on for Jackie Mac in the second half did tremendously well. As a unit our defence was truly heroic. Again, like the first leg we just couldn't get the ball and were trying to close them down as quick as we could, but it was near enough impossible because they were that good. At times we couldn't even string a pass together and it was just wave after wave of Barcelona attacks in the Nou Camp.

Another player who really stood up to be counted was a young Stephen Pearson. Pearo, for such a young lad going onto the world stage was outstanding. We got him from Motherwell for only £350,000 and what a signing that lad turned out to be! His nickname for us was the "white flash" because he would be everywhere on the pitch and at speed. Martin O'Neill was fantastic at doing that sometimes, looking at the young Scottish players who nobody had really heard of and bringing them through to make a mark in the Celtic team. The gaffer didn't mind taking a gamble on players that nobody had heard of before such as Didier Agathe for example. Martin brought him in the same time as me from Hibs for £50,000 which was out of the world to get a player of his calibre for next to nothing, especially as he signed me the same day for £2.75million. The Guinean Momo Sylla was another one he got from St Johnstone for £650,000 and he could cover a variety of positions in our team.

When you look at the stats for that game in front of 78,000, they were staggering. They had something like 37 shots at our goal and never scored once. We well and truly rode our luck that night at the start of Spring 2004 against the Catalan giants that's for sure.

We trained at the Nou Camp the night before that second leg which allowed us to have a nose about. The chapel in the ground was a special place and as I looked in, I could see where my hero Maradona used to kneel and pray in there which was quite surreal for me because I've watched a lot of documentaries about him. The Barcelona teams throughout the years have always been big into Catholicism and it played a big part of the club's heritage.

One thing I must say about playing in the two games against Barcelona is there really isn't any words that exist in the English dictionary to describe Ronaldinho. I actually managed to get to swap shirts with him after the game at Parkhead. I do often wonder if, when he's going through his unbelievable memorabilia of the games he's played in, if he sees my shirt and thinks, 'who the hell is Thompson?' (laughs). I think he'll remember the green & white hoops, I'm sure. I've got to say, out of all the shirts I've swapped such as Gerrard, Scholes, Giggs, Balakov, Ballack, Vieira, Nesta, Owen, Xavi and Yorke, Ronaldinho's is the most special out of all of them, not to mention I scored the winning goal in that game. My boy Zac has it up today on his bedroom wall. I tried to get near him in one of the games and I was just in awe of his presence. At that time when I came up against him in 2004, I would say he was the best in the world. The guy was strong, quick, skilful and it was like the ball was on a rope attached to his feet. I even tried to kick him, and I missed wildly then I had a 50/50 tackle with him and came off worst. He did me and he left stud marks up my inner thigh because I'd had a go at him, so not only was he a proper player but he knew how to handle himself. If you give it out on the pitch you've got to take it and that's what happened to me when I came up against the world's best. The man wasn't all about playing fancy dan football he could have a fight if needed so he had it all. He most definitely is the most complete footballer I've ever come across, easily! I've been lucky enough to play against Ronaldo in Roy Keane's testimonial, but Ronaldinho stands alone.

With us coming through the battering from Barca into the next round that brought us to the same stages as when we met Liverpool the year before, only now we were facing a very underrated Villarreal team. There number 10 was an Argentine named Juan Roman Riquelme and he stood out for me in the two ties. In the first game their captain gave a masterclass at Parkhead he was top draw. The first leg ended 1-1 at Celtic Park with Henrik getting his 35th European goal for Celtic in that game. The second tie in April 2004 I didn't travel with the squad because I was suspended so Liam Miller started instead of me, but we got well beaten 2-0 over there to go out 3-1 on aggregate and there weren't any complaints from us, the best team won and went through. I was surprised they didn't go onto win the full competition instead of Valencia that season. Villarreal done a number on us, and they didn't have the household names like the team we'd beaten before Barcelona but everything they did they did well.

For as much as everything was spoken about in our team, wanting our title back and a cup, the talk was always going to be around this being Henrik Larsson's last season. Maybe not by the squad but most certainly by the supporters. He had been the darling in the Celtic fans eyes for the past seven years, every Celtic supporter around the world would have sworn Henrik could also walk on water. Where do I start with talking about Henrik from playing with him for four seasons other than saying what a player he was!

That season we would go on to regain our title by a massive 17 points and even win the Scottish Cup. The final at Hampden in May against Dunfermline which we won 3-1, will always be known as the Henrik Larsson Cup Final and of course he went out with a bang getting two goals with the other coming from Stan Petrov.

Now, I have to go into great detail when talking about the magnificent 7 and say the fella was a total leader. Henrik was a great character, but he could also be grumpy, as grumpy as could be. None of us liked getting beat but Henrik would take defeat worse than most players I've played with. Henrik, I think has also gone public, saying that he would even swap his Champions League medal, which he won with Barca in 2006 against Arsenal, to have lifted the UEFA Cup with Celtic, so that just shows what Celtic meant to him. Losing to Porto in 2003 after scoring two goals completely shattered him. Everyone at the club was desperate for Henrik to stay on after 2004 but Henrik had made his mind up and he would leave us for Barcelona at 32. He finished his time with us with the double after giving Celtic the best years of his career. I dread to think of just how much Celtic could have got for him in his prime, but he showed his loyalty to Celtic Football Club and for that he's a God to the Celtic fans. I mean 242 goals in 315 appearances has rightly earnt him the nickname, 'The King of Kings' and he's adored by every Celtic supporter on planet earth. The man was just phenomenal. I remember when he fractured his cheekbone once and it meant he had to be out for a while, that when he got back into training, he had no fear. He was obviously that good of an athlete, like I said earlier, it was like he'd never been away from the game. He wasn't bothered about heading the ball going into his first game back against Rangers or a Champions League game. One of the most horrific injuries I ever saw was when Henrik broke his leg against Lyon away in the EUFA Cup, 1999.

Many have said Henrik being out cost John Barnes his job but to come back from that terrible leg break was nothing short of miraculous. John Barnes actually had a really good start to his Celtic career but obviously losing

Henrik in October played a big part in that season going Pete Tong. Of course, when Mark Viduka refused to go back out when Celtic lost to Inverness Caley Thistle the writing was on the wall for John. Can I just say now that Mark Viduka would never have gotten away with that if he'd have refused to go back out on the pitch for Martin O'Neill. Martin would have ripped his head clean off his shoulders, I'm sure! I dread to think of what would have happened and his career would have been over there and then, never mind joining any other club after Celtic.

Going back to the main man Henrik though, not only was he a goal machine but he was a supplier for great goals. He was very different to the average selfish centre forward because instead of it being all about me, me, me, Henrik was a pure team player! His work ethic for closing people down and winning the ball back was better than anyone I ever played with for a striker. It didn't surprise me that Henrik left Celtic at 32 to go on and do amazing things for Barcelona and even Manchester United at 36. Henrik going to United on loan for his holidays for a few months and doing it in the Premiership proved all the doubters wrong, and at the age of 36! Wayne Rooney said in his book that Henrik was sublime and that was at the end of his career! For years people used to say that Henrik could only do it in the SPL, but I think he proved the doubters wrong and he did it at the highest level when he was getting on. Also, you've only got to look at what he did for Sweden in World Cup's and the Euros that this kind of talk was nonsense, and he would have graced any team's eleven in the world. He was that good that when Henrik broke his leg again for Barca the club gave him another year's contract whilst he was in recovery and on the mend.

When I played in Henrik's tribute game against Seville in the May 2004 Celtic Park had 60,000 fans in floods of tears. I don't think I have any memories of that game other than the emotions at the end of the game. Henrik was a broken man once again in front of the roaring Parkhead crowd who were all in even more of a state than him. I think at the end of the game I even said to him, 'listen Henrik embrace all of this because you deserve it my friend.' There are not many lads who can get a send-off from Celtic Football Club like that. Larsson is to Celtic what Cantona is at Manchester United, Ian Wright at Arsenal or Alan Shearer is at Newcastle. Nobody deserved that night more than my friend Henrik.

Also, Henrik was the ultimate professional and he always looked after himself. Particularly his feet. We had this girl named Irene, a chiropodist who would come in once a week to look after our feet, but Henrik always had this strange obsession about it. He was totally right by the way because as a pro footballer your feet are your tools of the trade we were in. Some players feet I saw over the years were horrendous with black nails and all kinds of infections, but I followed Henrik's lead for looking after my feet. When I wasn't painting my toenails with ladies blue nail varnish of course (laughs).

Your diet for a modern-day footballer is important because skill can only get you so far in the game. When I first went to Celtic, and we would have our pre-match meals, I found most players have beans on toast, chicken & pasta or scrambled egg. Every player has their own little thing which agrees with them before a game, but I would always swap and change, always keeping it light though. I used to keep it light because I always knew whatever I'd had was coming back up anyway from my disorder. For all the years I played with Henrik he always chose fried egg on toast. That's what he did all those magical things on before every game. He was the only one in all the clubs I played for that chose that but who was going to tell him not to have it? He was never exactly carrying weight although it was maybe slightly unhealthy. Sometimes I wouldn't even have a meal I'd just have two bars of chocolate.

Away from the pitch Henrik was a family man who played a bit of golf, as a lot of us did. When the time was right the gaffer would let us play a few holes. Some say that golf could be quite harmful for a footballer, and I know when Gordon Strachan came in he had this rule that nobody could swing a club within three days of a match. In my time at Celtic Martin would usually give us a Wednesday off and he didn't mind us playing golf but as the Mark Twain quote says, "Golf is a good walk spoiled."

CHRIS SUTTON

Celtic Teammate

"I knew of Tommo from his Bolton days, I rated him and his thunderous left foot. I always thought he was this feisty all-in character but that he looked a bit daft, that was before I knew him. When I got to know him, I found my assumption was pretty accurate.

Tommo and I had a chat at the F.A Cup Final at Wembley in 2000, I can't remember what was said because I was warming the Chelsea bench and he'd been frozen out at Villa. I had no idea then that only a few months down the line we'd be meeting up again that year in a football sense in Glasgow for the same team. When Alan Thompson joined me at Celtic a couple of months after I arrived, we got to know each other, and we went on to have a close relationship as I really enjoyed his company. Tommo often describes me as his best friend at the club and I don't know where he's got that idea from as I was best friends with everybody because I was a very popular character (laughs).

Tommo and I lived close by each other, so we'd travel into Barrowfield together for training daily and that was always good fun. With me and him you never knew what prank was going to happen next, whether it was between us or on someone else. After training we would go to lunch together, usually to a place called Andiamo for a bit of pasta. One day I'd arrived before him, it was on a boiling hot day. Alan came in after me and asks me to get him a pint of cold water while he nips to the toilet because he is pissing with sweat. I notice that on our table was a vase with flowers in, only the flowers had seen better days and the water was bright yellow. I've taken the flowers out of the vase and poured the water in Alan's glass for him to drink. Alan then came in and did not give the glass a second glance. he's dogged the pint down in one!

Alan had a great personality off the pitch but on, his enthusiasm and drive was sublime. Some of the goals he scored for Celtic were absolute hammers. He also had wonderful awareness and was never frightened to play a pass. Maybe sometimes he would overreact in situations, but we always needed a player like Alan Thompson in our team. He was capable of doing things with the ball that other players just weren't capable of. His set-piece deliveries were phenomenal and overall, he was just a great footballer. He could also play a variety of roles which he did and was a major cog in that Celtic team. When Martin got him for £2.75million back in 2000 than you're talking about an absolute snip and he strengthened our team massively. When I look back at my time at Celtic and our successes domestically and in Europe, I'll think of the players such as Lubo Moravcik, but Alan was one of them calibre players. Tommo scored some big, big goals. He was just a big-game player. I love Tommo and throughout the years we had together you just never knew what was going to happen next.

CHAPTER 12

THE CALL UP... FINALLY!

It's fair to say I was a late developer in football. I would put that down to missing an important part of my youth career due to the car accident. I feel from then on, I was always playing catch-up, and nothing more gives you a good example of this than not getting to play for England until I was 30 years of age. For years before I got my England cap the press were talking about me and Chris Sutton and how we should be playing for England. Sutty maybe didn't have a sniff due to his refusal to play for the England B team in 1998 under Glenn Hoddle. In my opinion big Sutty should have had at least 25 international caps when you look at average players who went on to get double figures for England. You've only got to look at Chris' partnership with Alan Shearer in the 1994/95 season when the two literally won Blackburn Rovers the Premiership Title. If you want my honest opinion on why Sutty missed out on a decent England career I'd have to say that was political.

Regarding myself I was aware that the England boss Sven-Goran Eriksson had come to watch me a few times and in those matches I knew I'd done reasonably well. In the February of 2004 my youngest child Saffron was due when the England squad was going to be announced. Me and the Mrs had been planning on getting the baby induced, which is eventually what happened. I actually played a game at Celtic Park on a Saturday afternoon then had to rush off to the hospital to be with my wife Jo. By the time I arrived at the hospital Jo was well into her labour. When I was at the hospital I was walking in and out grabbing a coffee trying catch Sky Sports News on the telly in the canteen. After all this talk that month that I was going to be in the England squad I wasn't in it. Well, I was gobsmacked because my agent had been telling me for ages I was going to make the squad. The reason me and Jo got Saffron induced was because I was told I was going to be in this squad, so you can imagine I was pretty annoyed. Little Saffron didn't need to have come early at all. Thankfully, and better late than never I was called up in the next camp the month after in March with fellow new boys Jermain Defoe and Shaun Wright-Phillips.

As I said I was very much the late developer as a footballer and here I was in the England squad now in my 30's alongside Gareth Southgate, David Beckham, Wayne Rooney, Steven Gerrard, Jonathan Woodgate, John Terry, David James and Darius Vassell. Obviously, I knew Gareth and Darius from my time at Aston Villa, so I naturally floated around their company when having a cup of coffee. Gareth told me that he wasn't wanting to influence me because it was my first squad but after the game on Wednesday when we're flying back from Sweden, we'd have a beer on the way home and I could tell him my thoughts! Bearing in mind Sven was apparently on several million pounds a year but wasn't doing much. He was happy letting the players like Gareth and David Beckham do the talking. In fact, on the night of my first and only game against Sweden, Gareth, who'd been more or less in charge, wasn't even starting, it was John Terry who was the captain that night. Going on my first evening meal inside the England squad I found the set-up to be very strange because we were all put on this large table and even though we were as one, everyone was still divided. What I mean was the London players sat together, then the midlands lot and the Northwest and so on. There wasn't any real interaction from the Southern players with the Northern players. Me being the only player from a Scottish team I wasn't even sure where my place was, but I fell into the Northerners. Although I was the only one and I suppose you couldn't get more Northern than me.

As I said the boss Sven didn't do much and it was his assistant Sammy Lee that took charge of the training. Now this might sound farfetched but it's the truth, I actually found out on the Tuesday, the day before, that I was starting but it wasn't from the manager, assistant or even the captain, I found out from the England kitman. The Scottish lad who looked after our strips was a Celtic fan and it was him who told me. In my brief time with England, I used to go and have a cup of tea with him because he would just talk about Celtic Football Club 24/7. The day before England played Sweden it was the kitman who said to me, "do ya know ya starting Tommo?" That was how I found out I was going to play for England. When the time came later on that night the gaffer Sven pulled me aside and told me I'd be starting Tomorrow night against Sweden. I had to look surprised as he was showing me the number eleven shirt with Thompson on. Even though I knew it was still pretty much a 'WOW' moment. To this day I'm the only Celtic player ever to be capped for England whilst playing for the club. It was a massive honour in my life to have been capped for my country, even if I just got the one cap.

On the day of the game, we didn't train we all just went for a walk. The game itself was at the Ullevi Stadium in Gothenburg. During the day I was lounging about the hotel waiting for the game on the night. The goose bumps and excitement were now starting to set in because I'd dreamt of this moment since I was an infant in Wallsend. For our pre-match meal the English F.A didn't allow the Swedes to cook our food, so we took our own chef along for obvious reasons. The food in the camp was out of this world by the way and everything a proper athlete should eat. Myself and the rest of the team were really looked after I'll say that much. Gary Lewin was the physio for England, but he was also the physio for Arsenal. I remember him walking around all the players handing out this drink. We all had to take this drink before we got on the bus to the stadium which was a two hour drive away. "Do you use that drink at Arsenal?!" Nicky Butt shouted. "No, we don't use this at Arsenal" Gary shouted back, then Nicky told him if it wasn't good enough for Arsenal it wasn't good enough for England and he refused to drink it. I think that statement from Nicky just showed you the kind of rivalry between Arsenal who were flying at the time and Manchester United.

Of course, it's a privilege to play for your country so you shouldn't get paid, however you do get some sort of bonus from the F.A. Not a lot, maybe £500 or something. As a kid growing up in Newcastle I watched the England team at the 1982 World Cup in Spain, then the World Cup 1986 in Mexico, watching my heroes like Kevin Keegan, Bryan Robson, Peter Beardsley and Glenn Hoddle, now I had the chance to follow in their footsteps and the feeling was out of this world. I don't mind saying I was incredibly emotional, obviously some of that was the pride and elation of playing for England but mostly because of how far I had come since that terrible accident. The fears I once had that my dreams of ever playing football again were over then getting to a day where I was not only able to play but chosen to represent my country, I think anyone would have been emotional, it had been quite some personal journey to say the least.

Before the match Sven got us all together in the hotel for a meet to discuss the game. He then started giving his team talk in Swedish. This is to the England national team! It was then that his 2nd coach Tord Grip shouted down to him, "SVEN SVEN… ENGLISH". If it was done for a bit of banter, then it would have been funny, but it wasn't a joke. Sven was trying to address twenty-four England football players in a foreign language. Gareth Southgate was sat there giving me a nudge as if to say, this is the norm for the England national team now. Sven then gave out his team talk on this little magnetic board, and it was basically, "tonight boys we play 4-4-2 and we go forward as a 4-4-2 and we defend as a 4-4-2." I'm sat there thinking, 'wow, this is something I got taught for the under 9's at the Boys Club in Wallsend.' I was listening to this great manager and his instructions were like the team talks I used to get from the coaches who had day jobs and just helped out with youth teams in Newcastle Sunday football leagues. I was kind of amazed that I was hearing this from the England national team boss, it just didn't add up.

I started on the left of a four and Jamie Carragher was playing behind me. Now, no disrespect to Jamie but he was a centre-half, and he was right footed. I was playing on the left, but I didn't have the correct guy behind me which didn't let me see a lot of the ball. Had Ashley Cole been playing that night it would have been totally different and we'd have been overlapping each other. Jamie and I just didn't have that kind of communication because my view is that he wasn't really comfortable in that position. It wasn't as if he could have opened up with his left foot, so he was always cutting inside on his better foot. That's not a criticism of Jamie Carragher, it's just common sense. Look how much playing in front of Gary Neville did for David Beckham's overall game when he was at Manchester United for all of those years! I just wish Sven would have given me a left footed player behind me, my performance would certainly have been better than it was. I hope that doesn't sound bitter I'm just giving you lot my honest feelings about what went on in that England game.

In the opposing team that night was a familiar face I knew as "Dolph", better known as Johan Mjallby my Celtic teammate. I was taken off after an hour and swapped for Leeds United's Alan Smith and I knew my chance with England had been and gone. It was only a friendly, but I knew I hadn't performed to any level. After the game against Sweden, which we lost 1-0 to a Zlatan Ibrahimovic goal, I sat back, and it hit home I'd actually played for England and it was an amazing feeling. I sat there in the dressing room thinking of my time in the hospitals as a young teenager thinking I might never walk again, now I'd just played at the pinnacle of my profession. Astonishingly Sven got us all together after the game and said something like, "ok lads, we must improve next time so let's get showered and leave" and that was it! That was the team talk of one of the best coaches in the world who's managed clubs such as Benfica, Roma, Fiorentina, Sampdoria and Lazio!

We had a beer on the flight home. The plane arrived at Manchester first to drop off the northern lot, including myself and then flew onto London to drop off the remaining lads, we all went our separate ways and I headed off back to Glasgow. The one thing which did hurt and was a right kick in the balls was what I overheard after the game against Sweden. I was sat on the team bus by myself waiting for the rest of the lads coming out, I was maybe three or four seats away from Sammy Lee and Ray

Clemence. I was in a world of my own thinking about my performance and to be honest I was pretty down about it when I overheard the lads at the front. They weren't exactly slagging me off, but I overheard Sammy say to Ray, "he's a good player but not good enough for this level." I knew that comment was aimed at me, and I was just thinking, 'hang on Sammy have a bit of respect I'm sat only a few feet away from you here! If you're going to say it then say it where I can't hear it.' I knew if Sammy was sat there saying this and he was one of Sven-Goran Eriksson's biggest influences I knew my England days were numbered. I knew there wouldn't be any second caps forthcoming, and I just had to concentrate on my Celtic career. I was 99.99% sure that ship had sailed, and it turned out I was right.

Some have said Sven gave me a cap as a token gesture to get the press off his back because the media had been talking about me and Chris Sutton playing for England for so long. It's a real shame considering England were never exactly blessed with left siders for the many years that I was around. On the plus side, I got to keep this really upmarket Armani England suit which I've still got, although I might have to lose a few stone to get back into it. The bottom line is if someone would have said to me in September 1990 when I was laid in hospital with a broken neck, 'don't worry son because you'll play for England in fourteen years' time' the stress would have left me there and then.

SIMON FERRY

Celtic Reserve Team Player

"Tommo was brilliant when I was a lad coming through at Celtic. Him and big Sutty used to terrorise us all. One example was when me and my teammate in the youth team Paul McGowan were in the back cleaning the squads boots for the first team. Tommo and Sutty then opened the door to show us off to the full Celtic first teamers and they shouted, "OI LADS, COME AND SEE HOW FUCKING UGLY THESE TWO YOUNG KIDS ARE IN HERE." Myself and Paul must have been sat there, two 16-year-olds, and just been totally humiliated.

Back in that time as a young lad I was very much into my brand clothes i.e., Dolce & Gabbana. I was only on £350 a week but one day Tommo came in with two big bin bags full of Armani gear for me. I don't know if it was stuff he'd been sent and it was too small for him, but he came in one day and said, "ere ya go young'un, take them." That's what I meant by saying he was brilliant and even though he would torture us with his pranks, he sort of took us under his wing.

Around 2006 Tommo kind of got moved into the reserves with us but he played like an absolute beast still. He was a great example to me of how a modern day pro should train and had to be. If at any time I had a shot on goal or played an amazing pass he'd shout, "KEEGAN" or if any of us young lads took a few people on he'd shout, "IT'S FUCKING BEARDSLEY" because obviously he was a big Newcastle fan. One true story I must tell while we're talking about Alan Thompson, and this has to go in his book is of one afternoon in Celtic Park. Myself, Michael Gardyne and Paul McGowan were in the physio room lounging about, probably trying to wag off our tidying up duties when Tommo and Sutty came in. At the time we were just young lads and not on much money when Tommo shouts to us, "ere lads, al give ya £100 each if ya come and trash this physio room." Me and the other two were umming and ahhing but Tommo says, like a devil on our shoulder, "just fucking trash it man, it'll only take a minute, and nobody will know it's you." In the end the carrot which was dangling of £100 each was too great, so we were all like, 'ok Tommo no bother' and we proceeded to tip the room upside down. Whilst we were smashing the room up, Tommo runs to Martin O'Neill's 2nd man John Robertson's office and says, "Robbo I don't know what is happening in that physio room, but I'd take a look sharpish if I was you." The next thing wee Robbo comes running in and myself, Michael Gardyne and wee Paul McGowan stopped chucking tables about and Robbo started going fucking mental at us three. That was Alan, he was always trying to stitch some poor unsuspecting bastard up for his own entertainment. Another example of this is when Aidan McGeady had broken through into the first team. At the time Neil Lennon was the main man and all of us young players were scared of Lenny. None of us young lads would ever have the balls to do anything bad to Lenny or noise him up but Aidan, being the type of lad he was, nutmegged Lenny in one of his very first training sessions with the Celtic team. Well Lenny went off it and was screaming at Aidan, 'how fucking dare you' and that he should show a bit of respect. Lenny threatened Aidan saying to never fucking do that to him again or he'd regret it, then two seconds later Tommo runs over to Aidan and says, "I'll give you £500 if you meg him again."

Lenny was the top dog at Celtic in those days but often Tommo would say to some of the youth players, “if you man-mark Lenny all game there’s £100 waiting for you after training.” Alan was the first to have a laugh and a joke but at the same time he knew when to be serious. When I watched him as I was coming through at Celtic, I realised just how high the bar was to become a top player in the game. Alan was a big help to me growing up.”

CHAPTER 13

HELL AT FIR PARK & THE GAFFER'S LAST STAND

I had three full seasons as the main supplier for Henrik Larsson, Chris Sutton and John Hartson. That was one hell of a formidable forward line for any club in European football can I just say. What I'll also say is the three were all very different to the other. Larsson & Sutton were a total separate partnership to Larsson & Hartson. The only time Sutton & Hartson were together was when Henrik had a spell out in 2003 with a fractured cheekbone or when Henrik left. Larsson & Sutton linked up the play better because those two were so cunning with little 'overs' around the box. Henrik and Chris had an almost telepathic understanding the likes of which you see in twins, each knew what the other was going to do and it wouldn't even be worked on in training. Sutty could also head a ball harder than most players could volley it.

When you put John into the equation, who didn't have great movement outside of the box because it simply wasn't his game. Inside that penalty box he was so skilled that he could move one way to go the other way. Technically Hartson was as good as any striker I've ever played with and that's why he got the big money moves to the clubs he did. He could batter the best defenders in the Premiership for 90 minutes and not give them a moments peace. For me big John wasn't given the credit he deserved but if you look at the man's goalscoring record of 109 goals in 201 games then it's up there with anyone's. Away from the pitch big John was one hard man let me tell you, he could pack a punch. Sometimes when we would do boxing exercises in squad training, the one man you really didn't want to take on the pads was big John, Or Big Rab Douglas for that matter because both could seriously bang.

Sutty was the complete team player, and he wouldn't mind if we won 1-0 and he didn't score. With Hartson & Larsson it was all about banging the goals in so their names would be in the media headlines. Pound for pound Chris was as good as any player I've ever played with in my whole career. He was that good he could play in defence because his football brain was so good. Saying that Sutty would say I'm a bit thick so I'm not going to how he was a clever lad, but he was sharper than most footballers.

I don't know if Celtic Football Club, since its beginnings in 1888 have had three strikers of that quality at the same time, put it that way! Martin O'Neill knew, for those three seasons he had them together that he had the arsenal to sink any team in Europe. Out of the three I would say Sutty was the cleverest and he was good at pretending to defenders. He also had a bit of vision about him. When you look at the others in the team such as myself, Petrov, Lambert, Lennon, Agathe, Balde etc we were all so different to the one another and I think that's why we were so problematic to play against. Not only were our front lot something else but we were a very physical team. I remember Ronald de Boer once telling me that when he saw the size of us all in the tunnel then most of the Rangers team would be intimidated. When you think of the size of some of our lads like Balde, Mjallby, Valgaeren, Hartson, Sutton, Douglas, Varga, Pearson we were all big lads in height. Even myself I'm a 6-footer, albeit a poncy little winger (laughs).

If Henrik's last season was emotional, then this one was going to be harder for me because it was Martin's last season, although none of us knew it yet. In actual fact I started off that 2004/05 season in iconic fashion by putting my laces right through on the ball which smashed past Rangers goalkeeper Stefan Klos and it went in off his crossbar. It was the first Old Firm Derby of the season at Celtic Park, and we won 1-0 with my goal coming in the 85th minute which saw us snatch the victory. We had a great start to the season with a few new players in the team such as Henri Camara and the little Brazilian magician Juninho. If there was any pressure on the little fella coming to Celtic, then it was doubled when he was given the number seven shirt from the departed Larsson. Signing the Brazilian made a lot of people sit up because he was some player! In fact, it started great for him, and he was given the man of the match in his first game against Rangers but from then on, he seemed to fade away. Many said he was never the same as when he set the Premiership alight for Middlesbrough in the mid-90's and since coming back from an horrific injury whist playing for Atletico Madrid. He just didn't seem able to get away from his opponents like he once could. Maybe the style of play in Scotland was too physical I don't know but it didn't help his cause that a young Aiden McGeady was now knocking on the first team's door in his position. I found him a great little character who was always bubbly around the place, but it just wasn't meant to be at Celtic I'm afraid.

I'm not going to lie there was a big void in our team because Henrik was no longer with us, and our team was trying to recover as best we could. Henrik Larsson would have been a loss to any team in the world, so we were obviously going to feel it in that first season without him. Although we were going into that season as champions, it was going to be much closer now without our star man plus our Glasgow rivals had signed some top players such as Jean-Alain Boumsong, Gregory Vignal, Dado Prso, Alex Rae, Thomas Buffel, Marvin Andrews, Nacho Novo not to mention brought Barry Ferguson back from Blackburn Rovers. That kind of business by Rangers boss Alex McLeish made us aware that they meant business and were coming for our title.

We had to pick ourselves up and it was hard that season because the gaffer missed most of our pre-season due to personal issues. We didn't know it at the time but that was the start of Martin's better half Geraldine being ill which would eventually lead to Martin leaving at the end of that season.

Robbo and Wally took us to America to play a few games in the Champions World Series against Chelsea, Liverpool and Roma, we lost all three games fairly heavy. If we were inconsolable over the loss of Henrik Larsson then we really shouldn't have been, because who did we get in our first game in the Champions League at Celtic Park but Henrik Larsson's Barcelona. You really couldn't have made it up when we drew them in the group stages along with AC Milan and Shakhtar Donetsk. That September the 14th the prodigal son returned to paradise when he came on from the bench for Barcelona to a very hostile environment. Barca ran out 3-1 winners and of course Henrik being Henrik he got himself on the score sheet, but he looked devastated when he scored. To his credit he ran off stone-faced with no celebrations to rub our noses in it. He actually looked like he was walking to the gallows as his Barca teammates congratulated him. I'd scored the winner against Barcelona only six months earlier in the same team as Henrik, in fact it was Henrik who nodded it down to set me up. When Henrik scored against us it was my sloppy back pass to David Marshall that Henrik pounced on like a fox. Basically, he knew me that well and read very well what I was going to do.

If you're reading this Henrik then I'll say it wasn't really a mistake on my part, more an assist to pay you back for you setting me up the previous season. Henrik took advantage of my mistake because he had the instinct of a pure predator. Jokes aside I gave Henrik lots of assists over the years but that's not one of my favourite ones.

I could go on and on about that season but what people really remember about that season was 'Helicopter Sunday'. The last game of the season we played Motherwell at Fir Park with Rangers playing Hibs away at Easter Road. The day was May 22nd, 2005, and I'll never forget it as long as I live. There was a 13,000 attendance and all we had to do was win the game and we'd be crowned champions again. Big Sutty scored in the 29th minute. We were in a great position, and we missed some great chances to put that game to bed. One, off the top of my head, was when Craig Bellamy missed a great chance and then the tension set in. We really should have been out of sight, but we didn't take our chances and left ourselves in danger and that's what happened.

I must say a few words about Craig Bellamy though and on his time at Celtic. He arrived on the last day of the transfer window on January 31st, 2005. He came on loan because him and Graeme Souness weren't seeing eye to eye at Newcastle, which of course got him brownie points with the Celtic fans before he'd even arrived. Martin O'Neill said that because Chris Sutton doesn't like anyone's company, so if he likes Craig which he did, that was a major plus. If he passes the Sutton test, he should pass anything and he brought Bellamy in. I found Craig to be a bubbly character and although I didn't know him well, I'd heard bits about him from lads at Newcastle. When Craig first came people were saying he'd come along and cause all sorts of problems in the Celtic dressing room, but he was anything but that. Craig was nothing but respectful to all the lads in the squad. Craig had to be managed really closely though because he suffered with a few injuries so the doctors at Celtic were always keeping any eye on him.

As a player he was really quick like Didier Agathe, and he scored on his debut at Easter Road in the February. Craig's knowledge of the game was also something else and he loved football. He'd study the game like watching German, Italian and Spanish league games so he always knew who was who in the game. You wouldn't have got that impression with Craig until you got to know him. He worked his socks off for his team, was in the gym constantly and was always looking to be in peak condition for match day. He wasn't too dissimilar to Henrik in that he was quick, two footed, read the game well and closed the opposition down when he never had the ball. Often front players get bored or go missing when their team aren't in position. As a centre half you just didn't want to come up against players like Bellars because he was everywhere and just a total nuisance constantly. You probably already know he was mouthy and he loved a bit of verbal's on the pitch with whoever he was playing against. That was just Bellar's personality and when I saw him at Norwich City when he was young, he was already like that. Not only that but he genuinely loved Celtic, Martin and all the lads. He knew all about Sutty from his Norwich days and big John because of the Wales setup. I honestly think that if Martin would have stayed beyond when he left I don't think Craig would have signed for Blackburn Rovers in the July, he'd have joined Celtic on a permanent deal.

The league was coming back to Celtic Park until the 88th minute when self-confessed Celtic fanatic Scott MacDonald scored, then bagged another in the 90th minute to hand Rangers the title. It wasn't just freaky that we conceded one, but we got double whammed which knocked us into utter devastation. I've had lows in football before, but this was something from out of this world and I'd never seen or felt anything quite like it. I can understand ex Rangers man Terry Butcher going nuts as the Motherwell boss, but MacDonald celebrated like he'd just won the league. You'd have thought he could have taken a leaf out of Henrik's book when he scored against us for Barcelona, but the self-confessed Celtic nut MacDonald went crazy in joy when thousands of Celtic supporters were on the floor in tears in the stands at Fir Park. The way the Motherwell team celebrated was an absolute disgrace to football. There was no respect and as I said it was like Motherwell Football Club won that SPL Title.

Back to Easter Road, big Rangers defender Marvin Andrews said God was behind us losing the league in the last two minutes of the season. Well, I don't know what God was playing at if that was true because it was a stake through the heart to all of us on that pitch at Fir Park on that final day of the 2004/05 season. As this book is being written now sixteen years on, I still can't describe the feeling from it all. It was just horrific and if we thought losing in Seville and the league on the last day of the season in 2003 was bad this was tenfold. For me, to this day I'm still broken hearted, and it brings a bad feeling to my stomach. At least in the 2002/03 season we had great memories to take away from winning nothing at all.

After the game in the dressing room there wasn't a lot to be said because everyone was in a sheer state of disbelief of what had just happened. If it was a boxing match then MacDonald's 88th and 90th minute goals were left and right hooks from a prime Mike Tyson of 1986 and we all were K.O'd. It was impossible to think it could have got even worse, but it did. Martin then said, "listen lads the Scottish Cup Final next week at Hampden is going to be my last game in charge as the manager of Celtic." There were just no words to how I was feeling that day. I'd been at Celtic at that point five seasons and I never knew anything different than playing for Martin O'Neill and his gang of merry men John Robertson and Steve Walford. At that point I had no idea that Martin would be off because he'd given me a contract extension and wage rise not long before that. I'd built up this trust element over the past five seasons and now I was being told he was leaving.

The eleven-mile bus journey after the game back to Celtic Park from Motherwell was something else also. I'm not kidding you there were bodies laid around on the floor in green & white colours in a daze. If they weren't laid down crying, then they were sat up with their head in their hands broken. On the bus none of us said a word. When you actually think about just how close we came, we then lost the league and the helicopter had to do a U-turn from Glasgow to Edinburgh in mid-air, it tells you everything doesn't it?! As soon as the team bus dropped us off at Parkhead it was a case of us getting in our cars and going home. None of us were in the mood to even talk to each other by that point, I think most of us just wanted to go to bed. As you can imagine Martin gave us all the day off the next day but when we came in for training on the Tuesday you can imagine the atmosphere. We still had a Cup Final to win a few days from then, so it was incredibly hard for us all to lift ourselves up from it. We were flat but we had to win this game against Dundee United for the fans and of course Martin as it would be his last game in charge. The day before the game we didn't feel like we had a Cup Final in twenty-four hours' time. That feeling of what had happened at Fir Park never left me until I started getting my kit on for that Scottish Cup Final. We won the Cup Final against United and I scored the only goal of the game in the 11th minute a proper scruffy goal at that. It was a freekick from wide which travelled through a horde of bodies, it was nothing special. I wish I could sit here and write about just how we put a show on for Martin, Robbo and Wally but we just to say got over the finishing line, especially when Dundee Untied midfielder Barry Robson had an unbelievable effort from distance rattle off our crossbar towards the end of the game. I was actually brought off in that game with a torn calf and as Chris Sutton skied his penalty I was walking behind the goal. I know this sounds bad because I was in the same team as Sutty, but I had a little chuckle because I thought it was funny. Sutty didn't find it funny and nor would I if they'd have gone on to score.

I think God gave us a little bit of luck because he felt bad about what had happened the week before at Motherwell. I did have a laugh with Chris after the game when I told him I was laughing at him.

We won the Cup for Martin but if I'm honest we were 75% at our best, still shell shocked and obviously we needed the summer to get over it. Martin then went off into the sunset to look after his lovely wife Geraldine having won seven trophies at Celtic in his five years in Glasgow. It was an end of an era for Celtic Football Club and of course Robbo and Wally went with him.

What I will say personally is it should never be forgotten what the gaffer did at the club because when he first came in June 2000, five miles across the city Glasgow Rangers were in such a strong position in Scottish football and at the time were being backed with big money. I've heard over the years that people have said, 'well Martin spent big on the likes of myself, Lennon, Sutton, Valgaeren, Hartson etc' but Rangers were spending £12million pounds on Tore Andre Flo from Chelsea and we never got near those type of figures. In fact, the biggest signing Martin pulled off was for around half that amount. I don't want to put it in this book because it wouldn't be right, but I know what Ronald de Boer was earning to even come to Glasgow and it was double what Henrik Larsson was earning put it that way. We would have done well to compete in those years, but we didn't only compete, Martin put them firmly in their place. I think Chris Sutton summed it up when he first signed for Celtic by saying he knew signing for Celtic was all about winning the league and putting Rangers in their place.

After we'd won the Scottish Cup, we all went off on our summer holidays not having a Scooby-Doo who would be the new boss. It's fair to say that when Gordon Strachan was appointed many fans were furious. The bad feeling towards Strachan went back to the 1980's when one fan ran on the pitch at Celtic Park to try and punch Gordon who was playing for Aberdeen. When the guy was put in front of the courts the Celtic support all had a whip round to pay the attackers fine. It sounds crazy but it's a true story, so many of the supporters were upset that Gordon Strachan had been appointed. You can only imagine what the pressure was like on Gordon when he got smashed 5-0 in his first game over at Artmedia Bratislava, but we'll talk about that in the next chapter.

When you talk about that period of my career and also at Celtic Martin O'Neill was the figurehead behind all the success, not forgetting John Robertson and Steve Walford as well. I have to say that part of Martin being the top manager he was, was down to the two fellas he had by his side. Those two were the unsung heroes. Robbo was Martin's sounding board and the two had massive trust in each other. Wally was more Martin's Day to day man who did the sessions with us all. The three guys complemented each other terrifically well.

Thankfully I've never lost touch with the gaffer even after he left Celtic, and I'd left the club. I remember one occasion not long after I'd retired around 2009, I was in London for the weekend and I met up with him. Martin took me out and bought me dinner and it's little touches like that as well as phone calls that reassures you he's always there for you. He'll be my friend for the rest of my life and I'm forever grateful for everything he did for me in my career. If you look at the gaffer then, he looked like butter wouldn't melt in his mouth but let me tell you all, when he walked in that dressing room, he had my full respect and attention. There wasn't anybody other than Martin O'Neill I wanted to write the foreword for this book.

ALAN STUBBS

Former Bolton & Celtic Teammate

"I was with Tommo when he was a young lad at Bolton Wanderers from 1993 to 1996 then I was with him for a season at Celtic 2000/01. As a young lad at Bolton, he was finding his way whereas when I met up with him at Celtic a few years later he'd found himself and was blooming. He was out of his shell a lot more and didn't want to be the brunt of anyone's jokes like he was at Bolton. With him being such a young lad at Bolton with a temper he was easy to wind up. Me and Jason MacAteer used to love winding him up because Tommo had a bit of a short fuse. Me and Jason used to cast our rods at Tommo and entice him in and we knew we'd get a bite because he had such a short fuse. Sometimes we'd get close to Tommo's face and shout, "AAAAARGH" whilst laughing and it was like a red rag to a bull, and he'd be off. There was plenty of times in training where we'd wound him up that much he'd start throwing two-footed tackles around. As a Liverpool lad would do, if Tommo felt he was against it he'd put himself about in battle as a Geordie lad would do. He wasn't scared to look after himself whilst playing and he did that on a lot of occasions.

As I said when I played with him the second time at Celtic, he was far more mature and wiser in the sense of humour department if you like. He'd served his apprenticeship and I saw a notable change in Thompson compared to his early days. The young gullible Geordie lad was suddenly a main stay figure in anything that was going on. As a player also, I found he was more the finished article at Celtic because obviously he was older. In the early days at Bolton, I don't think he understood his talent, he just played football without a plan. When he was at Glasgow Celtic, he knew exactly what his game was about. As much as he loved giving out the pranks, he was never that good in a situation where the jokes were aimed at him. His short temper wasn't designed for being made fun of."

CHAPTER 14

THE GREATEST DERBY IN THE WORLD

I played in 26 Old Firm derbies, scored 7 goals and of course got three red cards so I got to know a little about the world-renowned fixture between the Glasgow giants. I was 26 years old and in my prime years when I arrived into the Glasgow goldfish bowl. Many players don't understand what that game means in the city but in all fairness, I knew a lot about it. I'd watched many games between the pair and although I grew up 151 miles away in Newcastle, I always preferred Celtic to Rangers well before I signed for them. My mam was Catholic and my dad was protestant but that never came into it. I'm not sure if I just liked the strip but I just preferred the green & white side of the city to the blue & white half, but I couldn't put a finger on why.

I remember well the incident in 1995 when Gazza pretended to play the flute in a pre-season friendly then acted like he was scanning the crowds for gunmen looking to shoot him in his head. If you talk about someone coming to Glasgow and not knowing what they're doing, then he's the perfect example. Then again, that might have just been Gazza being Gazza or perhaps he had been encouraged for the craic by some of the staff. Paul was checking under his car for bombs and was scared to open his mail for a good while after that, it's definitely not something to be joking about but he quickly learnt from his mistakes.

I had watched the Celtic v Rangers games for years before I went to Celtic so I knew what it was all about. Before my first game in November 2000, I was talking about it for weeks beforehand with the Glasgow boys and the intensity naturally built up as the date got closer.

Talking about when I'd just signed for Celtic, there's a story I'd like to add to this book. Now this might sound farfetched but its 100% the truth. This incident was only weeks after I's signed for Celtic Football Club and I thought my time in Glasgow would be over when I realised what I was being told. Around 1990 I was in Tenerife on a lads holiday with my close mate Peter Joynson. Peter and I went over to his parents place as young teenagers. It was my first lads holiday so you can imagine what my plans for the trip were, they included drinking in the sun and pulling girls. Well myself and Peter pulled these two lasses from Glasgow but before anything could happen I got too drunk and fell asleep. Nothing happens with myself or either of the girls other than they put me to bed for being a lightweight, some Geordie I am eh?! Baring that in mind, we fast forward a decade, the year is now 2000, I've just signed for Glasgow Celtic and I'm living in a hotel on the River Clyde. I was still in my honeymoon period at Celtic, so I ring my mate Peter Joynson to see if he fancies coming up to Glasgow for a bit to have the odd night out. Peter agrees and comes up to Newcastle on his own and he stops with me for a short time. Me and Peter go on this night out in The Corinthian Bar on Ingram Street, which is one of the city's most impressive buildings having five floors. Myself and Peter are having a great evening and enjoying a few drinks when we hear these two women shouting, "ALAN… PETER… HOW YA DOING, IMAGINE SEEING YOU HERE"!! I have no idea who these two girls are until

Peter says to them, "Ah, you're the two girls from Tenerife ten years ago aren't you?" Well I was amazed at the coincidence of bumping into these girls who had kindly tucked me up in bed a decade earlier. Everything was going well that evening, we were having a great conversation until one of them said to me, "Alan I've got a picture of you with a tampon up ya bum." I'm just stood there staring at her, and I was sure that I had misheard her, so I ask her what she means. "Yeah yeah, I've got a photo of you with a tampon up ya bum from when we tucked you up in bed." I hadn't misheard! I turn and look at Peter then it becomes apparent that what this girl is saying is true! I suppose she never expected to see me again and I never expected to make it as big as I had and now be playing for one of the biggest clubs in the world. As I'm sure you can imagine, this is a rather awkward situation to be in because if that photo fell into the hands of Glasgow Rangers supporters it would become extremely embarrassing indeed, worse still, could you imagine if the press got hold of this photo??? The only thing I could think of doing now was sitting this girl down and explaining the whole scenario of what damage could be done if she leaked this image she had of me. Thankfully she responded with, "ooh darl don't worry, I will never show anyone. I'm now married with weans", this does put me at ease, but I've got to admit as I'm buying her drinks in this bar I'm thinking, how on earth am I going to get this photograph from her? Thankfully and touch wood the lass was true to her word and it's never seen the light of day but if it does ever surface, then please remember I was just a young kid when it happened! I do hope this book doesn't bring this embarrassing photo out in the open but if it does surface, I'll put it in my next book (laughs). Could you imagine the laughs Ally McCoist and

Chris Sutton would have if they got that photo? Simply doesn't bare thinking about does it?!

I would spend seven years in Glasgow and I scored a goal for every one of those years against Rangers. I'd love to sit here and to just talk about those seven goals, but the reality is there were three red cards at Ibrox also that I have to address. When I look back at my time of being involved with the Old Firm games it's even bigger than what I thought it was at the time. When I was playing for Celtic I was living in Mearnskirk in Newton Mearns then later moved on to the Broom estate which was quite an affluential area of the city so you would have thought none of that sectarian nonsense goes on. How wrong I was. One night I looked out from my kitchen window when I saw these two teenagers spraying the words, 'FENIAN BASTARD' on the side of my house. I banged on the window and the pair ran off, so I jumped in the car to go looking for them. I must have drove around the streets of Newton Mearns for a good twenty minutes looking for these kids who just came to graffiti my home for no other reason than I played for a football team they didn't like, eventually I caught sight of them at the Shell garage. I couldn't believe it when I saw them in front of me messing around with the jet wash trying to clean all the silver spray paint off their hands. I drove over and stopped in front of them so they couldn't get out of the bay and I grabbed hold of the pair of them. I wasn't even sure what I was going to do with these two kids who were around 16/17 years of age. As luck would have it a police car pulled into the garage, and I shouted over to the officers for some assistance. The officers didn't take any notice to begin with, I think they thought it was just three youths messing about but when I told them I was being serious they came over to help. The police asked me what I'd like to do about it and I told them I didn't really want to press charges as they were just young lads, however I did think they needed a telling off so I asked if they could take them home and inform their parents of what they'd been up to, which is what happened. The police could see the evidence was on their hands still. Around an hour later my buzzer went at my home and it was both the boy's parents coming to apologise. In all honesty, they were mortified with what their offspring had done and they offered to get it cleaned off the side of my house. That just shows you what you're dealing with living in Glasgow when playing for one of the big two. You all know about Neil Lennon getting death threats and bullets sent to him in the post sent just because he was a Roman Catholic playing for Northern Ireland. I got some stuff like that too like people wiping faeces on toilet roll and sending it to me. To be honest I'd have rather had a bullet than other people's crap! I learnt from the minute I opened the first one and put my finger in it to be extra careful from then on. It wasn't always monstrous things that I got in the post because I got some lovely stuff but there was lots of bad stuff. One day I was walking around Glasgow city centre with the wife and we'd just had Saffron so she was in the pram when this transit van pulled up and as the doors opened, a couple of lads jumped out the back and came running over to me being hostile, this was whilst I was pushing the baby. I couldn't believe that in the middle of Glasgow in broad delight grown men were behaving like that. I jumped in the way of the baby and these lads were calling me every nasty name under the sun. Another time I was called a "fenian bastard" at a Snow Patrol concert. I had to remain calm and professional but unlucky for the perpetrator my good friend Geoff Stokes was there, and he went and put it on the culprit. Just to let him know that although I was taking it, he certainly wasn't!

I have to say though it wasn't all bad and many of the Rangers fans were very respectful.

To be quite honest I probably had more occurrences like that with my old sparring partner Fernando Rickson as I was on the left and he was on the right so we came up against each other for six years. Fernando, God rest him, was a good strong player and can I say how devastated I was that he passed away at such a young age due to Motor Neurone Disease. There's no doubt about it, Rickson and I had a rivalry that got quite nasty at times. Fernando was a Dutch international and when he was at Rangers he was one of their main men. He received joint player of the season with John Hartson in 2005. You don't win those awards in Scotland if you're not doing it in the SPL. I'll never forget when me and Chris Sutton rang big John up, putting on a Dutch accent pretending to be Fernando. I called big John up and basically told him although we shared the Player of the Year award I was keeping the trophy as he wasn't in my league. Big John was getting irate down the phone screaming that next season when we played he was going to kick me all over. John had to pull over in his car because he was that fuming with Fernando. Myself and Sutty could hardly breath trying not to laugh but we couldn't hold it in any longer and as soon as we started laughing the penny dropped for John who had realised that Sutty and I had got him hook, line and sinker. Big John saw the funny side of it but at one point was threatening to do all sorts.

Going back to me and Fernando, it's common knowledge that we had our battles off the pitch as well as on. On the pitch I can honestly say I never set out to hurt him and I think it's safe to say that he would have said the same but in the heat of battle myself and Fernando still wanted to leave our stamp on each other if that makes sense.

I never set out to hurt anybody in my career, I can say that with my hand on my heart. There were the players out there you had to be wary of because these people were capable of doing things with sheer malice in mind. Vinny Jones for instance is a perfect example of someone who tried to go out and intimidate opposing players. Fernando Rickson wasn't one of those players who some would call a thug though. Yes, Fernando tried to put it on me, but I could handle it because I knew how to look after myself on the pitch too and he knew that. I was the type of player who was prepared to go toe to toe in a fair manner. There were however two off-field incidents when it did turn sour for me and Fernando and I'll explain them in detail here. The first was in May 2003 on the night they won the league, the first Helicopter Sunday. Obviously, we'd just lost the league, so I had an early night and went to bed. I must have been in bed for a few hours when I was suddenly woken by the noise of a car pulling up. I lived on the same street as Fernando but around the corner six or seven houses along. You'd guessed it, the car that pulled up was Fernando Rickson. He walked over my flower bed, opened my letterbox and shouted, "LEARN HOW TO TAKE PENALTIES YOU ENGLISH NOBHEAD." Obviously, he was referring to me missing a penalty that day against Kilmarnock. Not only was he shouting and bawling but he also dropped some sort of firework then bolted. It wasn't hard to work out who it was when I heard the Dutch accent and Rangers had just won the league that day. I have to say that Fernando wasn't on his own when he did this, he had a couple of mates with him that he was trying to impress with his silly antics. That was the first time he called trying to noise me up. The second time was the following May in

2004. It was the night that we beat them 1-0 at Celtic Park to complete the whitewash of beating them five times in five games. That day Chris Sutton had scored the chip over Stefan Klos in the dying seconds. Chris then ran to the crowd and I ran over and jumped on his back going ballistic. We'd just wiped the floor with the Gers five times in one season and I don't think that will ever happen again. Although I never did what Fernando did by going to his home and invading his private space, I did wind him up however. After I'd been going nuts with Sutty and the fans I ran up the park for Rangers to kick off but on the way, I ran past Fernando and gave him a little tap on his cheek and said, "don't be coming to knock on my door ever again." I'll admit now that I did that to my old sparring partner for a reaction. Only seconds after Rangers kicked off the fulltime whistle went and as you've probably guessed, Fernando comes looking for me. He didn't get anywhere near me though as there's green & white hooped shirts in the way and we go off the pitch. He wanted a boxing match in the tunnel, but it was never going to happen because there were just too many bodies around. I go to the dressing room to celebrate with the lads. We've got our title back as well as doing our biggest rivals over five times in one season and life is good.

On that same night I go out to celebrate with Chris Sutton and the wives to a place called 1 Devonshire Gardens in the West End of Glasgow for a nice meal. My mam had babysat the kids while I was out with Chris and the girls and it was a great night. Later that night, again in the early hours, the doorbell goes and as I look out the window I see Fernando on my front with this Bullmastiff on a lead. I just remember the dog being absolutely huge. I shouted to him, "what do you want?" It didn't take a genius to know what he was after yet again. "COME ON

THEN BIG MAN WE'LL DO IT NOW" was Fernando's response with his very angry Pitbull growling aswell. It was if the dog had known what had gone on and he wanted revenge also. I told Fernando I was happy to come down and, as they say in Glasgow, 'have a square go' but he needed to take that monster home first. I wasn't rolling around the floor with him when this giant beast was in his corner, so I told him to get stuffed, but not in such a polite manner. "NO NO I WANT IT NOW" was his reply so I ring his mate fellow Dutch international Ronald de Boer who also lived in the same street as me and Fernando, in fact Ronald lived directly opposite to me with Rangers Norwegian striker Tore Andre Flo also in the same street. Ronald thankfully answered although it was in the early hours and I told him what was going on. I told him I had my little girl Saffron who was only three months old asleep and that his mate was again outside of mine wanting fun and games and that it was unacceptable. Ronald then opened his door to talk sense into his teammate which made Fernando even more irate. It was then I knew he was intoxicated. I don't know what Ronald said because it was in Dutch but whatever he said it worked and off went Fernando into his house and that was the end of the matter. Although he was a pain in my arse at times, that was Fernando Rickson's personality and as a footballer you probably wouldn't want to take that side of him away, although he was difficult at times. God rest his soul; I wouldn't speak ill of the dead but what I'm putting in this book is exactly how it was back in the day when two footballers played for opposing teams of the big two in Glasgow. I have nothing but respect for Fernando Rickson as a professional.

In the next old firm game Chris Sutton scored the winner the May of 2004, that game finished 1 nil. The old firm game after that was when I scored the winner. I put my laces through the ball and it went in off the crossbar, that was in the August of 2004. I made a point of not winding Fernando up that time as I ran off to celebrate my winner in the last five minutes, I think Neil Lennon jumped on my back in case I had any thoughts of getting up to any funny business but that was never my plan.

I've discussed my first red card at Ibrox in this book already, so we'll move on to my second red which was November 20th, 2004. We actually played Rangers twice in ten days and they did us in both matches, one being the league and the other was the League Cup. My name will forever be linked with Rangers Danish striker Peter Lovenkrands after that match. There was an incident in that game when myself and Lovenkrands went face to face in the 38th minute, then out of nowhere, he went down like he'd been shot, he was holding his face and writhing like he was in agony. To my absolute shock the referee Kenny Clark bought his bullshit playacting and sent me off and we lost the game 2-0. Peter went down like I'd hit him over the head with a wooden mallet it was embarrassing. As a fellow professional footballer, I was ashamed for the lad and it was totally unacceptable. Chris Sutton also saw red for a second yellow for handball, but what I got sent off for was absolutely absurd and I've never really forgiven Peter Lovenkrands to this day for the way he cheated me. At the end of that 2004/05 season I was at the Player of the Year Awards at the Thistle Hotel, Glasgow. I was sat with the whole of the Celtic squad and of course all the Rangers team were there also. Peter came over to me and said, "Tommo Tommo can I have a word outside?" I asked him what he wanted and he said rather sheepishly it was about what happened at Ibrox a few months back in the season. I told him to jog on because I wasn't interested in hearing any kind of apology. Maybe I should have been the bigger man, but it was still eating me away at the time and I wasn't going to pretend that it wasn't. Moving forward to a few years down the line when I was the under 23's manager at Newcastle United the boss Chris Hughton signed Lovenkrands. Peter came and knocked on the office door one morning at the Longbenton training ground on the first day he signed and said sorry. By that point it had been five years since the incident and a lot of water had gone under the bridge. I'd been retired for a year or so and Peter was now in his 30s, so we had a cup of tea together. In his defence he held his hands up and told me it was a stupid thing to do and how much he regretted it. I told him it was nice to hear that and that would do for me and life went on. There were no hard feelings although it's been reported in the press that I did call Peter a coward via Twitter in 2020. I was new to Twitter and didn't know a lot about it but somebody had put the video of our incident on there and I had written 'coward' underneath. It was a spur of the moment thing, I didn't plan on digging it all back up from sixteen years previously but the next thing I know is it had made the media that Alan Thompson had launched an attack on his old nemesis Peter Lovenkrands. Maybe I shouldn't have put it but if you want my honest opinion, I truly believe it was a genuine act of cowardness.

My third red at Ibrox was August 2005. This was Gordon Strachan's first Old Firm game and this time I bit the dust in the 23rd minute for a late tackle on Nacho Novo. At the time I thought it was an unfair decision but looking back I lunged into a tackle and paid the price. They say a picture can speak a thousand words and there's a picture of me on Google images helping Nacho up but at the same time referee Stuart Dougal is pulling out a red. When I look at that picture you can clearing see my mind saying, 'NOT

AGAIN'. At the time I was 31 years old and I should have been more mature as a player and I should have controlled my emotions more. Although Martin wasn't stood in the dugout this time as I walked off the pitch, I knew only too well that exact feeling as I walked past Gordon Strachan who was shaking his head in utter disbelief because it was his first Old Firm match. I have to hold my hands up today in 2021 to holding the record for red cards between Celtic and Rangers with all my reds coming in Govan. It's a record I'd love to change but I can't I'm afraid. I think my closest rival was the French man Stephane Mahe who had two but I told him to hold my beer and I'd show him how it's done. Jokes aside it's not something I'm proud of to be brutally honest but I've more fond memories of the clashes than I have negative ones.

I scored seven goals against Rangers and all seven were against Stefan Klos. Two of the goals were the game deciders and in the seven games I scored we never lost. My first goal was a 1-0 win in February 2001. As I said earlier in the book it was my first game after my first red card and although it was only a tap in with my right foot (how strange) it was a great feeling. You'd take any kind of goal during a Celtic v Rangers match that wins you the game.

One of my better ones was a dribble at Ibrox in September 2001. Myself and Stiliyan Petrov got the goals in a 2-0. I cut in from next to the dugout, played a one-two and slotted it in the far corner at the Celtic end past Klos with my right foot. Maybe the most impressive was in early January 2004 when I hit a 30-yard freekick which ended up in the top corner to seal a 3-0 victory. When I used to step up to take my trademark freekick I used to tell myself, 'Alan just relax, you've pinged these in all week on the training ground' and I would let my technique do the talking. When I used to watch myself back taking freekicks

I saw that I was very slow in my approach. I could generate a hell of a lot of speed even though it was a side-foot. Sometimes you can hit twenty of them on the training ground and only one will go in but practise is everything.

One of the most spoken of goals against Rangers was one the in August 2004 when it went in off Klos' bar. Poor Stefan must have hated me as he picked the ball out of the net seven times in under five years. Stefan was a top quality stopper as well who'd played at the highest level with Borussia Dortmund. He actually won the Champions League with my buddy Paul Lambert. In the build up to an Old Firm game or any game for that matter I would practice freekicks at the start of the week. I wouldn't do it too much because it can fatigue you, I'd do the start of the week, leave the middle out and then I'd practice again the day before the match.

Since I've retired I'm often spoken of because of my trademark freekick. I think I've always been able to strike a ball since I can remember. When I was a lad in the Boys Club at Wallsend I took everything, even goal kicks. It was just always one of my strengths.

In my opinion the Old Firm Derby is the biggest game in world club football. On paper it's only a game of football but then when you take the religion, deep history and rivalry it becomes people's lives. It's a real eye-opener to just how many people know of me just because I played in those games. Around 2017, when I was at Bury I was staying at The Lowry Hotel, Manchester with Lee Clark. Who walks in, Noel Gallagher because Manchester City were playing at home nearby and he was going to the game. Noel came over and asked if he could sit with us both and used both our first names. This is one of the biggest rock stars not only asking if he could join us but already knowing my name! It was kinda scary really that he even knew who I was and all he wanted to do was ask me about Celtic and Rangers because he'd been to several. I asked him if we could talk about music but he said no because he wanted to know about what it was like playing for one of the Old Firm! I met world boxing legend Oscar De La Hoya around the same time but unfortunately, he had no idea who I was, however me and Lee Clark did manage to get a selfie with him though. Whilst on the subject of celebrities a minute I can remember training at Rod Stewart's house when Gordon Strachan was the manager. Gordon was good mates with him so he got us all a gig playing at Rod's home on his full size pitch. Rod was there in his Celtic kit. I remember looking at his £500,000 smashed up Ferrari on his drive, 'what's happened there Rod? "Ah Tommo my wife Penny did it at a MacDonald's drive-thru" he told me in his extremely East End of London cockney accent. Although Rod is a proper fully blown celebrity and known worldwide, I think he was more starstruck having all the Celtic squad in his garden as he was like a kid. Rod even had two dressing rooms for the pitch nearby and inside he had a load of Celtic kits in one, and the Rangers in another. He had these because he would play a match every couple of weeks with all his neighbours or fellow celebrity mates and he'd make them play for Rangers.

Not only have people been murdered because of the emotions the Old Firm matches evoke, but even Mr sensible the civilian Joe Public can have is day ruined if his team get beat. Losing that game can ruin people for weeks living in Glasgow, people in England just don't understand the passion that comes from it. If I'd not scored seven goals against Rangers, had only red cards and not won most of our encounters out of 26 then maybe I'd be more upset about it today. I think the Celtic fans appreciate what I did against Rangers. Every time I meet one of the Celtic family anywhere in the world its always my goals against them that gets brought up. Sometimes fans bring up their memories of the games and you can see it in their faces that it meant the world to them. I go to Celtic conventions all over the world and it still fills me with pride to relay these stories. Today I still make a point of watching the fixture because it's such a special game. When I think of my time in the Celtic shirt battling away against our dearest enemy, I just think of my old rival Fernando Rickson. Me and him went at it like Tom & Jerry, cat & dog or hammer & tongs. Every time I got the ball he was on me closing me down and vice-versa. No matter who got the upper hand between us the other always knew it was going to be one hell of a battle.

STILIYAN PETROV

Celtic Teammate

"I knew of Alan Thompson before I played with him as back home in Bulgaria, the English Premiership is big news. All eyes in my homeland would be on your Aston Villa's, Manchester United's and Liverpool's. What I found out about him when he joined Celtic was that he was one of these character's you wanted in your team. He was a leader who you could always count on. Tommo never complained about left back, central midfield or on the wing. He was always there for the side and he was the heart of our team. I met Tommo when I was a young player but playing with him showed me the way you have to prepare for games. That fire and desire he had meant he was a very important player for us. Alan was a huge personality and if something wasn't right in our team, he demanded it to be changed. If ever he was below par he would address it. He was a big voice in our Celtic team and he demanded that everyone in the side did their job properly. It was great to have such a leader in our team that we could fall back on like Alan Thompson."

CHAPTER 15

THE STRACHAN ERA & THE END IS NIGH

It's fair to say that there were a few raised eyebrows when Gordon Strachan took over at Celtic in the summer of 2005. Before a ball had been kicked I was behind because I didn't do pre-season training that year due to my injury from the Scottish Cup Final against Dundee United. I did try to train the first day under Gordon, but my calf went again and after that I was playing catch up with the rest of the squad. As soon as the new gaffer came he sat me down and told me the slate was clean and that I'd be given a chance to get into the starting eleven. True to his word that's what he did and I was given a fair crack at the whip.

On the first day under Gordon and his assistant Gary Pendrey, we did a fitness assessment in a park in Glasgow. We all had to do so many laps of a 400-metre track in eight minutes and as I was doing it that's when my calf went, which wasn't ideal. Especially as Gordon had brought many fresh faces into the team such as Adam Virgo, Shunsuke Nakamura, Paul Telfer, Maciej Zurawski, Artuc Boruc, Jeremie Aliadiere, Mo Camara plus the young Aiden McGeady, Ross Wallace and Shaun Maloney were all fighting for my jersey. By the time Gordon's first competitive game came up over in Bratislava I'd only had around two- or three-days training whereas the rest of the squad had four weeks under their belts. I remember a couple of days before the Artmedia Bratislava game Gordon told me he wanted me to play. I told Gordon of my concerns and that it wasn't ideal as I was nowhere near match fight. The boss told me it was a big match and that he'd like me on the pitch none the less as I was one of the more experienced heads in the squad at that point. Although I told him I didn't think I'd be doing him, myself, Celtic or the fans any favours I would start.

I got through the game and my calf was fine, but we got thumped 5-0. I played 66 minutes before Jeremie Aliadiere came on for me. Also, in that game Chris Sutton fractured his cheekbone early in the game so it was a total disaster. We actually had a strong team out that night with Lennon, Petrov, Balde, Varga etc but nothing went right for us and the young David Marshall picked the ball out of the net five times and none of those goals were his fault. In the second leg a week later at Celtic Park the gaffer replaced Marshy in goal with the new Pole Artuc Boruc. We had a great chance at the end of that first let in Slovakia when Aiden McGeady missed with a header which would have made it 5-1. If he'd have taken that chance we'd have went through the tie as we beat them 4-0 at Celtic Park. I got on the score sheet with a penalty but it was a case of, close but no cigar, and we went out.

The failure in that tie meant there would be no European football for us that season so we only had the league and two domestic cups to focus on. The crazy thing is many were calling for Gordon Strachan's head after only one game and many were saying they wouldn't be coming back to Celtic Park until Strachan had been sacked.

I scored two in one game as we beat Falkirk at home 3-1 in the August. As I scored the second in that game, which was a freekick from outside the box, I ran off celebrating with my hand cupped to my ear. That was for the benefit of the Celtic boo boys who had been giving me a bit of stick, it was my way of saying, 'listen, there's life in this old dog yet'. It wasn't planned it was just a reaction that was borne from personal frustration.

If I'd had to work hard to get in Gordon Strachan's good books, then I did myself no favours in his first Old Firm Derby in charge at Ibrox the week after the Falkirk game. History repeated itself and I was sent off again for a rash tackle on Nacho Novo for the third and final time. It wasn't nice walking off the pitch at Ibrox past Gordon as he was stood there shaking his head in disbelief, it felt like walking to the headmasters office. Although I'd done it twice before, doing it the third time wasn't any easier. As soon as everyone came off the pitch from our 3-1 beating I apologised to all the boys as well as to Gordon. Rather than give me a verbal bashing like Martin did, Gordon gave me the silent treatment but I think it was because he knew where I was mentally. He knew that I knew I'd well and truly fucked up.

Like Martin and his merry men Wally & Robbo, Gordon came with his team which was Gary Pendrey, Jim Blyth and later on Tommy Burns joined the staff. The difference with the Strachan team to the O'Neill lot was Gordon liked to be out in his shorts and boots on the training ground. Gordon was more hands on and he liked to psychically set his teams up. Gordon told you where your game was going wrong and he told you the areas you needed improvement. Gary did a bit of coaching also and overall, it was so different to what we'd had with Martin, Robbo and Wally. Gordon was fanatical in having his players running all day and that pre-season I remember watching from the side-lines as he had all the lads running all day. Running drills were a constant theme and I think that's why Gordon Strachan played for Leeds United until his 40's, so he must have known something. Gordon was all about old school running, which was his style as a player so, regardless of which team Gordon Strachan managed he had them fit, fit, fit.

I must say one of the more impressive names Gordon brought in was the big Pole Artur Boruc. From 2005 - 2007 seasons that guy was world class and one of the best shot-stoppers in Europe. Gordon later said that after having the experience of managing Boruc for four years he'd have made Prime Minister. Big Artur was one hell of a character in the dressing room, although he could be temperamental. Big Artur loved his Polish lager and was fond of the odd cigar, in fact he would go in the toilets at half time and have a cigarette every game and the gaffer just let him get on with it. Out of all the signings Gordon brought in he was the guy who impressed me the most and the Celtic fans took to him as soon as they saw him blessing himself at Ibrox. Of course, his antics towards the Rangers fans also made the Celtic fans fall in love with him even more. I think David Marshall was unlucky that such a world class keeper had come to the club to fight for his No.1 shirt.

Although I was starting games for Celtic in the December of the 2005/06 season, I would say the writing was on the wall that my time at Celtic was coming to an end as soon as I was sent off at Ibrox in the August. Also, in the board room I knew that Peter Lawwell wanted to move me on because the last contract I signed was one of the more lucrative ones shall we say.

The two-year extension deal that Martin gave me was by far the best of my whole career and with the likes of Shaun Maloney, Ross Wallace and Aiden McGeady coming through I knew that Celtic would be thinking it would make business sense if I wasn't here anymore. I'm sure there must have been a conversation with Gordon Strachan and Peter Lawwell around my contract situation. I was tied to Celtic Football Club until the summer of 2007 and if I was surplus to requirements to the team it would free up an awful lot of money to ship me out and get me off the wage bill. Not only was my contract incredibly handsome but I was also on a bonus of £10,000 an appearance on top of my basic salary. If I played two games in a week there's £20,000 grand on top of what I was earning! Like I said, it was some deal. I'm sure they must have thought, 'hang on a minute we've had the best out of this fella and don't need to be paying him anymore so let's get him out.' I think the finance side of it was 50% to do with my Celtic exit.

I turned 32 years old in the December of 2005, so my legs weren't getting any fresher. It really saddened me that my end at Celtic happened the way it did. I felt I was kind of pushed out the back door like a thief in the night and Chris Sutton was treated the same. Maybe Gordon Strachan made the correct decision in football terms but I feel that if Martin, Wally and Robbo had still been at the club I'd have been treat better. Let me just say for the record that Gordon didn't treat me badly, in fact he was very matter of fact. He told me that if I stayed I'd be travelling away to stay in hotels and sometimes lucky to be on the bench. In the highlight years of my career, he told me it probably wasn't what I wanted to be doing but that's what was going to happen. Gordon sometimes told me that he was happy for me to stay at home because I wasn't going to be involved but I told him I wanted to play, even if that was for Kenny McDowall in the reserves with the young lads. Gordon was here and he wanted to put his own ideas in, so that season also saw the likes of John Hartson and Stiliyan Petrov leave the club.

Chris Sutton and Didier Agathe had already left for Aston Villa where they would meet up with Martin O'Neill,

Steve Walford and John Robertson again. Shaun Maloney would also follow Martin down to Villa a short time later. Gordon then shipped in Dion Dublin and Roy Keane for experience and it paid off because Gordon's team walked the league and League Cup that season. However, it wasn't without another bump because Clyde did us in the Scottish Cup on Roy Keane's debut. Chris Sutton, being typical Sutton gave a statement when he left Celtic in the October of 2005 which said, "I've had a great five years at Celtic." The actual truth was Chris had been at Celtic for five and a half years so a lot could be read into that statement. As I said Gordon wanted his own stamp on the team and as he was getting Martin's team out one by one, he was going for the more dynamic players. Celtic knew Stiliyan Petrov was going to fetch in good money going to join up with Martin at Villa and eventually he did for £6.5million. Everyone knew that was on the cards before it happened, it was a matter of when. The one player of the Martin O'Neill era Gordon kept for a couple of years was Neil Lennon for obvious reasons. Lenny knew what the club was about, he had the background and that was why he made him captain. It was my decision to join all the young lads in the Celtic reserves like Simon Ferry, Rocco Quinn, Michael McGovern, Scott Cuthbert, Gary Irvine, Joe O'Brien, Ryan Conroy, Darren O'Dea and Paul Lawson. Many players at that time in their careers probably would have refused it but it was my decision I wanted to play regardless of the level. I liked the reserve team coach Kenny McDowall and I had a good relationship with him so I chose to play for him. It wasn't only that, I know when I was a kid I enjoyed watching and learning from the veterans such as Roy Aitken and Mark McGee, so I wanted to give something back and to pass on some of my experience.

One big name who came to the club in the January of 2006 was Roy Keane. I remember being sat in the canteen at the training ground with Roy, he'd shook my hand and asked, "What's happening Tommo?" I told him that my time was up at Celtic and now it was just a matter of when I was going not if. When I asked him what had happened with him at Manchester United, he just laughed and said, "much the same as what you're going through now." He said that as footballers we were like pieces of meat and we all had sell-by dates and now we were ready for the skip. I remember going away from that chat with Roy and thinking, if Roy Keane can sit there and say that after the glittering career he's had then that puts my situation into perspective. Did Gordon Strachan sign Roy or was it really Dermot Desmond because of his Irish connection and the boost it would give the merchandise? The impression I got when Roy came in was that it wasn't Gordon that brought him to the club it came from above him.

It was tough the way I left Celtic in the January of 2007. I signed for Leeds United on a six month loan deal at first before winning myself a contract for the season 2007/08 which I'll go into in the next chapter. I did try to leave Celtic in the summer of 2006, but we couldn't agree anything with the clubs I was talking to. I didn't want to stay in Scotland and move down a few levels. I don't think I could have played against Celtic and in truth I just had that many fond memories up here, I didn't want to tarnish that. I'd played for the biggest team in the country so moving to a club in Edinburgh or Dundee wasn't an option. I couldn't have joined another club in the SPL then played at Ibrox and been a shadow of my former self whilst receiving pelters. Ideally, I wanted to leave Celtic Football Club on a high but it was anything but. For my last pre-season at Celtic we were in Boston, New York in 2006. We'd also been over to Poland to play, obviously to show off the Polish Artur Boruc and Maciej Zurawski. When I was over in the States I was training for a few days and Gordon Strachan could see I wasn't myself. I wasn't a hinderance or being like a Mariah Carey type because she didn't like her dressing room at a show, I wasn't causing a fuss like some players would have done. I think it was after a pre-season game in Washington DC when he put me on for five minutes at the end. The next morning Gordon pulled me and said he could visibly see my heart wasn't in it because I wasn't on the pitch hardly at all. At that point I had twelve months left on my contract but he was good enough to give me the option to fly home. I told Gordon that overall, that was the best route out and that I was happy to do that. I think Gordon, in reality, didn't want to look at my face tripping myself up so he told me that Michael McDonald, who was on the board at Celtic, was flying back the next day so I was welcome to board the plane with him which is what I did. I must say I was looked after and I was put in business class on the flight home to London. I'll never forget the feeling of being on the plane thinking, 'well Tommo that's the end of your Celtic career.' I don't mind admitting that there was a lot of tears as I sat alone on the plane journey home. I sat and had a couple of drinks on the plane and I started reminiscing about how the last six years at Celtic had been.

When I got back to Scotland I trained with Celtic for a bit but I was going through the motions. I wouldn't leave Celtic until the January of 2007 when everything was sorted out with my loan move to Leeds at 33 years old. As the saying goes, all good things must come to an end. It wasn't only hard for me to deal with but it was also tough on my wife and the kids. Scotland had been our home for the last six and a half years at that point and now we were having to having to uproot. It meant new schools and leaving behind close friends. The day I cleared my locker out at Parkhead was extremely real and the only two people I spoke to were the kitman John Clark and the laundry lady Angie. There was no reason behind that, they were the only two people about. To be honest I made a point of going in when nobody was around because I wasn't in the mood to be seeing people. At that point the only relationship I had with any of the team was with Lenny. Neil followed me out of the door only four months later anyway as he left for Nottingham Forest. After giving Angie and Lisbon Lion Clarky a cuddle, I walked out the side door at Celtic Park via the kit room and turned right into the stadium for one last look. As I was stood in the corner of this magnificent stadium, I thought of everything that had happened. I looked at the goals where I'd beaten Stefan Klos so many times with a smile. It was also the same goal where I'd got the winner against Barcelona. I looked at the empty stands where the masses of fans usually were holding aloft their green & white scarfs and it felt like the saddest ending to a film that you can imagine. I knew this was it as I was putting my boots, bits and pieces in my car, I knew I was driving away from Celtic Park for good, or so I thought at the time.

That would be the very last time I would be in Celtic Park until I came back with Lenny on the management staff years later. At that point I didn't have any idea that I'd be back for more fun and games. My journey with this great club wasn't over just yet, I just didn't know it!

PAUL BYRNE

Former Celtic Player

"I met Tommo when I was on loan to Bolton Wanderers. We just clicked straight away and he made me feel welcome. Alan ended up at Celtic a few years after I left and he went on to have great success there. I knew in the early days from the brief spell I had with him at Bolton that he would eventually become a special player. I could tell at Bolton he was fearless and a typical cocky Geordie with it. He just loved playing the game and he got his rewards from football with the efforts he put in. The success he went on to have at Celtic was unbelievable and the Celtic fans will never forget him for that. I can tell you he has friends up there for life.

Just before the pandemic started, I was over in Thailand with Tommo at a Celtic supporters convention. I was at a cash point with him over there when he asked me if these cash points spoke in English (laughs). He has a lot of funny ways about him but overall, he's one of the true gentlemen of the game. He's become so famous to every Celtic supporter around the world that it must have been hard to stay in control of the things that have gone on in his life.

CHAPTER 16

MARCHING ON TOGETHER!

My Leeds United career started at the grand age of 33 years old on a six-month loan deal at first. It was during those six months that I impressed enough to earn a 12 month contract for the following season of 2007/08, although we got demoted to the third tier of English football.

The last game of the 2006/07 season was against Derby County at Pride Park, which was my last game of the six-month loan deal. I didn't know then that I would earn another 12-month deal with the club so I drove all the way back to Glasgow after the game listening to Snow Patrol's song, 'Open Your Eyes' on repeat. I'm not kidding I must have listened to that song for three and a half hours continuously. All the way on that journey home I didn't know whether I'd played my last game of professional football at only 33 years old. Maybe the injuries sustained in that car wreck had finally caught up with me, I knew my body was ageing but I still felt I had something to offer. That summer was plagued with uncertainty, I didn't have a clue what my footballing future held for me. I was convinced that I'd just played my last game at Pride Park, but of course at that point I didn't know I'd have one more season.

Thankfully I struck a deal with Leeds, but it was for a fraction of the wages I'd been used to. I played that extra season for the love of football because the big money that I'd been bringing in for the last decade had well and truly gone. The money that put my children through private education and paid for flights to New York on Concorde, flash watches and the top cars was little by little drying up.

I knew enough about the Yorkshire giants because my old man has been a Leeds fan all his life. My old fella was from Newcastle but his mam was a Yorkshire girl being from Thirsk so that was the team he chose.

I joined Leeds during probably what was their worst time in the clubs history when they were in the third tier of English football. Dennis Wise and Gus Poyet were on the management team, but it was a fella named Gwyn Williams who brought me to the club. Gwyn was a technical director at the club, but he had a big connection with Chelsea, hence the reason Dennis and Gus were at the club. Many of the Leeds fans didn't like this because they thought the proud Leeds Yorkshire heritage was being overtaken by Cockneys. Another Londoner, Ken Bates who also had Chelsea connections was at the club too, so you can imagine that this really annoyed many of the Leeds hardcore. Being at the club at that time, there was a very hostile atmosphere if I'm honest, with relationships between the fans and the board being what it was, but it was still a real honour to pull on the Leeds shirt.

Gwyn Williams brought me to Dennis Wise's attention because Gwyn had known me as a lad when I had a trial at Chelsea while Gwyn was the Youth Development Officer there. To give you an idea of just how long me and Gwyn go back, he looked after me in 1986 as a 13 year old boy. Now here he was twenty years later still looking after me and sparking Denis Wise's interest in me. Gwyn had wanted to sign me as a schoolboy and even though that didn't happen, he'd followed my career with great interest so, when I became available at 33 years old, he moved quickly to bring me to Leeds. I'll never forget getting off the train at Kings Cross, London going for my trial at Chelsea and Gwyn taking me and John Watson, who was another young kid from Newcastle, for our first ever McDonald's meal. At the time we didn't even know what a McDonald's was because in 1986 we didn't have one in Newcastle. After training Gwyn took me and John and spoilt us with food we thought was from the god's because it was all new, then he dropped us off at our digs. It's ironic how I had dealings with Gwyn at the start of my footballing career and at the very end.

I'd never had anything to do with Dennis Wise and Gus Poyet apart from playing against Chelsea when I was with Bolton and Aston Villa, but I instantly hit it off with the pair when I got there, particularly Dennis the menace. It was Dennis who made me club captain for the 2007/08 season after my loan spell. When Dennis asked me to take the skippers armband, I was uncomfortable with it but very much like Gordon Strachan at Celtic when he took over from Martin O'Neill, he wanted to put his own stamp on the team, and he saw me as his leader. The reason I was uncomfortable taking the role as club captain was, I had a lot of respect for Leeds United legend Gary Kelly who was coming to the end of his Leeds days then and who I'd be taking over the role from. Gary was part of the furniture at Leeds as he'd been there since 1992 for fifteen years but he wasn't playing. I think his situation may have been very similar to what happened to me at Celtic as Gary will have been on big money, but the club were in financial crisis and possibly wanted to fade him out to save the money. Funnily enough I scored from around 35 yards at Elland Road in Gary's testimonial five years previously when Celtic beats Leeds 4-1 and I'd played against him a lot, but it was Dennis' decision. Apart from that it was a real privilege to lead my Dad's team onto the pitch.

It turned out that the 2007/08 season would be my last as a professional footballer and to be totally honest I hadn't planned on it. I was only 34 years old in 2008 and in hindsight I maybe had a couple of more seasons in my legs but what did me was that very same calf injury I obtained in the Scottish Cup Final against Dundee United in Martin O'Neill's last game. If I'm honest, that very same injury just kept niggling away at me for the next couple of years. For all the medical teams I had looking at that injury they could never get to the bottom of why it was still a problem other than maybe just wear and tear. I didn't play as many games for Leeds as I would have liked to have done, which was the reason I ended up going out on loan to Hartlepool United. Although I went to Hartlepool, I just couldn't stay fit long enough. At the time I was living in Newcastle, but I'd been travelling from Newcastle to Leeds training sessions at Wetherby daily which was a ninety-minute drive each way. Although it was over eighty miles each way, I was getting to training sessions early, but Dennis knew it was taking its toll on me. I was getting to training early so I could do my work on the exercise bike, prep properly and have a massage then stretch but my calf was constantly flaring up. I told Dennis that I was sure it was because of the amount of driving I was doing daily so he sent me out to Hartlepool on loan.

At the time Danny Wilson was the manager at Hartlepool and he was fantastic by the way. Danny had been a superb player in his time and really knew the management game extremely well. At the time Hartlepool trained at Maiden Castle, Durham which was only around twenty miles from where I was living.

In my time at Hartlepool, I played seven games in one month and scored maybe the best freekick I ever took on my debut so I got off to a flier. During my time at

Hartlepool on loan from Leeds, Dennis Wise left Leeds. He'd got the director of football job at Newcastle United. If Dennis had had a few issues at Leeds because the club was full of Southerners, he was going to get more of the same at Newcastle. The Toon Army were protesting saying the Cockney mafia had taken over Newcastle and Mike Ashley was the ringleader. By the time the month at Hartlepool was over and I went back to Leeds Gary McAllister had taken over the reins. It was Gary who contacted Hartlepool to inform the club that he wanted me back at Leeds, but I didn't want to go back to Leeds. I'd just played seven games in a month and I knew if I had to drive for three hours a day to training then my calf was going to flare up. Plus, I went to Leeds to play for Dennis Wise and not Gary McAllister. It was nothing against Gary but I knew he was close with Gordon Strachan so I was worried that would have had some input on me as a player. Low and behold when I went back to Leeds to try and impress Gary, because of the driving my calf goes again. No matter how hard I trained and conditioned my body my calf wouldn't heal and that was the end of my footballing career. I knew after the seven games in a month at Hartlepool, that now I was back driving longer distances again I wouldn't have managed another ninety minutes.

My last game for Leeds in the 2007/08 season was at Wembley in the Play-Off Final against Doncaster Rovers. Although I was in the squad I wouldn't play. I thought that was an incredible feat because Leeds United started that season on -15 points, yet we still reached the Play-Offs but fell short in an all-out Yorkshire Derby 1-0. Dennis really put his mark on that Leeds side which was very successful because we won our first nine games in that season. In that final against Doncaster Rovers Gary McAllister didn't even think I was worthy of a place on the bench. Although I wasn't the Alan Thompson of old, at the time of that game in May 2008 my calf was fine and I felt I could have contributed to the team, but it wasn't to be. My overall stats at Leeds were twenty-four games and five goals, which were all freekicks.

I have to say as much as I enjoyed my football at Bolton and Celtic, I loved it at Leeds. Loved it! I thought the fans were great and the whole club was magnificent. The training facilities, although far away from my home, were top notch. Everyone who worked at the club were so welcoming. Ok, it wasn't the mighty Leeds United that once got to the semi-finals of the Champions League only a few years earlier with some of the biggest stars in British football, but I could still see it was a classy club. Really it was a sleeping giant and I'm only too glad the sleepy beast has awoken and is playing where it belongs, back in the Premiership.

One of the first things I did when I joined the club was to go to my grandfather Thompson's grave nearby in Thorp Arch, Wetherby. Sadly, I never got the chance to meet him but low and behold, the church graveyard was just down the road from the Leeds training ground. I found it so surreal to think that I was playing so close to the final resting place of a member of my family.

For a while I hadn't made my mind up that I was 100% going to retire when Leeds got beat at Wembley. I decided to put a pin in it for a while in the summer of 2008 but when Dennis Wise got in touch to offer me a role at Newcastle on the coaching staff it was hard to turn down. Looking back, I wish I could have joined Hartlepool and had a couple of seasons there, as at 34 I felt I could have managed a bit more playing time, but it wasn't to be. At the time when Dennis rang me and offered me the role, I'd already done all my coaching badges. It wasn't every day you get offered a chance to join the Newcastle United Academy staff and have a career still in the game, so I took it with both hands. The chance to still be in work back in my home city of Newcastle with the club that I supported as boy was a no brainer then. Its only now as I write this book that I know I wasn't ready to hang my boots up for good. It was two years too early. If it had been any other club apart from Newcastle United and Glasgow Celtic, I know I'd have said no and continued playing for a few more years.

Towards the end of my career, I wouldn't say I was falling out of love with the game, however I knew I'd had my good times. From the highs of playing in the Champions League groups, European Cup Finals and scoring the winners in the Old Firm Derby I had a few down seasons towards the end of my career where I couldn't even make the bench, like in that last game at Wembley. My decline happened so quickly from 2004 to 2008 which is such a short space of time. I didn't take the decision to give up playing football for a living lightly, it was something I had long discussions with my family over.

The one funny thing was when I went back to Newcastle in 2008, Kevin Keegan was the manager and Terry McDermott was his number two, when I left Newcastle sixteen years earlier those two were in the exact same positions.

JOSH WARRINGTON

Leeds Warrior
IBF World Champion 2018-2021

"Alan Thompson came to our club during the worst period of our history. We were playing in England's third tier and our future was looking incredibly bleak. Saying that, it was probably one of the most exciting seasons ever when we were down there. Starting that season with a -15-points deduction made everyone fight that bit extra and Alan Thompson, as our club captain, epitomised this. Tommo led a team full of misfits or make-do's but Tommo had the experience to keep them inline.

To be honest I didn't know too much about Alan Thompson before he came to Leeds but at that time he was exactly what we needed. When I think of him what springs to mind was his trademark freekicks from a fair distance. You'd always fancy him to put one away, which he did several times. It wasn't only his freekicks, Tommo showed real fight and us as Leeds fans love a battler. We loved those David Batty and Alan Smith types who were rough and tumble and gave us something to sing about. Alan Thompson, as they say in Yorkshire was a 'ryt playa' who did a shift for our team in his time at our club."

CHAPTER 17

TESTIMONIALS & GOOD CRAIC

I was never privileged enough to ever receive a testimonial, but I played in a fair few in my career. Gary Kelly, Tony Adams, Roy Keane and Alan Shearer's to name a few. I also seemed to do well in scoring in many for some reason. It goes without saying with Celtic's fanatical large support that I'd play in my fair few because everybody asks the Celts to come to their ground and bring the massive travelling support. I played in Keane's and Shearer's back-to-back in May 2006 within 24 hours of each other. In fact, the night before Roy's we had a few beers, which to be honest is about the norm for a testimonial match because it's at half pace. The night before Roy's, as I said the Celtic squad had a few halves in the Worsley Marriott and a lot of our team were worse for wear during Roy's tribute game at Old Trafford. Roy played a half for each team and United ran out 1-0 victors with a goal from the very young Cristiano Ronaldo. What a player he turned out to be! I asked Cristiano for his shirt, but he said he'd already promised it to Chris Sutton which didn't surprise me. Sutty would get in where water couldn't. Although the outcomes of those games aren't incredibly important, they are fantastic occasions. The following night we played at St James Park in Alan's and some of us were rough again from after Roy's. In fact, I've got to admit that every player on that pitch was rough as Tarzan's feet big time! All of us were that rough from the night before that we needed an afternoon in bed in the hotel in Newcastle to recover. I've got to point out though that although I was never Gordon Strachan's favourite player in his time at Celtic it was a lovely gesture making me captain to play my home city. If the Celtic boys were stinking rough than I can assure you that the Newcastle lads were even worse than us. They'd all had a big function for Alan the night before and were in no state to be playing football for ninety minutes.

It may only have been a testimonial but it was great leading Celtic out at St James Park in front of a packed stadium with everyone I know watching. The only downside to it was I didn't last long and I was hooked at halftime for Stephen Pearson. I must have passed to a black & white shirt more than a green & white top. Gordon must have been stood on the side-lines thinking my play was diabolical and it was the right decision to take me off.

One funny memory from that game involved Derek Wright the physio at Newcastle. Wor Derek is one of the nicest men you'll ever meet and you've all read the bit he put about me in the start of this book. Derek is truly one of the nicest men on planet earth, however when Lee Clark was laid out injured, the Newcastle lads had taken all Derek's medical equipment out of his bag, then replaced them with bags of pies. Derek is a big lad and some would say, 'slightly overweight' so when he ran on the pitch and Clarkie was waiting for treatment, Derek's got down on one knee to delve into his magic bag only to find mince pies. Well, a few of the Newcastle team went over and started tucking into Derek's pies. Derek's face was a picture when he was watching all the players getting stuck into these pies and he didn't have a clue how they'd got in there. Derek, at that point, didn't see the funny side of all the lads stitching him up for the craic. It's the little things like that, that those benefit games are all about. Maybe the funniest trick of all was in 2009 during Sir Bobby Robson's testimonial in an England select v Germany select. It was Sir Bobby's last public appearance in the game to commemorate the match between the two countries during Italia 90. Sadly, Sir Bobby passed away from Cancer only five days after that match.

At the time I was coaching at Newcastle so that's how I got roped into playing which was a total honour by the way. That's the reason this book will support The Bobby Robson Foundation among a couple of others. Although I never played in the World Cup '90 I was in the England side among David Platt, Peter Shilton, Ian Wright, Les Ferdinand, Rob Lee, John Beresford, Steve Hodge, Peter Beardsley, Alan Shearer and of course the star of that very World Cup '90, Paul Gascoigne. I didn't start, I came on from the bench but as usual with Gazza involved, there was lots of funny moments. In the dressing room before the match we're all there ready to go out and give Sir Bobby one last show. Ian Wright was there holding court as he does and Les Ferdinand was taking the mick out of the people around in a friendly banter manner. There weren't only ex-footballers involved there were a few celebrities such as Robson Green, Ralf Little and Craig David. At that point Gazza hadn't come in the changing rooms. He then came walking in late with his boots in his hand because he'd been doing the rounds around the stadium. Knowing Gazza, he'll have been cracking on with all the punters and making the best of the free hospitality. When Paul enters the room, he goes around shaking everybody's hands. It's always great to see Gazza and many of the lads there hadn't seen him in years so they're all making a fuss of him. That's one thing about Paul, he's got this extremely infectious energy about him which you can't help but warm to. You just can't help but laugh at Paul even in the most serious of situations. Well when Paul's going around the team he's got to Craig David, Gazza then blurts out very loudly, "alright pal, what on earth were you thinking of going up in that glass box near the River Thames for 44 days?" Paul was confused and thought Craig David was the American magician David Blaine! When Gazza was told he just said, "sorry pal sorry pal" and went around the rest of the lads. Most of us were rolling around laughing, only Paul Gascoigne could come out with something like that and be so straight faced! What was really special at the end was when we were getting beat 1-0 by the Germans, we got a freekick in my favoured territory. It was around fifteen minutes before the end and many of the lads were tiring because most of us were getting on. The freekick was right where I like it and it was at the perfect angle. It was so special that I managed to whip one off the wall one very last time in a ram-packed football stadium and it flew in the top corner. The match finished 1-1 and I managed to fulfil a lifetimes ambition of scoring at St James Park. It may have only been a Micky Mouse game in all other aspects, but it was in front of a 52,000 sell-out crowd.

Sir Bobby came around one last time to say hello, and goodbye as he was in his wheelchair. Sadly, my very last freekick was also the last goal Sir Bobby would ever see in this lifetime as he passed only days later. It was very moving that on his way home from the game, Sir Bobby's lad Mark had asked him what he thought of the game. "How did Gazza do?" was Sir Bobby's reply. Sir Bobby once described Gazza as, "daft as a brush" before the World Cup Italia '90 but obviously that special bond remained between the pair almost twenty years later.

If there's a lot of humour in testimonials then I've come across the same in football in general. You don't half meet some comical characters in the game, you can end up doing the most outrageous things to your teammates for bants. If I had a partner in crime in my time at Celtic then there's no doubt that it was Chris Sutton. If someone was getting the Michael taken out of him then you can be assured that Sutty wasn't far away from it. With Chris and I living so close to each other in Newton Mearns, we used to share the same housekeepers because both our wives were friends. This one day I had this great idea that because his wife Sam used the same ironing company as us, I would pull the ironers to one side before he next visited the Sutton family. The guy who owned the company was called Bruce so I asked him if when his girls next did Sutty's ironing, could they iron some tremendously huge creases in his jeans? Now I knew Sutty didn't have many pairs of jeans, he maybe had two pairs if he was lucky. "But why Alan?" Bruce asked but I told him not to ask any questions and just to make sure that the girls did as I asked and not to worry as everything would be ok. I forgot about the whole thing until around a week or two later when Sutty came strolling into Barrowfield training ground one morning with big fuck off creases in his jeans! It was around 2001 so it was in the early days but the whole squad was in absolute stitches over this big plonker walking around with creases in his jeans. He looked like Rodney in Only Fools and Horses. I think the only thing any of the lads said to him that day was, 'you don't have creases in jeans' whilst laughing some more at him. Well, the one thing about Chris Sutton was he was good at giving it out but he didn't receive it back very well, maybe a bit like me. He was not happy at all that day and he spent the day walking around scowling. In the end Chris is a bright lad and after he had done a bit of detective work Sherlock found out I was the culprit behind his humiliation and he wanted revenge. I knew Sutty would have his revenge but I didn't think it would be so quick.

That very same day after training there was a few of the lads going for a meal to an Italian restaurant called, 'Andiamo' in Giffnock just outside of Newton Mearns for a bowl of pasta. On the way there I stopped off for fuel at a garage. As I was in the queue to pay for the petrol there was this very attractive woman near me. As I put my wallet on the counter and opened it up to pay, all this pubic hair fell out of my wallet onto the counter. The woman behind the counter is staring at me as well as this model like woman who must have been thinking 'what the hell is all that that's just fallen out of his wallet.' To be honest it was fairly obvious what it was and I'm mortified! I'm now trying to brush all this hair off the table and sweep it into a pile but at the same time I'm paranoid thinking, 'does she know what that is because by now I'm aware of what it is and who's behind it. To cut a long story short Sutty was that fuming that during training he'd sneaked away into my locker, shaved his own bollocks and put the remnants in my wallet. He'd got his revenge around one hour from me publicly slaughtering him in front of the Celtic dressing room which is pretty impressive going. The only thing which kind of spoiled the evil genius' plan was Chris had planned for me to open my wallet in the restaurant in front of him so he could scream with laughter to add to my humiliation. It took some explaining to the watching girls in the petrol station that unfortunately I was the victim of the Celtic Football Clubs no.1 prankster. Thankfully they saw the funny side and I was surprised, but I shouldn't have been, that Sutty had wreaked his revenge as quick as he did. I have to admit he got me good and proper.

I'm sure that Chris Sutton was definitely Martin O'Neill's lovechild as the two loved each other. Martin would always let Sutty off from his pranks and Sutty could always be found around the gaffer's office.

Things like that went on in that Celtic dressing room all the time with Chris usually behind it. I remember playing golf with him once over in Florida on a winter break with Celtic. The gaffer was quite happy to let us play the odd round of golf as long as we were on buggy's. I was playing against Sutty on Lake Nona which is where all the famous golf pro's live, in stunning mansions. In fact, it was only because of Martin O'Neill pulling a few strings with Celtic owner Dermot Desmond that we had the privilege of even getting on that green at all. Well, this day on this round of golf it was Chris' shot but there was an alligator in the Tee box but Chris wouldn't take his shot. "Oi its 15yards away you big girl" I told him but Chris took his ball in his hand and scurried off to the next hole. Chris wouldn't even get out of his buggy he was that scared, it was never going to run for him. All the way around the course I didn't let him forget it. The way Chris tells the story was he avoided a huge man-eating 'gator like something out of Indiana Jones but in reality, the croc was laid asleep totally chilling out in the sun. In the end the big fella wouldn't even get out and surrendered the hole to me.

I'll always remember playing A.C. Milan away at the San Siro in 2004. We were trailing the match 3-1 and badly in need of a goal toward the end but I'd gone off. I remember sitting on the bench and saying to one of my teammates, 'look at Sutty, he's following Paolo Maldini like a sheep dog.' In the last few minutes wherever Maldini was then Chris followed him which was unusual because he was a striker and we needed a goal. After the game in the shower, I asked Chris what he was up to and he said, "I wanted his strip didn't I."

I've made a lot of good friends in football but one of my best mates in the game is ex-Everton winger Peter Beagrie. 'Beags' is from Middlesbrough and as crazy as they come. I first met him many years ago on holiday and we've just been close ever since. The guy literally never stops talking because he's got so much energy. His trademark celebration after scoring was running and doing a couple of backflips and that's Peter all over. He can't stand still, I'm sure 'Beags' even does star jumps when he's in the shower, he's just a constant ball of energy but I have great love for him.

There were quite a few jokers at Celtic apart from Sutty, Paul Lambert was a dark horse. Lambo comes across as this serious guy but he had many a victim he played pranks on. Chris was the main culprit though!

It wasn't all fun and games though because I'll never forget the day that Bobo Balde was having a shocker. It was half time and we had gone back to the dressing room. In this game Bobo couldn't help but give the ball away in every pass he made so Stiliyan Petrov was giving him both barrels. Stiliyan was rabbiting on relentlessly, "BOBO STOP GIVING THE BALL AWAY... WHEN YOU GET THE BALL JUST KEEP IT SIMPLE AND DO YOUR JOB PROPERLY" he was ranting rather angrily. Bobo, you could tell, wasn't liking being publicly ridiculed in front of everyone so he tells Petrov to button it! Stiliyan would not give up and even Martin O'Neill butted in in fear for Stiliyan's life shouting, "Stiliyan shut up" but big Bobo had had enough. Bobo then walks towards Petrov and as he's getting closer and closer he's becoming bigger and more menacing by the second. Big Rab Douglas then comes over because he senses that Stiliyan Petrov is about to die and even little John Robertson gets in the way. Well Bobo throws Robbo away like he was taking off a tracksuit top and even the treatment table goes flying. As it's all going off in Bobo's attempt to murder Stiliyan Petrov I've noticed just how close I am to the pair of them. I don't mind admitting that I decided I wasn't going to get involved so I jumped in one of the lockers and closed the door behind me. I was hiding for my own safety; it was like being in a coffin but if you've ever seen the Guinean giant Bobo Balde about to kick off then you would understand why I hid in there. Chris Sutton has then stood up to try and save Stiliyan but Bobo's just pushed him into his own locker and he went flying. Bobo pushed Sutty so hard the locker doors caved in. I don't know how but Bobo didn't get the pleasure of ripping Stiliyan's head clean off his shoulders that day. I think that was as close as it ever came to fisticuffs during my time at Celtic but I saw a lot of things like that.

You often got bust-ups on the training ground but that was because you've got a team of professionals demanding 100% from their teammates. There was that other incident when the young Aiden McGeady, who was only coming through, nutmegged Neil Lennon in training and Lenny threatened to kill him if he did it again. Me and Sutty offered Aiden £500 each if he did it again so he did it again and, as you can imagine, there was hell on. Quite recently Aiden told the story on the Simon Ferry's Open Goal Podcast that I chased him down London Road in my car and he still had Adidas Predator football boots on. Some of the boys had bet Aiden, who was only a kid at the time coming through into Martin's team, to pull one of my windscreen wipers up. I eventually caught Aiden in the boot room and I had Rab Douglas hold him down whilst painting his face completely black with boot polish.

Playing for Celtic Football Club was a great honour and I took it very seriously but there was just so much humour day in, day out with stuff like that. Martin, Robbo and Wally, all knew it created great team spirit and would often turn a blind eye to these certain types of behaviour if the laugh merited it loudly enough.

STEVE STONE

Former England International and Premiership Player

"With Alan being a fellow Geordie I knew who he was before I played with him at Aston Villa. I've even lived next door to him for a spell so I know what he's all about. He used to light up the football pitch, but he would also light up the room he was in off the pitch. He used to express himself playing and he was no different when you went for a pint with him. I always loved going out with Alan because I never had to take the limelight, I didn't have to do anything because Tommo used to lead the night with his silly antics. When I used to live next door to him, I used to leave our front door unlocked. I think Tommo knew this as when I used to go to bed he used to come around and help himself to what was in the fridge; usually wine or beer in Tommo's case, if he'd ran out at midnight as we lived in the countryside. He did that time and time again and he'd leave me with nothing. I'd wake up most weekends to an empty fridge and I knew he'd helped himself to whatever he fancied. He would always deny it was him the next day and I think he still denies it now to this day. It was always around midnight on a weekend when these robberies would take place. I think because we were so far out and he couldn't be bothered going to the shop he used to think, 'aah I'll just burgle the Stone's again they'll never find out it was me' and that's when things would go missing. To this day he doesn't know I knew it was him all along. On a serious note, Alan Thompson was generous to a fault and I never begrudged him stealing anything because he gave out far more than he had away off us. Alan would buy anyone anything and that's what the true Alan Thompson is all about."

CHAPTER 18

BACK AT THE TOON

If hanging my boots up was hard then moving into coaching was a natural progression. I actually decided to do my coaching badges when I was still playing in 2004 because I knew they'd come in handy for a rainy day. I did my UEFA B licence with Stephen Craigan, Neil Lennon, Ricky Gillies and Phil O'Donnell (God rest him) at Fir Park. Lenny and I decided, as our legs weren't getting any younger, to do the UEFA A licence in Northern Ireland. I also added the UEFA Pro licence so you could say I have the full shebang in football. I mean, it's something I've done my whole life, and as the saying goes 'you can't teach an old dog new tricks', I assumed my future in later life would still be in football which to a degree it has been. The licences I have will never run out and I'll always be qualified for any kind of work if the right job comes up. In actual fact the UEFA Pro licences are incredibly expensive, I'm talking a ridiculous amount of money but it's imperative if I wanted to work in football. The Pro licence I did with Lenny, Sutty, Eddie Howe and Neil McCann. It's not really about coaching if that makes sense, it's more about learning how to treat players as a manager and not as your mate. There's a heap of psychological stuff I took away from it and if anyone gets the chance to do it I would highly recommend it.

With me having all of these coaching badges which get you work; Dennis Wise was aware of these and that's why he offered me the job at Newcastle in 2008. It was sad my playing days had come to an end but I was more than delighted to go into Newcastle and work with the youth setup.

I started off at the under 18's with Kenny Wharton who'd played for the Toon himself and I got on really well with him. After a while in the job the reserve team coach left and I was offered the role to step up and be in charge of Newcastle reserves. At the time Chris Hughton was the first team coach and his assistant was Colin Calderwood who I played with at Aston Villa. I worked with some wonderful people when I was starting out in my coaching career. It was great picking bits and bobs up from experienced footballing men and I learnt a lot in such a short space of time.

As I was doing my reserves/under 23s whatever you want to call it at Newcastle, my old mate Lenny was doing the same position 151 miles up the road in Glasgow. With me and Lenny being so close it worked well for us in football. I mean I took a team of under 23s up to Lennoxtown training complex and he brought one down to Newcastle. In certain circumstances in football its who you know. Listen I've just given you an example there about me and Lenny pulling a few strings in the game purely because we were best mates. I'd definitely say for sure many times it helps you if you've got an old pal who is at some club who can get you a foot in the door. There are managers out there getting jobs in the game that they never in a million years should be getting, however it's been down to people behind the scenes networking.

I have to be honest with you all reading this and say that I'm not the best networker. I have mates out there who could sell snow to the Eskimos, but I've always struggled in that aspect. Maybe that's why I was so chewy as a footballer on the pitch to the refs. People often get the impression because I was fiery as hell on the football pitch and I'd tackle a brick wall that I'm like that in real life and that's so not me. Even the author of this book was taken aback and said I wasn't what he expected me to be so how many other Celtic fans have this false idea of me? You've all read the stories about me, regarding drink and women, which I'll go into further in the book, but they're farfetched stories. I think some of the tabloids in Scotland have me down as this Richard Harris/Oliver Reed hell-raising drinking character. I have to admit that when I first went into the coaching side of things I really missed playing, at the same time I was in my mid-thirties so I could run about with the "young uns" and I was a match for some of them. Let's just say I had more uses than just putting cones out and collecting bibs and was still the king of the crossbar challenge. At the start of my coaching at Newcastle it was like I was playing again because the lad who I was working with, Kenny Wharton, was a bit older and had bad knees so I was a spring chicken compared to him. Kenny was always asking me to show the lads bits of technique, crosses, freekicks or even how to walk off the field when you've had a red card (laughs).

Back in 2008/09 I had no problems playing 8 v 8 or a 9 v 9 on the training field. The first couple of years I would go home and deep down I missed it, but I knew it had to be over. Today and kicking on for 48 as I write this, I don't miss it but I get asked to play in charity matches which is something I don't like. I think footballers who go on that bit too long can make a fool of themselves and I was always petrified of it happening to me. Fair play to the boys who do it for charity but it's awful when you see a former great playing absolutely woefully on the pitch who only a few years previously would have gone around everyone on that pitch like they were training cones.

Nothing could ever be as good as scoring a "worldie" and the masses of fans chanting your name but going on the coaching side is the nearest thing you'll ever get when the fat lady has warmed up her vocal cords and is calling time on your career. Even now when I'm back in the game I just love being out there on the grass trying to develop young players. I have a lot to give in a football sense and I love trying to make kids better players. It was a joy doing one on ones with players and passing on my experiences. I'm not saying I was the world's best but I did pick up a few tricks of the trade in my time in the game. There's nothing better to me than seeing these young lads totally green around the ears like I was looking up to the older Newcastle lads when I was coming through. I can remember seeing the old pros and being in awe and I can see a few have been like that with me. What I've found is when someone like myself comes in and talks to these young kids they really do pin their lugholes back and sit and listen.

In my days at Newcastle, I was looking after the young kids such as Sammy Ameobi, Paul Dummett, Shane Ferguson, Kazenga Lualua and big Fraser Forster. It was me who actually recommended Fraser to Lenny when he took over as the Celtic boss. I knew the big fella very well and just how good he was so it was me who brought in 'The Great Wall of China' as the Barcelona players branded him in 2012. I'm not looking for any special praises but if you spoke to any of that lot now I'd like to think old Tommo played a part in their turning out as a pro.

When I was at Newcastle United one of my best mates was Steve Stone but he was out of work at first. It was me who went to the academy director Richard Money and said, "do you mind if Stoney comes in and does a few bits and pieces with the lads?" Richard told me to get Stoney in for the experience, but the club wasn't in any position to pay him anything. They say life is about taking your chances when given them because Stoney then got off his arse and started coming in. He would watch me taking sessions and learning the trade and because of his will to win the club gave him a full-time job. Stoney's working at Burnley now and he played for England in Euro '96. Stoney went on to get some cracking jobs in football but purely down to getting up and making something happen himself. Steve Stone saw the long game and that's very much how this life pans out. I think we could all learn a bit from Steve Stone's attitude and he's a great lad I love him to bits.

Maybe the saddest thing of all in my time back in Newcastle was the relegation from the topflight. Even Newcastle's most favourite son Alan Shearer coming back for a couple of months couldn't save us from the drop. To be fair to Alan he arrived on April 1st, 2009, for the remaining eight games taking over from Chris Hughton and Jesus Christ our Lord himself couldn't have saved us. When Alan came in he brought Iain Dowie, who's a renowned coach, in with him and he really did roll his sleeves up, dug deep and tried to save the club. I mean, nobody was more hurt on this planet than Alan Shearer when we dropped down to the Championship. At that time, I was Under 23's coach and when Shearer came in he involved me more in the first team, however if you want my honest opinion, he was let down badly by the players. The very last game of the 2008/09 season Newcastle needed to go to Villa Park and get all three points. At that time Martin O'Neill, Steve Walford, John Robertson and Stiliyan Petrov were all at Villa, so it wasn't going to be a happy reunion. The week of the last game Alan sent me to

Goodison Park to watch Leighton Baines because he was on Alan's radar. Alan asked me to fill a match report in on Leighton from the stands. For anyone who doesn't know how it works when you're checking a player out then you've got a sheet of paper with all the credentials on. You've got to assess certain skills in boxes and at the bottom you'd tick sign him, carry on monitoring or not for us. After watching Leighton Baines for Everton, I drove on to the hotel that the Newcastle United squad were staying at in Birmingham.

It was an honour that Alan wanted me to be there as part of his setup for the crucial game at Villa Park. One of the major talking points from that day was Michael Owen saying his hamstring was too tight to start. He eventually came on midway through the second half but made little impact and didn't break a sweat. That's what I mean about a few of the players letting him down as we as a club were fighting for our lives. The day before the match and we're in the hotel and Alan names the team. We have a team talk among the staff and Alan likes to have a couple of glasses of wine before going to his room. A little story about Alan Shearer is that he's not too keen of the dark so he always leaves his light on in his suite. This night when Alan's asleep in his room he's woken by a strange man playing a piano and singing in his front room like Elton John. Alan didn't have a scooby doo who he was. In the end Alan screamed at the guy to get out and even when it was investigated by the security in the hotel nobody had any idea how the nutter got into his room. The funny thing about it was when Alan screamed at him to get the hell out of his room, the crazy stranger said, "just let us finish this song." Like it was his right to be in there and it was like something from a Stephen King horror movie. It was sheer madness and if it wasn't bad enough then it happened the night before the biggest game of his career. Another scary factor was the man could have been some knife maniac. If it wasn't scary what happened in the gaffers room, then the 1-0 loss to Villa which ended Newcastle's 16 year stay in the top flight of football was. It wasn't nice to go down in any event but us going down at Martin O'Neill's place was extra hurtful. Martin has a lot of respect for Alan Shearer because they've worked lots together for the BBC but in those times there's few words that can be said to ease any pain. Normally when I see Wally and Robbo I make a fuss of them but with us going down we just wanted to go home and go to bed. The reality of it was if Newcastle would have beat Villa that day we'd have stayed up but it was a really good Villa side at the time against the likes of Barry, Petrov, Carew, Young and Agbonlahor etc... Words can't describe how all the Geordies who had travelled felt in Villa Park that day. The full experience was heart-breaking and I've never felt such agony since those two Helicopter Sundays in 2003 and 2005. Nothing really was said to Martin, Wally, Robbo and Stiliyan so we just got on the bus and got back up North all pretty miserable.

As of today, that's my pal Alan Shearer's only stint in football management but I know one day he'll be back as some kind of ambassador I imagine, and he'll do brilliantly. I don't think you have to be Nostradamus to figure out what club he'll be back at. I'd say for sure Newcastle's most famous No.9 has unfinished business at the club he loves in my opinion.

STEVE HARMISON

English Cricketer / Talksport

"Before I went onto play for England as a cricketer my plans were to be a footballer. The first time I met Alan Thompson was at the Newcastle School of Excellence when I was 11 years old. At the time of me meeting Alan, he'd just had his horrific car crash accident. Tommo was always a hero of mine as I was growing up in the training ground at Benwell Training Ground. Even though in those days he had this neck brace on, every time I saw him, he'd be doing keepy ups with this small football like he was Diego Maradona. His best mate Steve Watson had just broken into the Newcastle first team and Tommo would have been in had it not been for his life-threatening injuries. Even though the lad was going through a bad time, Tommo was always laughing and joking.

I suppose the reason Alan Thompson was my hero in life was because he was the first professional footballer I ever knew. Although he didn't do a lot for Newcastle United on the pitch, I always followed his career everywhere he went. If ever I met Tommo over the years, I would divert back to that 11-year-old boy being starstruck and this guy doing kick up's with a small Italia 90 World Cup ball. Over the years I've become great friends with Tommo as I've played golf with him. I admired how he had to go away from the Northeast to carve out his own career. I know he'd have loved to have had that same hero status in the Toon like his best mates Lee Clark and Steve Watson have today but of course he's achieved that in other places. He's very much a

Geordie legend in the football world although not in the black & white stripes for any length of time.

Thankfully, although I've been on a few drunken escapades with Alan I haven't been at the brunt of his jokes. The man, when he's in full flow and on form, can wind the best up.

I know I'm a cricketer, but Alan Thompson is someone who I would have loved to have played sport with because he's so infectious. I would imagine he would be a joy to be in the same dressing room alongside. You know when Tommo's around because there's something happening with him being the life and soul of the party."

CHAPTER 19

REUNITED WITH LENNY; CUPS, COURTS & SHAME NIGHT

At the end of March 2010, Tony Mowbray's disastrous eight-month spell in charge of Celtic came to an end. Losing 4-0 away to Kilmarnock was the final nail in his coffin. Tony's time at the club wasn't great, even with the world class striker Robbie Keane on loan from Spurs in the side it just didn't gel for Mogga, it summed up his time as Celtic boss when he was pictured by The Daily Record with his head in his hands on a rainy night at Rugby Park. That miserable evening would be his last. I think like Alan Shearer at Newcastle in the previous chapter, big Mogga was badly let down by some of his players.

When the time came for the Celtic board to look for a new gaffer, Neil Lennon stood up and was counted in the clubs call to arms, after all it was the club he loved. At the time Lenny was the reserve team coach, but he stepped up to the plate and did a great job. In my opinion Lenny did that much of a fantastic job that when he went public and said he wouldn't be interested in going back to manage the reserves, he made it impossible for the board not to give him the position on a full-time basis. The hardcore supporters saw Lenny as one of them and with him getting some decent results on the park he'd put himself in a great position. Lenny had showed the Celtic board he had steered the club in the right way at the end of 2010. At the end of our first full season, he uttered those immortal words in May 2011, "this isn't the end, this is only the beginning" and the crowd went nuts as we beat Motherwell 4-0 but lost the league on the last game of the season.

Going back to 2010 though, I can remember Lenny ringing me up when he was the caretaker and saying, "listen Tommo I've not got the job yet, however should I get it full-time I'd like you beside me in the trenches." Lenny saw that I'd served my apprenticeship at Newcastle looking after the under 23's and wanted me to come on board with Gary Parker and Johan Mjallby if things panned out. Although nothing was promised I told my old former partner in the midfield he had my word and I would join him at Celtic, if and when he got the job. Before I made any announcements regarding my future, I sought advice from a Newcastle colleague who I had a lot of respect for. He asked if I really wanted to stay at Newcastle United looking after the under 23's when I could go back to Glasgow and be involved in the Old Firm games again? That question sort of really put things into perspective for me. He also asked me if I wanted to go back working alongside someone I had so many great years with and that decided it for me, and I thanked him for his sound advice.

A few weeks went by, and Lenny still hadn't been given the role, but I received a message telling me I needed to go to St James Park ASAP to have a meeting with the Chief Executive Lee Charnley, along with the acting chairman Derek Llambias. I had no idea what it was all about but as Newcastle United were my employers I needed to be at this meeting. When I sat down with the Newcastle Board they just came out with, "we hear you're off to Celtic to be back with ya mate Lenny?" I had no idea where these guys had got this from because I'd only ever spoken to the wife and Lenny about it, and he hadn't even been confirmed as the manager yet. Then it suddenly dawned on me, that Newcastle legend who'd been a bit of an agony aunt a few weeks back had told them exactly what I had spoken to him about. I told the Newcastle guys my case and that nothing had been made final, but they told me it wasn't good enough for them. They basically told me that I hadn't been loyal to Newcastle United, and I was to close the door on the way out. I was fired there and then and told I would no longer be needed at Newcastle United Football Club. The club paid me up with a year's salary and legally I didn't have a leg to stand on. There was a period in the summer of 2010 that had Lenny not actually got the post at Celtic, I'd have been in limbo going nowhere fast. Fortunately for me, Lenny did get the job and together we were able to put Celtic back at the top of Glasgow's football world.

I'm not wanting to open a can of worms in this book with a certain Newcastle legend, but I have to question where the board got their information about me from? I don't think it was down to my ex-wife Jo or Lenny, so it was him who obviously shafted me. I can't actually prove anything, unless he admitted it, but it's gone now. It's water under the bridge and if you hold onto resentment then you only harm yourself so its ok and I've given it to God. I have to put it down to football being the dog-eat-dog world that it is. Maybe he just wanted my job, who knows!

In our first full season at Celtic together, Neil Lennon was the gaffer, Johan Mjallby was his assistant, and I was the First Team Coach. Gary Parker came along a little while later but if Lenny was playing the role of Martin, me and big Dolph (Johan) were his Wally & Robbo. Lenny loved coaching on the training field as did Dolph as he would normally take all the defenders separately. I really thrived when I was back coaching at Celtic daily as I would take probably 60% of the sessions. I was back on planet football, and it was what I was put on this earth for. Lenny, Dolph Gary and I were a very close-knit gang. Nothing got out to the press unless we said so and we trusted each other implicitly.

For that first season in 2010/11 the club heavily backed Lenny in the transfer market. Decent money was spent bringing in players such as Emillio Izaguirre, Fraser Forster, Gary Hooper, Efrain Juarez, Beram Kayal, Anthony Stokes, Daryl Murphy, Kris Commons, Charlie Mulgrew, Joe Ledley, Du-ri Cha, Daniel Majstorovic and Freddie Ljungberg. Lenny had started to build his own team which had predominately been Tony Mowbray's group of players. One of the players who Mogga brought in was Paddy McCourt. Paddy was just unbelievably talented but often the critics would have a pop at his fitness levels. I loved Paddy and he was a lively bubbly character to be around but physically he probably wasn't the best. Had he been athletic like Didier Agathe and Jason McAteer with the same skill then undoubtedly you're looking at another Ryan Giggs. Paddy wouldn't even have been at Celtic because he'd have been in the Real Madrid or Barcelona teams but in life and football, we can't have everything. Paddy reminded me of Aiden McGeady who'd left Celtic by then for big money, however he was gifted with ridiculous amounts of natural talent. Another character I had a lot of time for in the Celtic dressing room was Georgios Samaras aka big Sammy. He was always a very quiet lad and I used to say to him, "Sammy where are you going on holiday in the summer?" He would tell me he'd be back off home to Greece. He would say, "Tommo when I have a homeland as beautiful as Greece then why would I go anywhere else?" Sammy would come in, do his training and slip out very quietly and was almost unheard of again until it was time to come back in and then he would do the same all over again.

Life at that time was brilliant again for me because not only was I around first team football, but I was also back in Glasgow and I was with a club close to my heart. Before I'd gone back to Celtic as a coach, I'd only coached the Under 18's and Under 23's but now I was back to working with elite players. It's what you yearn for as a professional football coach. Think of a skilled tradesman working with the best tools in the world then this was exactly the same for a coach. You have the buzz, pressures, highs and lows of football which is what I absolutely lived for.

There was a downside to it though, I was back at Celtic from June 2010, but I would be living by myself as Jo and the kids stayed in Newcastle. I was having to travel backwards and forwards so much as we didn't feel it was right to up sticks and move the children again. I had this plush 2-bed apartment in the Westend of Glasgow. Looking back on it now, it was the first time I'd be living away from Jo and the kids and I began living the life of a single lad. I'd like to point out that I don't mean that in a womanising kind of way, although its well documented in the media that I did go on to have an affair. At that time, I constantly had cameras following me, the other woman in question and even my wife Jo. Jo then did an article in The Daily Record giving me both barrels. The way it came across in the papers was as if I was out hitting on every female I came across every weekend. I'm going to hold my hands up here and say that when I said I was living the single life it was more to do with the drink. I know now that I was consuming far too much alcohol than I should have been. I'm not putting the blame on anyone other than myself but when you look at my fellow coaches Johan and Lenny, they had their wives and kids with them. When I'd finished at Celtic and I got home to an empty flat I had no one to keep me in line. Gary Parker and I were both living by ourselves so it then became too easy to go out and have a bite to eat which was often then accompanied by a bottle of wine. Then going out for a few pints after that became a bit too regular and on top of that, I wasn't playing anymore so I didn't have to look after my body like I had for my previous spell in Glasgow when I was still playing. I had started to drink more days of the week then not. My local was The Drake, Kelvingrove which wasn't far from mine and not far from Gary's flat. Many a time the place would let myself Lenny and Gary stop back if we wanted a bit of privacy to let our hair down. The Drake became somewhat of my second home, and I would definitely say I was going out way too much, which obviously I shouldn't have been especially as I was the coach at Celtic Football Club.

Going back to the football side of things for a bit. In that first full season, we brought the title down to the last game of the season that Rangers would ultimately go on to claim. However, Celtic won the Scottish Cup beating Motherwell 3-0 at Hampden. With the highs came the lows though, as is mostly the way with football, and we lost to Rangers in the League Cup Final at Hampden. Nikica Jelavic got the winner as we lost 2-1 in extra time in what was Walter Smith's last ever cup as the Gers boss. Surprisingly we would lose the same Cup Final the following year to Kilmarnock. I'll never forget that Liam Kelly, who played for Killie, lost his father after that game, he sadly died of a heart attack. The poor lad was just sat in the tunnel with his head in his hands devastated after losing his old man whilst his teammates were out on the pitch celebrating as they didn't find out until after they had collected their medals. That put things into perspective that day for us all. We'd only lost a cup final, that poor lad had lost his dad on what should have been the greatest day of his life. RIP Jack Kelly.

One of the main talking points of that season was the Lenny v McCoist battle in February 2011. The first game at Ibrox was a classic which ended 2-2. It was a great result for us because we finished the game with ten men with big Fraser Forster getting sent off. That game was also the birth of, "The Broony" which became a very iconic celebration as Scott Brown scored in the 65th minute and stood with his hands in the air directly in front of El-Hadji Diouf, almost face to face! Scotty said afterwards that it was the best yellow card he had ever received in his whole career! I knew first-hand what a terrier Scott Brown was when I came up against him as a young player for Hibs. He was relentless in winding people up and would even go after Lenny on the pitch looking for him to bite. I knew he would go on to have a big future in the game and at the club before he did.

The Scottish Cup 5th Round Replay in early March was back at ours and if the first had been ill-tempered, then this was to be known as, 'the shame game' with players almost getting locked up by the police off the pitch and of course a few red cards thrown in for good measure. Celtic advanced into the quarterfinals with a 1-0 win, a goal coming from Celtic full-back Mark Wilson. Mark said after all the fiasco, "I hit the best half volley of my life which was quickly followed by the worst half volley of my life." Rangers' defenders Madjid Bougherra and Steven Whittaker both saw reds with El-Hadji Diouf getting up to his old tricks and trying to run into the Rangers end. Thankfully the police stopped him and redirected him back to the pitch, and he saw red also but overall, the game from start to finish was absolute mayhem. It's not as if these games are normally good tempered but this particular night it was extra spiteful.

The Rangers boss at the time pointed the finger at Lenny regarding what happened between them. He said Lenny acted over aggressively, which wasn't the case in my opinion, and I broke them up. What really started it off was Diouf gave our physiotherapist a hard shoulder and it escalated from there. Scott Brown took a few kicks and Kris Commons got clattered in front of our dugout which sent our emotions sky high. All the way through the game Diouf was dishing out verbal assaults on everyone in a hooped shirt and even directed a few to myself and Lenny on the side-lines. Don't forget it was Lenny and me opposing him exactly eight years previously when Celtic played against Liverpool in The EUFA Cup match at Parkhead. You look at El-Hadji Diouf and he was pretty decent. The guy had been with some good clubs but in my opinion the only reason Rangers brought him in on loan in January 2011 was that he was the biggest c*** they could have found on the planet to wind the Celtic fans up. That might sound a bit, 'pot-kettle-black' with my track record regarding old firm discipline but he was brought in by Rangers for the shock value. A bit like Mo Johnson signing for Rangers in 1989 after saying he was going back to Celtic, but on a smaller scale. Mo was never forgiven by the Celtic fans and it's the same for El-Hadji after he spat at the Celtic fans in March 2003. As I said Diouf was, 'on one' that night and I told him many times to "do one" away from our area as he was constantly trying to sneak in closer to our area to noise us up. Incidentally, El'Hadji bought my old house off me when he went to Bolton around 2005 time.

When the final whistle blew and we had won the game all the staff went over to shake hands with the opposing team as you do, when Lenny went to shake Coisty's hand. I was stood so close that I clearly heard Ally tell Lenny, "And don't you be speaking to my fucking players like that", only for Lenny to tell him, "They're not you're fucking players, they're Walters." It's never been disclosed what was actually said in over a decade now but I'm telling you that was the spark that lit the fire and Hell was hot. Lenny was right because Walter was the gaffer and Ally was only the no.2 at that time, Ally didn't take well to that. The Rangers boys were all trying to say it was our fault but any team who receives three red cards in one match need to have a long hard look at themselves! After a while everything calmed down and we were all delirious in the dressing room celebrating. Ian Jameson the press officer then came into mine and Lenny's office sniffing about for some kind of reaction. Well after what had went on at Celtic Park that evening there was no way that Lenny could have done some kind of reaction however Sky Sports were demanding it. In the end Lenny pushed me to walk the plank and I had to go out in front of the cameras to face the worlds media who were now like vultures flying over Parkhead for people's scalps and looking to blame someone in the papers the next day. After speaking to Ian Jameson, I told him I would go out and try to dampen the flames a little bit. I never minded speaking to the press, but I was asked by certain people to box clever and try to dull it down. It was clear the press wanted to make more of it than handbags, but it was going to be my job to try and play it down a bit, either way they were going to make a fuss about it in the papers the next day.

Anyone who watches my interview today on YouTube will see it was an incredibly hard task to do. After the interviews I had a shower then went into Lenny's office but as I got there, I was the only one in there from Celtic. Barrie McKay, Ian Durrant and Kenny McDowall were already sat in there. I already had a good relationship with Kenny from my time at Celtic, so I just broke the ice, 'lads what do you want to drink?' which I think caught them off guard. Not only had I just given an interview worthy of an Oscar, but I was now kidding on that nothing had even happened to the Rangers boys. Although I was playing it cool on the outside, inside I was thinking, 'where the hell's Lenny, Dolph and Parks?? It had literally just been like a bad day in Bosnia an hour ago and now I'm sat with three slightly pissed off Gers, so the silence was deafening. If you're thinking it couldn't get any more awkward than think again because Coisty strolls in. I'm not sure if he's come for more of same but this was turning into a very hostile teddy bears picnic, and I was the odd one out. All I could think of saying was, 'fancy a beer Ally?' God above must have heard my stresses because right on cue the three musketeers arrived. Lenny, big Dolph and Parks were here so it was as if it was now four onto four, or a square go as they say in Glasgow, was about to happen! I have to admit there was a bit of an awkward moment or two, but Lenny and Ally then shook hands, walked out of the office, into another room, shut the blinds and had it out with each other like men and then kissed and made up. It was all put to bed that night regardless of what the Scottish media were trying to stir up to increase paper sales. From our point of view, it was done and dusted and into the Scottish Cup quarter final we went, which of course we went on to win against Motherwell in the final.

If Lenny thought it couldn't have got any more heated than that Old Firm shoot-out then he was sadly mistaken. Only a couple of months on from that night at Tynecastle, a Hearts supporter ran from the stands and tried to attack him. My memories of it were that I was stood watching the game on the touchline next to Lenny with a pad in my hand when out of the corner of my eye I saw this unfamiliar figure. As I took in what was happening, I saw it was a fan in a baseball cap and scarf, he had something in his hand and was going for Lenny in a violent manner. It's scary because for all we knew that guy could have been carrying a weapon. My instincts then took over and just as he was about to get to Lenny, I sort of reached out at the last second and grabbed him around the neck. The fella was sort of running so fast towards the gaffer that when I caught him it ruined his momentum and lifted his feet off the ground. To be fair to the Hearts stewards and Edinburgh police they acted so quickly, got on top of him and held him on the ground. As this nutter started screaming, "YOU FENIAN BASTARD… YOU FENIAN BASTARD"! Thankfully what was in his hand was only his mobile phone, but I dread to think of what could have happened that night. I don't mind admitting that it may have looked as if he was given a few digs, but we only used sufficient force to keep him on the ground.

The whole episode was a weird incident to be involved with and of course it was a seriously ugly night for Scottish football which dragged on for months and ended in a lawsuit. I was there for two days in the dock at Edinburgh courts. This may sound really silly, but I found that whole court case horrific. I felt like I'd done something wrong as I'd never been in a court in my whole life. It's like when a shop alarm goes off and you feel guilty even though you haven't stolen anything. I was the closest witness to the full incident so it was inevitable I would have to swear an oath and give evidence. Nonetheless I found it very strange. "Mr Thompson do you see the accused in this courtroom today?" The judge asked, and I just replied, 'no your honour' without even thinking. "Well, I suggest you turn to your left and have a look" the judge told me. It wasn't something I really wanted to do as all the twelve jury members, punters and journalists were staring at me so it was quite off putting. In the end I stopped being a big girl's blouse and said to the judge I could see the accused and pointed in his direction.

I've no idea why that lad Wilson did what he did and what his end game was by trying to attack Lenny! Why did that guy Mark Chapman shoot John Lennon? All I can tell you is just how much that attack and the death threats and things in the post had an effect on my mate Neil Lennon's mental health. One particular time myself and Lenny where drinking in the Drake alone at the bar. We were on our first pint when two guys came in, walked straight up to us and said, "lads put your pints down and don't ask any questions." Before we could say anything back they said, "we're both plain clothes detectives and both your lives are in serious imminent danger." I was now being dragged into it but in reality, I knew Lenny's life was far more at risk than mine so we both followed the coppers out and got in separate cars each to a safehouse. I was thinking what on earth is going on. I'd only gone out for a quiet pint with my best mate and now I'm being whisked away to stop someone, "whacking us" as they say in the American Mafia. The story behind that incident was that the authorities had been tipped off that something bad was about to happen to both of us that day. I think the correct term used in those situations is an Osman Warning and for me to now be involved in that was absolutely terrifying, and I only had a fraction of it compared to Lenny. Neil Lennon has been a constant target since he rocked up in Glasgow and he had to develop skin like a rhino, however he is only human like us all. Let me break this down to you all about Neil Lennon.

Now I have never seen Lenny in tears, but I knew when he was down. Neil Lennon has suffered more abuse than any footballer I ever knew in my whole career. Neil Lennon suffered from clinical depression or as he called it, 'his black dog' as a young player. I was lucky and that black dog never found me until I was in my late 30's. The experts say that something in life can trigger it and mine came when I was sacked by Celtic, but Lenny's was from his younger days, when by his own admission, he'd been a bad lad at times. Lenny told me it's just something he's learnt to live with, and he gets on with it, and now I've had to do the same. If Lenny wouldn't have signed for Celtic, then would he have had all his problems then absolutely not is my opinion. There's no way all this crap would have followed him throughout his life if he'd have only stayed with Glenavon, Manchester City, Crew Alexandra, Leicester City, Nottingham Forest and Wycombe Wanderers. I knew it was hard for Lenny many times and often myself, Dolph and Parks would protect him from a lot of things as much as we could. Even the club doctor Roddy MacDonald would chip in and keep certain things from him that he didn't need to hear or see. Also, as a group it was our job to lift his spirits when his black dog was off the leash. I know the Celtic doctor Roddy was always a great listener to his problems and would also try to maintain that balance and try to hold him back from going too far under that black cloud. Roddy was just terrific with him he really was, and I'll come back to Roddy in this book a little while later and when I started having my own black canine at my heels.

Now switching back to the football side of things, the one thing I'd like to say is that when I was back winning things at Celtic on the staff, that was better than lifting cups as a player. That may sound slightly absurd because essentially it wasn't even my team, it was Lenny's team, but

I felt a part of it. I was part of the big Celtic family when we secured that first of nine titles in 2012. I'm pretty sure that had we not won the title that second full season Lenny, myself and all of us would have been sacked. We knew after coming close the previous season that anything less than first was a disaster. You can only imagine the relief when we finally did it and in that very same season Glasgow Rangers died in the February. Ironically it was on Valentine's Day which made the Celtic fans fall in love with Rangers new owner Craig Whyte even more. I can promise you that as much as people want to lynch him in the blue side of Glasgow, he would never have to put his hand in his pocket in the Celtic Bars down the Gallowgate. Please believe me I'm not looking for any cheap shots at all the Rangers supporters, but you can't put it any other way than the club completely folded. This proud club born in 1872 and steeped in great tradition was no more after 2012, some would say after that it was only a tribute act. I mean no malice when I say that I'm just stating facts.

Now I have to be honest here, when we'd just won the league in May 2012 everything was going swimmingly well, or so I thought! I had no idea that weeks later in June I would be out the door at Celtic after only two years on the management staff. They'd been a few issues with myself away from the club which were well publicised in the media but nothing that I thought was worth me being fired. Looking back at it now there were signs that I should have seen something like that coming. One day I remember particularly was Lenny coming into the coaching office to see me at Lennoxtown Training Centre. "Tommo, can I have a word please?" Lenny asks out of the blue. It sounded all rather serious considering we were best mates but of course I told him he could. Lenny then comes out with, "Tommo I've been asked from certain people above me to ask you this, although I already know answer, I have to ask you if you are you taking drugs?" Well, you could have knocked me down with a feather as he went on to say that certain members of the Celtic board had heard I was taking cocaine. Anyone who knows me will tell you the answer to that. I told Lenny straight that I was offended that he'd even asked me that. Then I told him to ring downstairs to the doctors and I'd take every single drug test in the world. I told him that even though I was petrified of injections, the club could take whatever they wanted from my body to test. If I never see my three kids again, I have never touched any drugs in my life! For as stupid as I've been in drink, taking drugs has never been my game. Ever! I've seen a hell of a lot of people within football doing it, with some it's common knowledge and others won't admit it. Once I was even having a few beers in my flat with a very famous singer from Glasgow when he pulled a bag of cocaine out. I didn't even know what he was doing and when I found out I chased him out of my home because it's just not my thing. Of course, I told him he could leave the crate of beers. Substance abuse is something I've never even come close to doing. Honestly, I think people just assumed because of how loud and bubbly I was that I was taking drugs. Gambling was another form of addiction which never really appealed to me. Some of my close mates like John Hartson have done it but I never saw the point of it. I was brought up listening to my old man telling me, 'You'll never see a bookie driving a Skoda son because they always win'. Also, I didn't and still don't get the odds i.e., 5/4, 8/13 or 15/2 etc and I'd rather it stay that way. I'm not saying I've never gambled because I've been to Las Vegas. When I've been there, I've gone in the casinos, if I lost that £100 then it was time to move on. Big John Hartson is a long time clean from that addiction and I've even played golf with John and suggested we have a daft £20 on who wins the game. He's always told me that he couldn't play for money, however the loser has to buy lunch.

Regarding Lenny asking me that I considered it as him putting a chink in our friendship if I'm being honest. I think I lost a little bit of something for Lenny that day when he asked me that because there weren't many people who knew me inside out on this planet but Neil Lennon was one of them. I also didn't like the way he did it in a manager's office, it was all too official, as a friend he could have asked me away from Celtic.

As I said, away from the club I'd had a few incidents such as the drink-driving one which was around that same time. I was driving to Lennoxtown one morning after an Old Firm game. I know I shouldn't have been doing it but I was on the phone which is something I never do because I normally use Bluetooth. Anyway, the police have pulled me over because they saw me with my phone to my ear then they've just asked me to blow in one of them testers and I still had alcohol from the night before in my system and I received a ban. That didn't look good on me, and it didn't look good for Celtic Football Club and it made the papers. Many were making out that I'd just been boozing then got behind the wheel which is utter crap, it was from the night previously, I didn't know I was over the limit and I made a mistake. Peter Lawwell obviously didn't want these things attached to the club, so it didn't do me any favours, and then the story broke in the papers about the affair with the other woman. The fling lasted under a year with a Britney Spears lookalike (or so the media said) which we both had a giggle about. I'll never forget getting off the team bus at Celtic Park and this woman came running up to me saying, 'Alan I'm a reporter for a major paper and tomorrow we'll be running a story about your affair so do you have any comments?" I quickly walked away but I'm thinking, 'WOW'. I couldn't believe this was happening to me but yes, I did bring it on by myself. It wasn't a nice feeling to know my marriage with Jo would be under the world's media spotlight in the next 24 hours and it would be another nail in my coffin with Peter Lawwell. That reporter was as good as her word and the world was reading about it the next day, which was horrific for my whole family and my friends. It was also tarnishing Celtic Football Club yet again.

All this then dragged on for weeks with the papers now sniffing around my wife Jo for comments and she gave them want they wanted. Jo told the papers that I was having mid-life crisis and I could get on with it by myself. Away supporters also jumped on the bandwagon, and it was used against me whenever we went to away grounds. In fact, the day Jo's interview hit the papers we were playing at Ibrox of all places, so you can imagine what I was hearing. Funny enough it ended up being a bit of a giggle for Lenny and Ally McCoist as the verbal attacks were aimed at our dugout from the home supporters. I can remember being on the touchline and I'd just told Lenny that Sammy (Georgios Samaras) needed to stay behind a little bit to stretch the defence and he agreed. Lenny told me to stand up and shout them exact instructions at Sammy which I did. After I've finished, I've walked back to the dugout and this bluenose has stood up and shouted, "OI THOMPSON, NAE WONDER YA MRS HAS LEFT YA YOU UGLY ENGLISH BASTARD." I thought cheers for that mate and as I looked up, I could see Lenny and Coisty stood laughing their heads off. It wasn't funny for me but obviously it was to some.

It wasn't only Lennon and McCoist who were laughing that day let me tell you because the whole stand was, as well as the 4th official, although he had the good grace to look away from me to laugh. Listen folks, I did do wrong with that one affair, but can I just say to everyone out there that I wasn't the serial womaniser that I was made out to be by the Scottish press. I put mine and Jo's 16-year marriage severely on the rocks but I wasn't a serial womaniser. The affair with the other woman was the first thing of that nature since I'd been with Jo. Even when I wasn't with Jo, I'd never been out of long-term relationships for very long so that puts to bed (pardon the pun) that I was some kind of bed hopper.

The day I was fired by the club it was totally unexpected and came out of the blue. I'd been to the Derby at Epsom with my wife Jo, ex player Steve Stone and his wife Judith who were close friends. Although I'm no horseracing fan I'd enjoyed the day out. London was busy that weekend because it was the Queen's Jubilee, not to mention the London Olympics. I just remember getting on the train at Kings Cross to go back to Newcastle when I received a text from Lenny asking if I was still in Tyneside. I thought that was a bit of a strange text so I said to Stoney I wouldn't be long because I needed to go give Lenny a ring. I called Lenny and he answered with, 'alright Hooch?' Hooch was the nickname given to me by a goalkeeper from Bolton called Aidan Davison and it was because of the dog from the 1989 film, Turner and Hooch. Aidan used to say I wasn't the best looking lad in the world so he named me that and it followed me around the clubs and obviously any piss takers at clubs would call me it. Aidan and Celtic's Tommy Johnson were best mates, in fact both were each other's best man at their weddings. It was Aidan who told Tommy when he was at Celtic my nickname was "Hooch" so that's how Lenny got hold of it and ran with it for a few years. Lenny calls me "Hooch" even up to this day. Getting back to the text, Lenny asked where I was and that if I was in Newcastle then he was going to come down and see me. I asked him why he would be needing to come down and see me but he wouldn't tell me over the phone. He told me he needed to talk to me face to face but now alarm bells were ringing. I told Lenny, "Whatever you've got to tell me then you can do it right now" so he told me that Peter Lawwell and the rest of the board wanted me out of Celtic. It didn't surprise me when he told me this with the drink driving, cocaine allegations and affair in the press so I asked Lenny what his take was on it! "I don't have any say on the matter Hooch". I told him that we're best mates and that he was the boss of a team we'd both just won the league with surely, he was going to back me? Surely, he could have told Peter Lawwell that I was an important part of his staff but there was just a deadly silence coming from him. I think Lenny must have known for a few weeks I was going to be axed and he said nothing or didn't warn me of what was to come. He could have given me the nod so I could hand in my resignation to save me the embarrassment of what was to come but he didn't. I told Lenny that although I wasn't too happy with the news, I got that it was because of what had gone on in my personal life over the last few months. I also told him not to come to Newcastle because I didn't want to see him and put the phone down.

What was a great weekend had now just been ruined as I walked back into the train carriages to meet Jo, Stoney and Judith to tell them I'd just had the chop at Celtic. From that minute on that train, I was an emotional wreck and it continued for many years after. Losing my job at Celtic took some getting over. I'd never had depression before that day but I'm pretty aware that looking back on it now that opened the door to a world of anxiety, depression and darkness. I was also out of work for such a long period from that day onwards and my drinking only escalated. I would drink to numb the pain and then spend full days in bed in a dark room. If I'd thought my world had just caved in on that train journey home to Newcastle and that life couldn't get any worse than I was sadly mistaken. There was so much more bleakness heading my way.

AIDAN McGEADY

Former Celtic Teammate

"I was only a young schoolboy when Alan Thompson signed for Celtic. I was first introduced to him when I was 16 in my first year as a full-time player when I got to train with the first team now and again. Mostly I had to do all the odd jobs like clean the boots and sort bits of kit out for the first team. I've got to be honest, it was the likes of Tommo, Lenny and Sutty that were brutal with us younger lads coming through. With the way the world is now you probably couldn't say the things that Thompson, Sutton, Lennon & co got away with as it'd be classed as bullying now but I thought it was character building. It's something that is definitely missing from football now, a bit of tough love to the younger players. It helped me sort of become a man although that might sound crazy. Even when I got into the first team regularly, although I was one of them, I still had to take my stick because I was just a young lad in their eyes. It's only after playing a while that you earn their respect.

Towards the end of Tommo's career, I used to travel in with him as he stayed close to me in Newton Mearns. Tommo, by that point was on the way out under Strachan's reign but I had got quite close to him by then. It was only at the start that I couldn't have been further away from that, in his eyes anyway. Tommo's antics were brutal; however, it was just banter. He wouldn't be harsh on people for the sake of being nasty. Everything he did was with a laugh at the end of it. The Christmas do was always very fun for the players if Tommo or his sidekick big Sutty was around.

I enjoyed learning and being around the older generation of players of that Martin O'Neill side. Thompson's sidekick Sutton is the opposite of how you see him on tv as a sports pundit by the way.

Alan Thompson first and foremost was a top player for Celtic. When he was sent to the reserves after he'd been a long term first-team established player it must have been hard. I've been there myself when you're going back down the rankings and then you can't be bothered anymore but Tommo never let that get to him. He was prepared to put in the graft even playing with the 18-year old's. The only time I ever saw Tommo being put in his place was when Roy Keane had just signed in early 2006. We were at training and Tommo, this particular day, was just arsing about and not being serious. He wasn't tracking his runners etc, so Roy turned around to him and said, "Tommo if you don't want to be here then fuck off!" Tommo never said a word back to him and it was the only time I've ever seen Alan take that because usually he always had something to say back. I think Tommo knew he couldn't actually say anything back because he knew he was pissing about, and it was something he never usually did.

I played a joke on Tommo once by messing about with his window wipers when I'd just got on with the first team. He found out and demanded to know who I was, and he said that he was going to tell of me to the gaffer. I told him I was sorry and that it was just a joke because the older lads dared me to do it. He asked me who the fuck did I think I was and told me that there was going to be consequences for my actions. I'm now shitting myself thinking I'm going to be done here and Tommo told me he was going to grass me up to Martin O'Neill. For the next week when I saw him the only thing he would say to me was, "PFFFT, YOU'RE DONE HERE LAD" and he would walk off in the direction of the manager's office. Another day, as one of the young lads I was putting the first teams boots out etc, this was away at Dundee United when Tommo kept coming up to me and staring at me then he'd walk up to Martin O'Neill, John Robertson and Steve Walford. He'd then put his arm around them and let me see him whispering in their ears, every now and again he'd look back at me as if to say, 'your time at Celtic is finished mate' before it had even really started. I'd be sat there thinking he was fucking telling on me. Obviously, nothing happened for a bit and I'd started to think that I'd got away with it but then Tommo would come looking for me to remind me of just how much shit I was going to be in. I didn't know it at the time because I was a young player, but he was just using me for his own entertainment by prolonging my agony. Today at 35 I know better; what manager is going to get rid of a 16-year-old kid because he messed about with one of the first team players window wipers? When I was 16, I was thinking of what I was going to say to my parents because I'd just been kicked out of Celtic. For ages I used to have nightmares about Alan going to tell Martin O'Neill about this bad thing that I was put up to by Neil Lennon, Chris Sutton and Paul Lambert in the first place etc. Tommo did eventually get his own back, not by telling Martin but by painting me from head to toe with boot polish. He even coloured my arms, hands and feet. Boy did he get me good. I learnt my lesson and I never wound Alan Thompson up again, although I was told by some of the older players that I should tie tin cans to his car, but I was too scared. I needed to keep my head down because he was a first teamer and I was a youth player coming through. Today if a young player did that to me, I think I'd quite enjoy it now. Tommo I'm sure enjoyed it but in a quite sadistic manner to say the least (laughs).

When I was coming through at Celtic Tommo was always the guy who seemed flash. Henrik Larsson had a Ferrari so Tommo got a Ferrari. I used to look at him in his Bentley and his big house in Newton Mearns and I'd think, 'I'd love to be like you one day!' Before I got up to the first team Alan was somebody I really looked up to, that's when he wasn't scaring me of course.

I was there that time that Tommo has mentioned, when Bobo Balde wanted to kill Stiliyan Petrov in the dressing room. I saw Bobo lose his temper like that twice. It was also Tommo who, when I 'megged Lenny in training and he threatened to rip my head off, was there straight away saying, "Aidan do it again and I'll give you some money after training."

A MESSAGE TO AIDAN FROM TOMMO, *"I was only ever hard on you lad for tough love. I saw the potential in you as soon as you came into the first team squad at Celtic and I knew a bit of tough love would help you to become the player you've gone onto be."*

CHAPTER 20

MY VERY OWN BLACK DOG

Depression was only a word to me before 2012 and nothing else. Obviously, I knew what it meant but I never truly understood anything about it because I had no experience with it. After the way I'd been sacked at Celtic, which wasn't nice for me and the family, it really took its toll on me. I now had my own black dog which I had to feed daily just like Lenny used to talk about. In the months after being given the boot by Celtic was when my world really turned into a bleak place and I couldn't really imagine that there was any light at, what seemed to be, a never-ending tunnel for me. Thankfully my family never turned against me, even after having the affair Jo and I had decided we'd try and make it work, at least for a little while. Even though me and Jo tried to give it a go, the repercussions of what I had done and the stories that appeared in the newspapers had an effect on my marriage, no matter how good things seemed at times, it was always there, like an elephant in the room that we were desperately trying to ignore. So, though Jo had given me another chance, even though I felt like I didn't deserve it, it was actually the dismissal from Celtic that I couldn't shake off, I fell into a rut.

I started watching telly until the early hours and then I'd not wake up until midday. Drink never really got a hold of me then, that came further down the line, but I had the body clock of a vampire. At times I tried to keep active playing golf and even spending thousands on cycling gear which was something I really got into for a spell. On my good days I was doing 35-40 miles a day when the weather would permit. No matter how much I tried though I just couldn't stop this anxiety from seeping in.

One evening Jo and I had taken the dogs for a walk when I turned to her and said, "you know, I don't feel well". I put my head on her shoulder, and that was the last thing I remember before coming around in an ambulance being taken to hospital. The whole situation was freakish. I didn't know why it happened because I was still relatively fit but here I was with wires strapped to my body and on a heart monitor. I then had to have all kinds of tests and there seemed to be a lot of questions asked but I really didn't understand the situation myself. I had my driving licence taken off me for a period of six months because I was now blacking out. At the end of the six months I was given my driver's licence back, but the medical experts couldn't put their fingers on what was causing these blackouts. I even bit my cheek once when I was fitting it was horrendous. After a while the doctors told me that because they couldn't find anything wrong with me physically, they put it down to stress. Everything that had happened in my life over the last few months had all added up and my body had reacted by shutting down. It was a build-up of everything that I had been through is what I was told by my doctor.

Although Jo and I worked at our marriage for another five or six years, we were both kidding ourselves. Overall, it was my affair that killed our marriage and I have to hold my hands up to that. Even when I was working away towards the end of our marriage in Birmingham, Bury and Blackpool I was on my own, once over she would have been by my side. I was away a lot, but I did try and pop back for the odd night but as tough as it was to come to terms with it, the spark had well and truly disappeared between us.

It's so bizarre to think of all the hate I've received in my life from Rangers fans, but I never had any mental health issues in that time. People were sending me the worst kinds of things in the post at Celtic Park, and it was so easy to deal with, whereas after 2012 I'd finished playing but struggled for so long with the simplest of things. It was an effort just to walk to the shop and buy a pint of milk at times. Any of the struggles I now walk around with have come from the age of 38 onwards. Breaking my neck never left any kind of mental issues on me other than a hesitancy to go up for an aerial challenge mid-air whilst playing which I always got around. My life changed for the worst in June 2012 in my late 30's and ever since then It's been a constant struggle for me. Only now as I'm putting everything down on paper in 2021 is my life showing any signs of going back to what it was before that time. In all those years when I sort of vanished away from the spotlight and away from football, they have been the worst times of my life. I can honestly say that walking off at Ibrox three times from red cards and the crowd shouting the worst kind of obscenities towards me affected me less. Over the years, from 2012 onwards, many of my close friends noticed I wasn't the same Tommo anymore. My good friend Peter Joynson reached out to me and offered words of care. Another family friend, Ian Watson a wealthy businessman in the Northeast saw the deterioration in me and pulled me aside for a word. At the time I didn't appreciate his views and was a bit snappy towards him but now I know he was doing it only out of consideration.

Ian noticed that I was now starting to have problems with drink, and it was him who first introduced me to Sporting Chance. It was a place for former sports stars to go if they needed any help with mental health issues and the problems that often come with that. At first, I didn't take Ian's offer up for a while because I didn't see myself as having a problem. I considered getting in touch with an organisation like that as a sign of weakness whereas now I know it's not. To admit you have a problem is actually an amazing sign of strength. For a lad from Battle Hill in Wallsend to open up and talk about his feelings was unheard of. Thankfully its more accepted now that mental health issues exist, even with the people who outwardly seem to have it all. Depression doesn't discriminate. Unfortunately, though it took us losing too many people like Gary Speed and Caroline Flack for it to become something that is acceptable to speak openly about. I'd like to say thank you to Ian Watson for his concerns and for helping me to see the light. I don't think I would have woken up without your push, so I'll be forever grateful.

For all of my problems around those few years I didn't just lay down and feel sorry for myself, I tried to pretend my problems didn't exist at all. At times I tried to get back on the horse and weather the storms like joining up at Birmingham City with Lee Clark. Clarkie had been there a while when he got me a post as Under 23's boss for four months. It was a job I would only be in for a short time as when Clarkie moved on I would be out of the door with him. It was a shame that job was so brief as I'd been out of the game for two years but of course when Lee and Watto, who was his no.2, were moved on then of course it meant they'd be no place for me as it was them who'd brought me in. I took the job at Birmingham in a heartbeat but in reality, there was a part of me that didn't want to go. This time it was nothing to do with anyone else other than my confidence wasn't what it was. At that time in 2014 I didn't have any belief in myself even though I could do the job with my eyes closed, I mean, football was the only thing I knew. I knew that I was in a rut, but I tried to put aside all the anxiety, depression and negativity which had swum around my head for the last few years and I went down to Birmingham and gave it a go anyway. I didn't get the job just because I knew Clarkie and Watto, I had to have an interview with about four other candidates. When Clarkie rang me to tell me I'd got the job I was over the moon. As I said the reason the job was only for four months was nothing to do with me, it was because Clarkie and Watto had left.

Although I was only Under 23's coach, on a match day Clarkie wanted me around the First Team to help him even though he had Steve Watson and Richard Beale as his First Team Coach and that was good for my confidence. Not only did Lee want me involved but he wanted me to watch from the stands to view the game, so I had a different perspective of the game from him. Ironically, we had a home game at St Andrews against my old club Bolton Wanderers, the Bolton Wanderers that my ex- best mate Neil Lennon was now in charge of. At this point I'd not seen nor heard from Lenny for over two years. I'm not going to lie; I was nervous about bumping into Lenny again. Although we weren't best friends anymore and he wasn't my favourite person on the planet at that time, I didn't want to say anything stupid because I had too much respect for him to go to that level. The tunnel at St Andrews is in the bottom corner near the corner flag. The reality of it was I was now going to bump into Lenny again whether I liked it or not. I knew the cameras will have been focusing on us two because it was public knowledge that we no longer spoke so that's why I made a point of seeing him before we were in front of the cameras. I waited in the tunnel for Lenny hovering like a would-be mugger waiting for his intended victim. Well before I could come across Lenny who did I bump into first but big Dolph and Parks. Big Johan Mjallby and Gary Parker were part of his staff at Bolton. I shook their hands then Lenny came strutting down and we then shook hands. We both kind of just said we'd have a chat after the game and that was that. To be honest that day Birmingham battered them, but Bolton went away winners 1-0. After the game I was in the manager's office with Lee Clark and Steve Watson. At that time not only were we working together but we all lived together in a place just outside of Birmingham called Lapworth. Most times after the game I would drive Clarkie back because I'd let him have a few glasses of wine. In that office big Dolph and Parks were the first ones to come in, so it was the same old spiel, I offered them a drink and we made small talk. I have to admit I was annoyed at the pair of them, because when I was kicked out at Celtic I never got a call from either of them. Not only was this me meeting Lenny for the first time it was also me bumping into them two again, so it was awkward x3. At one point myself, Lenny, Dolph and Parks had been so close and not to get even so much as a text wishing me all the best for the future from any of them hurt. It was uncomfortable if I'm honest, in fact more awkward than it was between me and Lenny as I sat and asked how both of their families were. I don't know if they were embarrassed but I didn't get a lot back from Dolph and Parks. Lenny then came in and he shook my hand, but he was more interested in chatting to Clarkie as both managers do after a game. Before Lenny left, he shook my hand again and said, "give us a bell Tommo", I said yes, I would but probably had no intentions of doing so as I waved him, Dolph and Parks off. About an hour later me and Clarkie are going home when he turned and said, "Tommo what did Lenny say to you as he was going?" I told Lee that he said I should call him and Clarkie said I should. I told the gaffer I haven't got his number anymore. At that time my brother-in-law Dave Lee still worked at Bolton, so I got in touch for Lenny's number. As soon as I asked, he said, "ah why what's up now?" I told him it wasn't anything to worry about. We've just sort of made up and we needed to chat, so he sent me it. I rang Lenny that very same night as Clarkie went in our flat we shared. I told him I'd wait in the car as I got this out of the way. That evening myself and Lenny had a long chat and spoke about everything about what really went on. I told him my feelings that I felt like I'd been fed to the wolves. Alive! Lenny was fairly understanding about it all and showed me real empathy and as I thought he might be he was a bit sheepish. Lenny even suggested that I could work at Bolton with the under 23's and be closer to Jo and the kids as Birmingham was a long way from Tyneside. As nice as it was for him to say that I couldn't help thinking, 'are you kidding me?' All the friendship, trust and respect had been obliterated with what happened to me at Celtic. I told him no thanks and that we couldn't ever be the same as we were once over. Even though I was once ranked 12th greatest player in Bolton Wanderers history by a fans poll and was looked upon as some kind of legend at the club, it never entered my head for a second to go back working with the three of them. Yes, it would have been a dream job and who knows what the future holds but to Lenny's suggestion it had to be a straight no.

Since then, in 2014 Lenny and I have spoken several times about certain players over the years and he even got me tickets for a Scottish Cup Final game at Hampden recently. These days we're ok but I don't think we'll ever be as close as we once were. There's a lot of water under the bridge these days with myself and Len so who really knows for the future as I'm not into holding grudges because life is too short for that. You only hurt yourself when you hang on to resentment.

It was sad, the way I left Birmingham. One day I had a game for the Under 23's and that very same day Clarkie got a call from the directors to go in for a chat. Lee knew what it was and when he came back he got all the staff together to say he'd been given the chop. I knew there and then I'd be surplus to requirements, but I still had to take charge of this game because I had a load of young teenagers to look after that day. Before Lee left Birmingham, he took all the staff for a drink at a nearby pub and Lee took care of the bar bill for the evening. The first team at Birmingham had a game against Preston North End the following night and Malcolm Crosby, who was a chief scout, was asked to take over the team for that game. Malcolm asked me if I would go and give him a hand, but I told him sorry I wouldn't be able to. I stood loyal to Lee Clark because he was the one who brought me in. There was no way I could be disloyal to him like that and Malcolm, who's a great man, totally understood my predicament. So, I packed my flat up and went back to Newcastle with Lee Clark. Birmingham City were superb also and understood I now couldn't be there if Lee wasn't. They understood and even gave me the next three months' salary which they didn't have to do so that was a nice touch from them. I have nothing but good things to say about Birmingham City, unfortunately I just couldn't stay after Lee had been given the boot.

Clarkie wouldn't be out of work for long, in fact it was only a matter of around two weeks until Blackpool came calling. Jose Riga had only just been sacked and the seaside club came looking for Lee Clark's services. The sad thing was that Blackpool as a club were falling to bits and at that point were very far away from the Premiership status that they'd been only a few years previously. They came to Lee and knew what he'd done at Huddersfield Town and Birmingham City. Lee kept the latter in The Championship on hardly any budget which was a great feat, so he had great pedigree. When Lee took over the reins at Blackpool his first port of call would be to bring myself in. At the time Blackpool was in great conflict between the fans and ownership. To say it was a hostile atmosphere was an understatement. Lee showed his loyalty to me again when he brought me in as Assistant Manager. When Lee and I took over its fair to say there was a lot of dead wood there in the team and the stadium was half-empty. If there were only half the fans there then I can assure you that they weren't there to support the team. They were there to scream bad things at the owners, so it was a mess from day one. Lee and I thought we could change it, but we realised that same season that this was undoable. If Blackpool had never brought in Lee Clark & Alan Thompson and went for Pep Guardiola & Jose Mourinho instead then they still wouldn't have improved, seriously. The matchdays were tough and one supporter on Lee's first game in charge ran down the stand, looked into our dugout and shouted, "OI CLARK... YA WORSE THAN PAUL INCE"! I'm not kidding you that was Lee's first game, and the game hadn't even kicked off. The supporters were already on his back before he'd literally started. The alarm bells rang for me then on what turned out to be an unpleasant time. Fans would be continuously making these protests outside the ground, even windows were being broken. Smoke bombs were getting thrown into the foyer of the main reception it really wasn't nice.

Mine and Lee's last game in charge was the last game of the season in May 2015. I'll never forget it as it was the same night as Floyd Mayweather beat Manny Pacquiao, but the pitch was invaded and the game against Huddersfield Town was abandoned after 48 minutes. The fans took over the ground baying for chairman Karl Oyston's blood. The funny thing is the game was still 0-0 at the time and we weren't even losing and they were behaving like that. We knew then that this was more than football, and nothing could be salvaged. The club didn't need a football manager, they really needed B.A. Baracus, Hannibal, Murdoch and Face from the A-Team to keep them safe from the fans it was unbelievable.

That night I remember saying to Nash that we now really needed to nash. Nash was Lee Clark and it's what I've called him since we were kids. It was a Geordie thing when you're going to do a runner from somewhere that you need to, 'nash.' It was fitting as Lee was always in a hurry and nashing off. Terry McDermott also used to call him it, so it stuck. It was also an incredibly fitting name for the situation we were both in and thankfully he took my advice. I told Nash that of course I'd always stand by him but it was impossible to work in that environment. We were getting spoken to from the club's supporters like we were paedophiles, and I wasn't used to it. The blue half of Glasgow were nicer to me than our own fans were at that point. Even though we had some good results on the pitch it didn't matter to the supporters, they just wanted Blackpool staff's heads on a plate. Considering Nash never had any money given he did a great job with loans in etc... Myself and Nash put it down to experience and lessons learnt in football and life in general. We both resigned and moved on with both our lives whilst we still could.

Dr RODDY MACDONALD

First Team Doctor at Celtic Football Club

"I had been the club doctor at Newcastle United when Kenny Dalglish was the manager so that was when I first heard the name Alan Thompson. For my master's degree in sports injuries, I had to study players injuries so I had done a bit of research on Tommo's injury. I got more familiar with Tommo when he came to Celtic whilst I was there. My best mate Derek Wright was the guy who nursed Tommo back to his feet after his accident and he told me all about the injury Tommo had sustained.

It was actually Kenny Dalglish who brought me to Celtic as the club's doctor and that was a dream come true for me because they are my boyhood club. In my second year at the club Martin O'Neill took over and Alan Thompson came to the club, it was me who did Tommo's medical in fact. It helped that I was already familiar with the whole story having been at Newcastle and from being Derek Wrights pal so I could put the rubber stamp on the deal. From the moment Tommo came to the club we have gotten on well and we formed a close bond. Back then in that era the players were great with the medical staff, and we really integrated and supported each other. The medical team was influential in how things got done and the players responded to that. What I mean was we had a good department in physiology and the players really bought into it.

A lot of Thompson's strengths while on the pitch were in terms of his leadership but the number of important goals that boy scored as well is there on record. Off the pitch however, he was very much a prankster, forever jovial and he was someone who kept the dressing room going in that sense. Alan was great with all the staff at Celtic Park and a real lynchpin in terms of mixing with both sides. Alan Thompson, regardless of how high he was on life sometimes, would have periods of massive self-doubt too. He used to get anxious and that's where the doubt crept in. I had many conversations with him about his confidence and trying to keep his mind positive. That's why the link between the medical staff and the players was important under Martin O'Neill, it was really encouraged. Martin's team placed a great amount of trust in us and likewise we did in them.

The problems that Alan has encountered now, never happened when he was playing, it's been more in recent years. As the years have gone by since he hung his boots up his issues became more profound, which had been worrying from my point of view and I definitely had to get myself involved with Alan's issues. I reached out to him to get him to talk regularly because it was extremely worrying for a few years.

I'd like Alan Thompson today to know that one day in the future he will make as much as an impression as a coach as he did as a player, I have absolutely no doubt about that."

CHAPTER 21

A BAD INVESTMENT

Nash, for as good as he was on the pitch in his playing days he was equally as good in his managerial career. Clarkie was offered the gaffer's role at Bury in February 2017. As usual, or maybe it's just a Geordie loyalty thing, he brought me in as his assistant. It was a role I would do for the next eight months until the October of that year. During this posting, my stress, anxiety and depression was at an all-time high. It wasn't just your everyday life things which were eating me away I also had this big legal case going on, which was taking its toll. I'd had this hovering over me since before I'd even taken the manager's job at Birmingham City, and it was all to do with some bad investment advice I'd been given. I'll never forget, not long after I'd left Celtic in 2012 that a well-known big-name manager in English football had rung me with his own worries. "Tommo you know this big investment thing we've been put into. I hope you know it's going to get messy!" When he said that he wasn't meaning Lionel Messi either! To be honest it went in one ear and out of the other and I didn't take any notice, or at least for a time. I had absolutely no idea what lay ahead in the long grass of life and that it would escalate to the point that I would start having sleepless nights, see me go bankrupt and have everything I'd worked so bloody hard in my career for stolen. I also never envisaged I would be lumbered with a massive tax bill. All I did was play football during my professional days, I earnt big money from it in my prime and I didn't think it was something I'd have to worry about.

During my time at Bury my mind was elsewhere, I was busy thinking about what would eventually drive me to bankruptcy, but on the football side of things the facilities were amazing. We inherited Manchester City's old training ground in Carrington. It was nowhere near as bad as it had been at Blackpool but still the fans were against the owner Stewart Day who was only a young property entrepreneur who'd specialised in building development sites around Lancashire. Even though he was just a fan himself the Shaker supporters just wouldn't accept him. The fans thought he should have been running the club in a different manner but away from that, football-wise Bury was great. Stewart let us bring in our own staff like Jim Henry who'd been our fitness coach at Celtic, he would turn out to be a huge addition to our staff. Lee Clark then signed some good players such as Jermaine Beckford, who he had played with at Leeds United. The young Irish defender who'd been at Celtic Eoghan O'Connell was another one who was brought in. I'm not making excuses, but when your top signings pickup injuries in pre-season or at the start of a season then it is always going to really set the team back, which is exactly what happened.

With our big signings out, as a team, we just didn't recover for the rest of the season. At the start of the season, we were contenders for promotion with the calibre of players we'd brought in. It was nothing like that though and we struggled in the mid-lower table which would essentially see myself and Nash sacked by the club. Again, it wasn't nice to smell the glove and since then the chairman at the time, Stewart Day, has even said that maybe he 'pushed the button too quick' but that's football in these modern times. Even the likes of 'The Special One', my old mate Jose Mourinho gets fired from time to time. Another source told me that the appointments after Lee Clark and I weren't any better either, which will always be the case if a football club's in trouble for various reasons. That was the last time I worked in professional football to this day.

After leaving Bury in October 2017, that's when everything came to a head with this legal case. Not only was this a drain on my mental health but because it had been dragging on for so long it was also costing a hell of a lot of money. At this point I was still with my wife Jo but we were hanging on by a thread. Almost everything that was happening around that time was placing a massive strain on our marriage.

Towards the end of 2017 I had a court date for this very expensive legal case along with a tax bill for £1,800,000 through no fault of my own. As it got closer to the court date it became more daunting. If I had been scared about standing in the courts being a witness for Lenny's attack at Tynecastle then this was so much worse because I had every reason to be scared. This was very much about me, and a lot of my future would depend on the outcome. The top football manager who was linked with my investment settled out of court and not long after another football manager settled so they were both happy. It was now dawning on me that these two had settled away from the courts, but I hadn't settled. Did I settle like the other two, on a decent sum of money or do I take the risk in going to court and possibly walking away with nothing? In the end I felt I couldn't take the risk of this being played out in court, so I ended up settling out of court. The bad thing was that the figure was nowhere near enough to cover that £1,800,000 by any stretch of the imagination, so I was now financially crippled too. As if that wasn't bad enough myself and Jo had now split after being together for over twenty years and so I'd also be needing a legal team for a divorce settlement.

I find it really difficult to even start to try and find the words to describe just how much of a shambles my life was back then. I hadn't signed up for all that shit, it must have been in the small print of life's contract which I never got around to reading.

From getting sacked at Celtic in 2012, now to getting divorced in 2019 it all compounded into what felt like a living nightmare. At times my thoughts were that black that I struggled to breathe and the only way to make it seem ok and for everything to make sense was to drink! If I pretended I was ok and put a bit of loud music on, had a beer and a dance, then everything would be ok, wouldn't it? It was far from ok.

I was as low as I could possibly be without having the balls to try and top myself. Most days I would lay in bed and think, 'I don't wanna be here' and I'd stay in bed, I felt an indescribable numbness, every day seemed like a monumental effort. At times the only thing that kept me going was my three kids Scarlett, Zac and Saffron. I've seen the aftermath of suicide and I've had friends who've done it, so I wasn't going to do that to the people I loved. I didn't know Gary Speed that well, but I knew his family. I know what they've been through as my boy Zac is good pals with Gary's lads Eddie and Tommy Speed. Suicide just wasn't an option but if God had decided I wasn't to wake up one morning I wouldn't have been that bothered at the time. Certainly, those few years after the bankruptcy and divorce put me through the mill.

Jo and I finally got divorced officially in the summer of 2019, I didn't come out of it particularly well financially, and certainly not well enough to cover that whopping tax bill I was now liable for. The pay out that I did get from my divorce was a nice six figure sum but of course that was swallowed wholly by HMRC which is what made me bankrupt. On top of my marriage of 20-odd years collapsing and the fall out of that, I also now had to deal with the hardships that come with being broke. At that time in my life, I seemed to be on an endless Merry Go Round of bankruptcy, divorce and being sacked! There didn't seem to be any light at the end of the tunnel appearing anytime soon. To be completely honest with you, I feel like I'm only just now coming out of that dark place, maybe having the chance to put things down on paper has been cathartic for me. When my life felt like it was at its bleakest the only thing I could do to keep myself going was to focus on my three beautiful children, I had to think of them to see some days out. I just knew I needed to be around to see them grow up and be happy, even be that grandad Thompson that I never had so I could tell them about when grandad scored the winning goal against the best team in the world Barcelona.

There was never any indication when I was playing football, getting sponsorships, driving Bentleys wearing a Rolex, getting signed to clubs for big money and everyone wanting to know me, that one day I would live such a lonely existence. Luckily, one of my best mates who's been mentioned in this book a few times Steve Watson had been through the same. Watto had been divorced and been attached to the investment schemes like I had. It wasn't that we were both trying to make more money or avoid paying taxes, we were badly advised as naïve footballers. My wife Jo's father was looking after my finances, and he oversaw everything. He passed the investment and gave me the go ahead to put my money in telling me the investment was solid. Many years later he also saw the fall out of that bad investment. I've been the one that's been left to pick up the pieces still to this day. Most people don't have any idea just how many bad investments have ruined many a sportsperson to this day. I won't name any, but I know six ex-high profile Premiership players have suffered the same fate as me from listening to bad advice. This has been going on for decades, which is tragic because it's ruined a lot of people's lives. If I hadn't been through all that and if I'd never made those bad investments, then the sad thing is I'd have been made for life. When I finally hung my boots up from playing in 2008, I had no idea of what was to come. I just thought I would enjoy a life of coaching footballers for the love of the game and a bit of 'pocket money' as I didn't need to work really. I didn't think I'd have any money issues or the stress that came along with that, but how wrong I was! Any young footballers who may read this, please take my advice and be very careful about the financial advice you take from people. Follow your gut feelings, I wish I had.

On the mental health side of things, with the anxiety I suffered I would become very short of breath, and I'd just want to curl up in a ball to hide. That's happened fairly often since around 2016 and if any of you are going through any problems then please, you must talk to someone. If you see someone having a tough time of it, offer to listen. You could be someone's saviour when they are in dire need of someone to hear them. Having a listener there means the world to someone who is in a dark place.

In hindsight, property investment would have been a better move for me in my Celtic days. When I was in my prime, I owned a 5 bedroomed house with a swimming pool in Orlando, Florida. I even got my old man over there purely because the local supermarket sold Newcastle

Brown Ale. When I sold that one, I bought a home in La Trinidad, Marbella and ex-Liverpool boss Roy Evans was one of my neighbours. Ian Watson my mate, the businessman who I mentioned earlier who's helped me out at times was also out there. Goalkeeper Shay Given, Andy Melville, Tim Sherwood and big John Hartson were also out there. I know it's a long way from home, but we had a lot of wonderful holidays there and that's the type of thing that's gone now. It's crazy that I had such wealth compared to what we grew up with in Wallsend. Once upon a time I was in a position where thankfully I could lavish my family with whatever they needed but today it's all gone apart from my pension.

If you read several of the football forums about me it'll say that Alan Thompson is a bit of a hellraiser. I like a drink absolutely but so do many ex-pros of my generation. In reality though I'm not really that interesting. I know a lot of the stories online have me down as a full blown alcoholic who is on the drink from morning 'til night but that's not the case. I'd like to set the record straight and say that over the last 8 or 9 years I probably have drunk more than I should, but I have always been able to keep it under control. Drink has never caused me to take days off work. I've got my problems, but I've never been arrested for kicking off while drunk or getting into fights like some of the forums say. I think many will look at what I was like on the pitch and think that I'm like that 24/7 which is just not true. I have however used alcohol as a tool to mask a lot of my problems that have seen me hit rock bottom. As stupid as I've been, I've only ever caused myself problems through drink, not anyone else.

Drink has never been an everyday thing for me, but it was something I went to, to help me feel better. There are days when I can have 2 or 3 glasses of wine and then leave it, but then there have been days that it's been 2 or 3 bottles and I'd drink till I fell asleep. I've always been quite partial to a glass of red with my dinner, or white wine overall. I very rarely drink beer and I like a Bacardi. Apart from that I don't bother with any other forms of alcohol.

Now with this book I've put some demons to bed, and I'd like to think that life's on the up now. I'm only interested in being around positive people and I don't get involved in any drama. It's imperative I keep carrying on climbing that mountain. The experts say that depression is never totally cured but just like Lenny I've had to learn to live with it. I know there's going to be times when I'm going to have bad days and it's just about giving yourself time. I'm not on any medication at the moment but there was a time around 2017 when I'd been talking to Steve Harper, the ex-Newcastle goalie and he had seen a change in me, he told me I should speak with someone about it. It wasn't just Harps that had been saying I wasn't myself; Hayley had mentioned to me also, further down the line, that I should perhaps look at getting some help. I took on board what Harps and Hayley told me, and I rang the doctors in Ponteland, Newcastle. I told the doctor about some of what had been going on and my daily thoughts and she told me it was blatantly obvious I was suffering from clinical depression and that I should be on medication. She then prescribed some tablets which I picked up but didn't take. I left them in the glove compartment in the car. It may sound ludicrous, but I felt better without even taking them because the doctor had told me it wasn't my fault and there was some kind of underlying disorder I was dealing with. I wouldn't take one tablet and whether that was the right thing to do or not I don't know but I soldiered on without them. As soon as she told me there was something wrong with me, maybe a chemical imbalance in my brain, it helped to know that I wasn't imagining it, that I wasn't just being miserable, I felt a weight lifted after speaking with that GP and I didn't need to take the tablets but that was me and sometimes that is important. I think it's about the individual finding out their own way of dealing with it and there is no shame in having the medication, I just felt it wasn't for me. There is no wrong way as long as it's making you feel more able to cope with life.

One ex-player I played with at Villa when he was a young lad was Lee Hendrie. I've been in touch with Lee quite recently while writing this book because of my own issues. Lee went public with his own demons and it's so heart-warming that he's now doing well on Sky Sports and he's an inspiration to myself in my own battle.

One of the things I love to do is cook. I'm very passionate in the kitchen. I also still try to get out and play golf. I've always thought of myself as a bit of a player and maybe was even the best at my time at Celtic, that was until Gordon Strachan signed Paul Telfer. What Paul could do on a green took some beating and he wasn't far off pro standards. Lambo and Henrik weren't too shabby either. Alan Shearer is something else with a 9 iron in his hand, but Sutty wasn't the best. I played against Chris Sutton in Barbados. Ryan Giggs was staying in the same hotel as us so me, Sutty and Giggsy had a few rounds and Sutty spent more time hitting thin air and taking chunks of grass out of the green. Big Sutton was a greenkeepers nightmare, and he could wreck every putting green on a course, no dramas! With Chris being an outstanding cricketer, I thought he'd have been this total all-rounder as a sportsman but it was the opposite. If you're reading this Sutty then you swing a golf club like a cricket bat with no hips.

Jokes aside I feel like I was on the ropes for some time and I felt like chucking the towel in on a few occasions but I'm confident I'm over the worst years of my life now. I haven't been a saint in this life, by any stretch of the imagination, but there's more bullshit out there about me than actual truths. Football has brought me good, bad and dark times but overall, its brought me far more good than bad. As that song by Florence and the Machine says, 'the dog days are over'. There's also a song which means so much to me, it was relevant then and it's still relevant. It was released in 1989 by Michael Bolton. A lot of people might cringe, but I love Michael Bolton. The song was, 'When I'm Back on My Feet Again. If you listen to the lyrics of that it meant so much when I was laying in hospital with a neck brace on and still means a lot to me even to this day. These days who I listen to morning, noon and night is a guy called Gerry Cinnamon from Glasgow. Gerry's a one-man-band who does everything himself and basically has come from nowhere these last few years to now having an army of hardcore followers including myself. The guy writes, produces and promotes himself and he's become a bit of a hero of mine as I've been pulling myself out of the darkness. A lot of Gerry's lyrics really mean so much to me also such as,

This is the beginning of the rest of your life
You better start movin' like you're running out of time
The realisation coming over your mind
That it should be a canter
If you were just a wee bit less of a wanker
More than half ae' the time

And it goes on from there. I really feel Gerry's lyrics and his music puts me in a good place. If you're reading this Gerry

Cinnamon, then thanks for your music mate and keep up the good work.

ALLY McCOIST

Rangers Legend

I'm absolutely delighted to have been asked to be included in this book. Alan Thompson is a fucking top boy he really is. I've known Tommo since he was a young boy starting to play the game.

I know the area where he's from really well also as there was a hotbed of talented footballers that came from there around that time. I suppose I really got to know him when he came up to Celtic. Kenny MacDowall, who ended up being my assistant manager when I was manager of Rangers, knew him well also. Kenny had nothing but good things to say about Alan Thompson from his time managing him at Celtic. Kenny told me all about the high standards of Tommo's training, work ethic and professionalism which rubbed off on the younger boys about the place. Alan Thompson, being from Newcastle in many ways is like him being a Glaswegian. What I mean is both cities just love their football. Newcastle folks are working class people who love their football, and you can tell that's the way Alan Thompson has been brought up when you get to know him.

Tommo coming to Celtic and playing in the Old Firm games, the guy just got it from day one! There's been so many Italian and English boys who have come to Glasgow and when they've played in a Celtic v Rangers game they've been like, 'FUCK ME, WHATS THIS ALL ABOUT?!' Whereas Alan Thompson just took to the Old Firm, he took to Celtic, and he very much took to Scottish football. Don't get me wrong, Alan Thompson got caught up in the game several times but having done that myself it doesn't make you a bad person.

I'll never forget the time Tommo came to Ibrox in 2012 as part of Neil Lennon's staff because it was priceless. I can still see Tommo on the Ibrox touchline pointing at Georgios Samaras, who by the way, probably still doesn't understand his instructions to this day. You could have told Samaras five hundred times and he wouldn't have got it, but that boy always did well against the Rangers (laughs). Tommo that day was telling big Sammy where to be then all of a sudden, it was as if our place fell silent on purpose to make this one fan heard all the more as this boy from the crowd stood up and didn't half give Tommo both barrels shouting, "No wonder ya wife left you Tommo you ugly English Bastard". Tommo turned around as if to say, 'did anybody else hear that?' He looked around to see me and wee Lenny in tears pishing ourselves laughing. I could see it in Tommo's face he knew we'd all heard exactly what the guy had shouted. It was brilliant (Ally is really laughing as he recounts this story). Jokes aside Glasgow is the same as the Northeast man, there's no hiding place in times like that on the big stage. If you dish it out you've got to be able to take it back. Tommo to be fair took it well, even the 4th official couldn't help but laugh at what had just been said as well as the full stand behind us at Ibrox. The place was howling with laughter and that's typical of Glasgow, it has a wicked sense of humour.

On a serious note, I would say Alan Thompson was born to play in the Old Firm Derby. I can still see him going head-to-head with boys like Rickson & co and I loved it. The one thing we always had, and I'm sure Tommo was the same was a real healthy respect for the Celtic boys when I was playing. We were going into battle with the likes of Paul McStay, Danny McGrain and Paolo Di Canio and boys like that. We would go in to win the game, however we appreciated them and respected them immensely. Tommo came into that category man, and I've got to say, when I used to watch him winding up his left foot outside the box I'd think, 'ooh nooo, here we go'. There weren't too many Celtic players that when they got the ball near our goal would scare me, but Alan Thompson was one of them. That boy played in 26 Old Firm games, that's a lot of Celtic v Rangers ties to have played in by the way. If you can't handle those games, then you don't play in four or five because there's been many from down South who just couldn't handle it. Of course, Alan Thompson got three reds but Christ almighty, so did Terry Butcher, Chris Woods and Graeme Souness. All those boys got their game as well but they suffered reds, so Alan Thompson was the same.

Alan Thompson was someone who, no matter how reckless or emotional he was at times, you wanted him in your side for that game. Listen, there is absolutely no getting away from it that Alan Thompson played in one of the greatest Celtic teams ever. People understandably and correctly talk about the Lisbon Lions, and I get it. Scottish football will never see the likes of a team like them again, all born within 30 miles of Celtic Park. Martin O'Neill's team from 2000 – 2005 was an incredible team also. To get to that European Final against FC Porto and win the league titles they did was magnificent. That team were powerful and could play. Alan Thompson fitted into Martin O'Neill's side perfectly because of what he was, he was very much Martin's type of player. He had no shortage of talent, and he was a grafter. He was a player who did his shift and worked up and down in both boxes. He could go one way only to go the other. Tommo played in a proper Celtic team with Sutton, Larsson, Hartson, Petrov, Lennon, Lambert, Balde, Agathe, McNamara etc…

A lot of people have this misconception of Scottish football down South. They think it's easy to come up to the SPL, play with Rangers and Celtic and win things with your eyes closed. It's not the case! There are so many players who've come up for big money and this outstanding reputation with it and done nothing up here. Then they've disappeared in the next transfer window with their tail between their legs. Alan Thompson was not one of them. He's a player who came up and handled it well. The best thing I could say about Alan Thompson was, and this is the hardest thing to do in the world, I really mean this from the bottom of my heart, was he was the best after an Old Firm game to defuse situations. Win, lose or draw, after the heated battle which got ugly at times, he would want a bottle of beer with you. He just wanted to relax with you and have some banter and discuss the game in an adult manner. Let me tell you now there's been a lot of members of Celtic and Rangers management staff who've come and found that difficult to do for years and years. Whether it was at Celtic Park, Ibrox or Hampden, we'd beaten them, or they'd stuffed us, Tommo was there shaking your hand, asking for a bit of craic and my thoughts on the game blah blah blah… That's my abiding memory of Alan Thompson although clearly, he was a giant in Glasgow. I'm so glad he's done this book I'm looking forward to a wee bit of blather with Tommo on TalkSport."

PASSING THE BATON - SCOTT BROWN

Former Celtic Club Captain

"I suppose I have a direct link with Alan Thompson because I took over his No.8 shirt at Celtic when he left. I remember playing against him for Hibs aged 17 years old and I had a few running battles shall we say, with him for two seasons. The banter we had while playing against each other was brilliant and then when he came back to Celtic for a few years with Lenny that's when my friendship with him started to blossom. To be fair, before I got to know him me and him were a car crash because we only kicked lumps out of each other. If we ever spoke it was only to wind each other up. It was never anything nasty, it was only ever football banter. We had respect for each other but for ninety minutes we wanted to kick the living shite out of each other.

When he was a coach at Celtic, he used to make the lads on the bus play a game which was called, 'the managers a c***'. In this game you had to shout on the bus, "the managers a c***" and try and get away with it without said Manager hearing it. Tommo used to tell us all he would make people play it when Martin O'Neill was manager, and he would ask who had the balls to play it with Lenny. Tommo said we had to shout, "the managers a c***" and get as close to Neil Lennon as we could and say it as loud as we could without him hearing it. Everybody used to shite it whilst playing and the last man standing was the winner and Tommo would be there winding everyone up and stirring the pot. If the manager gets on the bus, he should have that aura about him where he demands respect but Tommo used to encourage us to give Lenny grief. He'd call us a bunch of shite bags, but he was great for the wee bits of banter.

When I was a young lad coming through at Hibs, I used to love watching Tommo in the Old Firm games. I used to love watching his fiery character exploding like a volcano among it all. You don't see a lot of guys playing that game like Alan Thompson did anymore and he had a bit of arrogance which I like also. Not only could he do the hard work, but he was also technically very gifted. He was good on the ball, off the ball and could be nasty and that's what that Celtic team under Martin O'Neill was. Take it from me it wasn't a nice team to play against because they were all big monsters in the team from the front men to the goalkeeper. They were fucking horrible and if you weren't dealing with the monster Bobo Balde, you were facing Alan Thompson who had the biggest mouth in the team. If you ever had to tackle them, they'd be in your face and Tommo would usually be there saying, 'WEE MAN FUCK OFF YOU'VE GOT NOTHING SO DO ONE'. Playing against them, Tommo was at the heart of winding people up so can you imagine him in the Celtic/Rangers games. It was him and Rickson that had the biggest beef on the park for like six years.

Alan Thompson helped me a lot when I was a young player at Celtic through his coaching and mentoring. As a coach he was very hands on and knew his stuff. There was nobody who messed about more than Alan Thompson but see when he went on that training field, he was 100% focused and a man on a mission for the whole squad. He was great for Neil Lennon as a coach because he had his back always.

Taking over the No.8 shirt from Thompson I knew I had big boots to fill because Tommo is an absolute global hero among the millions of Celtic supporters worldwide."

PETER BEAGRIE

Former Everton & Manchester

"I'd like to pay tribute to Wor Al! The boy had a wanderful left foot & has been a wonderful friend.

I've always loved words as Al will testify and he is always bitching that he can't get a word in...so he won't find it a surprise that I've penned this bit of verse just for The Karaoke Kid, The Kitchen Party King, Ladies & Gentlemen I give you Super Alan Thompson.

'Ode to a Geordie Bhoy'

A Geordie Bhoy born & bred
Who never let fame go to his head,
Played the game with such ease & grace
A solitary England cap a fucking disgrace,
'Jobs for the boys' springs to mind
Coz wor Al was certainly one of a kind
Poetry in motion such skill & style
Best left foot in football by an absolute mile
Decided to write my thoughts in verse
Controversial nay different but definitely not a first
Tommo will read this and a smart arse comment he'll make
About me being strange, a nutter, a proper fruitcake
Seriously though I love his hospitality, kindness & totally weird ways
Went for one night ended up staying four days
He's a geezer, a sort, his own special creation
Can calm things down or set fire to a nation
His confident air is sometimes an illusion

Coz by his own admission at times he's a mass of confusion
We've nursed each other through thick & thin
One things for sure I can rely on him
If there's one person I could choose to always have by my side
It'll be wor Al my best mate, my very own Jekyll & Hyde

Love you pal P.S. You will always find me in the kitchen at parties…Love Beag.

Peter went on to say…

"We got on brilliantly from the day I met Alan Thompson in Dubai. I knew of him from playing against him over the years in England but became super close since that holiday. When my Mrs sadly passed away Alan was always on the phone making sure I was ok. Alan was there for me when I went into my shell too, he was there sending me messages telling me he was there for me when I was ready. Together we've shared some funny times which normally ends in him being naked, usually when he gets drunk! Maybe it's his party trick but he's not blessed in the manhood department so it's always baffled me. He's even done it abroad in Marbella. He did it once over there and walked into these patios doors thinking they were open and even though he fell flat on his back, he still never dropped the two tall glasses of champagne which he was holding. There are many other tales of him getting naked which are very similar that I could fill a book alone with. I think after five or six drinks his brain just thinks it's a great idea to get naked. Even when you think he's gone to bed he'll pop out from somewhere stark bollock naked! Usually, it's with a drink in his hand and a tea towel like he's a butler.

Every time we get together, we just spark off each other because of our love for football, families and silliness. If you looked at Alan Thompson on the pitch then you'd think he was this supremely confident guy, but nobody knows what goes on behind the scenes like me, we've both been through the mill shall we say.

If Al and I are out, everybody's going to have a good time, whether that's because we're winding others up or we're slaughtering each other. When I'm with him we can forget about everything, which we both did for 90 minutes when we were on the pitch during our careers and that was our stage. We had to have this mentally playing the game where you'd have to think, 'I actually feel sorry for anyone marking me today!' That takes a hell of a lot of focus when there's other little things in the background going on off the pitch.

Alan is very grounded because like me he's a Northeast lad and we've both come from humble beginnings. Alan and I were over privileged to have played a sport which most lads would have absolutely died to do for free. I would like to say that through Alan's career it was an utter disgrace that he only got one England cap. It's well-spoken of just how good his left foot was and often when I say, 'Al do you have a bottle opener'? He'll always reply with, 'no but I've got my left foot'! He really was a magician with it. As a person I really can't speak highly enough of the guy. My mate Al is such a warm-hearted spiritual individual that if you meet him, he'll take you and your family under his wing. Being a warm guy is just his nature and underneath all the bravado he's just a big soft teddy bear. He might think he's not and pretend to be different, but he's got no bite, in fact he's hardly got a bark"!

CHAPTER 22

THE DOG DAYS ARE OVER!

Looking back on my life these days, rapidly approaching 50, I'm not so sure it's right to have any regrets, maybe I could do with losing a few grey hairs. No, seriously you can't change the past, but you can learn from it for your future. Often people say, "aah Tommo you must regret not signing for Manchester United" Had I gone with Sir Alex Ferguson's offer though, I might not have gone on to play for Glasgow Celtic. I'm sure I'd have picked up a few trophies at United, particularly as that year they went on to do the treble but no doubt I'd have warmed a few benches as my direct competition would have been Giggs, Scholes, Butt, Beckham, Neville, Keane etc... Yes, I would have got big money and picked up massive bonuses here and there, but I wouldn't have been part of a team as a regular. The one slight regret I might have is hanging my boots up for good at only 34 at Leeds. I probably jumped ship a year or two too early because once you're retired, you're retired. In football there's no going back to the sport, not like when you see these boxers coming back for one more shot at glory. If I could turn back time, I'd have stayed at home in the Northeast and had another season or even two at Hartlepool United or even at Carlisle United. I know many might frown upon me saying that as I left for a club the size of Leeds United to Hartlepool United but sometimes the devil is in the detail. Hartlepool was a club I had connections with, Joe Allen and Lee Clark's brother-in-law

Paul Baker played for them. I even went to watch the Monkey Hangers as a kid at times. Although I was only there for seven games and scored one goal, I really was welcomed with open arms by the fans and it's a great little club, the likeable Jeff Stelling will tell you that most Saturday afternoons on Gillette Soccer Saturday.

Most people know me for what I did at Celtic, but I played equally as big a part at Bolton Wanderers. If my spells at Newcastle United and Aston Villa could have been so much better then I wouldn't change a thing regarding my time at The Wanderers. I joined just as a young lad not knowing much about life in general and had some of the best years of my life there. I didn't walk into that team, I had to work hard and show Bruce Rioch and Colin Todd what I was about, establish myself and I did that with some good Cup scalps at Everton and Arsenal both away. Bolton Wanderers will always have a special place in my heart forevermore and I'm sure I'll go back to the Bolton Stadium over the next few years. I always look out for their results on the vidi-printer every Saturday afternoon.

Although I'm a bit of a fossil regarding social media I do try, via Instagram and Twitter, to interact with old sets of supporters of my clubs. It's great that after all these years people still remember you for what you did at their clubs. Even the Rangers fans always pipe up for an engaging conversation from time to time and it's not always abuse. I only started my social media platforms (@alantommo8 on both if you'd like to follow me) because of someone abusing The Toy aka Jackie McNamara, some toad was abusing him after his brain surgery. If it wasn't for that I wouldn't have gone anywhere near it but I have enjoyed it at times and it's nice to catch up with some old faces. If social media is used in the correct manner, it can be a great tool to have because it puts you in touch with people from many decades ago. Without it then you would never come across these people again. Although I'm not the greatest on it, I do try. My old gaffer Martin O'Neill has even joined in on the act and is on Instagram so if he's doing it approaching 70 then I'm sure I'll be ok.

At the end of the day because of the life football has brought me I can't go anywhere in the world without meeting a Celtic who wants a chat, and that's great. Australia, Thailand, South America and parts of Europe, I've been all over when suddenly, I've heard, "hang on a minute, there's Alan Thompson", then they've came over to talk about the beautiful game. It doesn't matter to them that I'm now a middle-aged man well finished because the Celtic fans are everywhere in the world and their support is phenomenal. The Celtic family always shower me with love wherever I am in the world and I'm so grateful beyond words for this. If I can make someone's day with a quick scribble and a picture, then it's the least I can give back for the great years when they paid my wages and put me where I am today. I think every ex-footballer in the world should be the same and that's how it should be. After all, I was once the very same as them looking up to my football idols.

Did I waste lot of my wealth? I don't know. At the time I was passionate about cars, but I would change a car these days at the drop of a hat. It just doesn't seem as important to me now as it did then. I never bought them posh motors because I wanted to be flash, I just had a thing about nice cars, and I could afford them. At the end of the day, I'm from a council estate in Wallsend and I never forgot that but I did appreciate the things that my career could bring in its day. Sadly, that lifestyle doesn't last forever and obviously it didn't for me, but I'm ok with that. I've lost a few keepsakes over the years like my Barcelona Xavi shirt,

Seville Cup Final top and a medal from the youth World Cup from playing in Australia for young England. Thank God I received the latter back as it was returned to my parents' home in Newcastle. Some guy had been trying to sell it on the internet and my old man found out. To cut a complicated story short the medal was then returned to my family home. Losing a few memories over the years can hurt but it's memories that I'll never forget and thankfully I got to live the dream first-hand.

The deepest and darkest days are thankfully now well and truly behind me as I sit here mid-2021. Thankfully the bow of my ship has changed direction and it's up to me to remain positive and set off towards happy times. My partner Hayley is by my side, and I won't be stalling again on the journey they call life. In the foreseeable future I'd like to get back into football because it's what I do. It's the only thing I've known since I was around 5 or 6 years old. Sadly, playing isn't an option any longer as the legs and ticker don't work as well as they once did, saying that my wand is still there and I can still whip a pretty effective cross into the box at pace, with precision and accuracy. I still think I could beat anyone at a crossbar challenge. I do hope I can get back into coaching in some capacity, whether that be with youngsters or full-time pro's it's what I enjoy doing. Mentally, technically and tactically I love to improve lad's games. I'll be looking to go back out into the deep end of the football world in 2022, a new man and put what I've been through to use to help others who are suffering. I'm no longer a young kid who can just keep making excuses for the obstacle's life throws at me. As I said earlier in the book, the dog days are over and with the help of Sporting Chance things are happening for me.

My old Celtic doctor Roddy MacDonald has been a tower of strength and allowed me to use his shoulder to cry on. I've had some great chats with him, one because he's a close friend, two I can trust him and three he's qualified in what he's talking about. He was the one who said, "Hooch I think you need a bit of help" he then contacted Sporting Chance on my behalf and got the ball rolling. If any of you reading this book can take one thing away from this book, then I'd like it to be that you can talk about things and things can get better.

I do see myself working for the next twenty years and I do hope it's in football. I'm fully aware I'll need to start at a bottom level club and I'm very much prepared to work at it like all the great managers do. Over the next few years, I'm going to be out there full of energy and I'll see what doors open up. The one thing that I've got going for me is I have some marvellous contacts in the game. You don't get anywhere in life if nobody gives you a break and that's all I need. Watch this space for the new and improved version of me being back in football for 2022. Who knows, down the line I may end up at one of my favourite clubs Hartlepool United.

I couldn't do this book, without giving the woman who's stood by me through all my rubbish these last few years a mention, my rock Hayley. We first met in the summer of 2017 in Lymm, Cheshire. We were friends for a while as I was still with my ex-wife, and I wasn't going to put Jo through everything I had done years earlier with the other woman in Glasgow. It was just friendship at first and at one point we did sit down with a coffee, and I told her that it couldn't go any further as I was married. Hayley understood that I'd already put my kids through enough, so we were going to have to put some distance between us. The last thing I wanted was for the newspapers to start following people because of my actions like they had only five years previously in Scotland. We did bump into each other from time to time but there was never anything more than a hello, how are you doing and a goodbye. It wasn't until much further down the line when my marriage was no more that myself and Hayley became an item. We've been together now for four years, and that woman has the patience of a saint. She's stood by my side when probably she'd have been better off not getting involved with me because of my mental health baggage.

For all of those years that I was playing in front of the cameras I've been told I came across as being confident. Deep down inside I was anything but what I appeared to be. Having low self-esteem is the real reason why I've never done a book until now even though I've been asked several times. There was a time when Martin O'Neill had a few books on him written then all the others such as Neil Lennon, Chris Sutton, Stiliyan Petrov and John Hartson, all brought theirs out but I've been in no state to do one until now, about 15 years after all the rest. At times I didn't even think I was worthy of a biography. All the flash cars, Versace suits and fights with Fernando masked who I really was and that is a man who has had very little confidence throughout his life, apart from those 90 minutes on a football pitch that is. Funnily enough I read an article the other day on ex-Liverpool player Danny Murphy. Danny's gone public lately and has been so open about his problems, such as a high-profile divorce, drugs, drink, court cases and gambling and it was like reading about myself, minus the gambling and drugs of course. The list is endless of ex-players who've gone to the wall.

Hayley also took on the aftereffects of my divorce, which wasn't even anything to do with her. I know now that in my future whatever I do with regards to rebuilding my life she'll be a big part of it. She's stood by me at my worst so she more than anyone deserves me at my best.

There are not many women who would have put up with the things she's had to endure just by getting involved with me. She was the one nursing me through the blackest days. Bless Hayley after getting with me she had no idea of just how well known I used to be, that was until she was on the phone one day. She'd been on hold to one of them call centre's when finally, she was put through to a guy with a Glaswegian accent. I don't know how but she must have told the guy on the other end of the phone that her partner used to be at Celtic. When she told him it was Alan Thompson, she was met with all the, "get tae fuck, on ya go, no way for fuck's sake Alan Thompson's a God up here man" etc, etc blah blah blah. Obviously, this guy was a huge Celtic fan and I think that's when the penny dropped that I used to be a somebody once upon a time. In fact, when I've been up to Glasgow with her, she's seen me getting mobbed at games. She couldn't get her head around that even the homeless people living on the streets knew who I was but that's Glasgow I suppose and no matter your choice of colours, the city takes its football incredibly seriously. It's a city like no other in the world!

It's not only Hayley I have to thank for my rebuilding, but Hayley's family have also been so supportive and there's always great humour around them. Particularly Hayley's mother's Debz and stepfather Pedz. This day I was in The Wine Kitchen in Lymm with a few of my mates. The footballer Jlloyd Samuel came in, I knew Jlloyd well because he was at Aston Villa as a youth when I was there. Jlloyd lived in Lymm because he'd been at Bolton which isn't too far away. Hayley and her mum Debz then came over and I introduced Debz to Jlloyd, well Debz got all excited so much so that she phoned her partner Pedz and said, "ere Pedz, you'll never guess who I'm with in the Wine Kitchen" there was a long pause before she blurted out, "Samuel L. Jackson." Seriously she was all straight faced and everything. Pedz wasn't feeling up to going out as he'd had a busy week at work but how could he not, now the actor from Pulp Fiction was around the corner. A few minutes later Pedz comes into the bar looking for Samuel L. Jackson but is sadly disappointed when I say, 'Pedz, this is Jlloyd Samuel who I played with at Aston Villa'. For the rest of the day, even though she was now enlightened with the truth, she just could not stop calling Jlloyd Samuel, Samuel L. Jackson. We still laugh about it now and have a giggle, but Jlloyd took it well. God rest him in Heaven. Sadly, Jlloyd died in 2018 aged only 37. I went to his funeral and met Emile Heskey and Gareth Barry there and he's greatly missed. He's survived by a young lad, Lakyle at Manchester City now with a big future ahead of him.

Football has given me a great life overall. I must have played my first match as a seven year old for Battle Hill First School and then went all the way through playing Champions League games as well as a full England cap.

You've read my story, it's been full of highs and lows with some humour added into the mix. I'd like anyone out there who reads it who might have had any of the issues I've had to learn from my mistakes. When you finish playing at whatever sport you do then there's a cliff to drop off. My councillor John at Sporting Chance has dealt with so many Alan Thompson's from all of the many different sports out there. He sees all the downfalls for sportsmen and women coming to the end of their careers and so many of them far worse off than the issues I've had too. Once they've been at the pinnacle of their sport and then it finishes, it's often the case that they then chase that same buzz which they can't get from their sport any longer. That's why people fall into drink, drugs, gambling, depression and having affairs. One or two of those examples might seem far-fetched, but you'd be amazed at what people become addicted to when the limelight has gone. Also, when you're in the public spotlight like I have been there's so many bad people who just want a piece of you. You need to have good people around you and have positive influences to show you the good, bad and the ugly because there's a hell of a lot of wicked people in this world trust me.

I've had a lot of good people looking out for me over my years, too many for me to mention them all in this book. It's a bit of an art if you're one of them folk with a built-in sixth sense who can work out who the wrong people are along the way. When I was doing my UEFA Pro licence with the Irish F.A in Belfast I was taught an invaluable lesson, I only wish I had known it a quarter of a century earlier. A psychologist came in and he gave me a sheet of A4 paper. He told me to draw a line down the middle and on one side of the paper he said to write the word, 'energiser' then on the other he said to put, 'de-energiser'. On the energiser side I was told to write a list of people who I trust, like and love to be around, then on the other side I had to write a list of people who drained me, who I couldn't trust and who I found it hard work to be around. When I was finished, he told me to rip the page in half and the energisers he told me to put in my pocket to take home, and the other side of the paper, the de-energiser's, he said they needed to be put straight in the bin and I should keep out of their company forever. It was so simple, but it worked and going forward in life we should all do that no matter what our occupation or circumstances.

For all you young footballers out there earning ridiculous amounts of money I'm telling you all now there's a lot of blood-thirsty sharks out there who can smell you from miles. The football world is brutal, and it can be a nasty environment where if you turn your back for too long then someone will make a move to get your job. These people pretend on the surface but deep down they want to portray you in the worst light possible to the club you're working with. I know that people in the game will go sit in the stands and be pictured by the paparazzi, purely because that manager is under pressure, and it will throw some fuel on the burning fire of the flames which is rising around him.

When I was asked to write my life story with the author of this book, I was determined to do it as honestly as I could. I may have opened myself up to the world with information that could be used against me but if that happens, so what, it's the truth and you're hearing it from me, not second hand. I can't do anything about my past now but only apologise for my mistakes to those that I may have hurt along the way. I may have been rocked, wobbled and on the ropes during the last few years but this Geordie Bhoy has NOT thrown in the towel. I'm up before the count of ten (unless I'm up against some bloke from a boy band, some will get that, some won't). Everything in life is a journey and is not to be feared, only to be understood. I came from nothing, and I've been left with nothing but it's been one hell of a ride. Thank you all so much for taking the time to read my story. If I can make a difference to just one person out there by airing my laundry in public then it will have all been worth it.

Tommo x

“God grant me the serenity to accept the things I cannot change, the courage to change the things I can, and the wisdom to know the difference.”

-Reinhold Niebuhr

ALAN THOMPSON
CAREER STATISTICS

1991 – 1993	*Newcastle United*	
	Appearances 20	*Goals 0*
1993 – 1998	*Bolton Wanderers*	
	Appearances 198	*Goals 42*
1998 – 2000	*Aston Villa*	
	Appearances 58	*Goals 5*
2000 – 2006	*Celtic*	
	Appearances 227	*Goals 51*
2007 – 2008	*Leeds United*	
	Appearances 25	*Goals 5*
2008	*Hartlepool United*	
	Appearances 7 Goals 1	
2004	*England*	
	Cap 1	*Goals 0*

HONOURS

Bolton Wanderers –

Football League First Division: 1996-97

Football League First Division play-offs: 1994-95

Football League Cup runner-up 1994-95

Celtic –

Scottish Premier League 2000-01, 2001-02, 2003-04, 2005-06

Scottish Cup 2000-01, 2003-04, 2004-05

Scottish League Cup 2005-06

Scottish Cup runner-up 2001-02

Scottish League Cup runner-up 2002-03

UEFA Cup runner-up 2002-03

Individual

PFA Team of the year: 1996-97 First Division

GREATEST EVER XI PLAYED WITH:

Peter Shilton

Didier Agatha John Terry Gareth Southgate Jackie McNamara

Peter Beardsley Stiliyan Petrov Steven Gerrard David Ginola

Henrik Larsson Chris Sutton

GREATEST EVER XI PLAYED AGAINST:

Peter Schmeichel

Cafu Tony Adams Carles Puyol Paolo Maldini

Ronaldinho

Paul Gascoigne Dennis Bergkamp

Christiano Ronaldo

Thierry Henry Alan Shearer

THANKS

To my big sister Jane, her husband Tony Richardson and their two sons Sam & Joseph, love you guys to bits.

I'd like to thank my old schoolteachers David Scott, Kevin Vale, Graham Netherton, Alex Giacopazzi and Rob Kitchen.

My coaches Peter Kirkley, Stan Nixon among others

All my teammates

All the fans at my clubs

Jamie & Shirley-Anne Boyle for welcoming me into their family home a few times during the writing of this book. I couldn't have done it without their drive behind me. Also, to all the guys at WarCry Publishing.

And last but not least my partner Hayley who's been there for me during some of the worst times of my life. I know I must not have been easy to live with. The woman is beyond patient, giving and positive towards me and had it not been for her I wouldn't have had the encouragement I needed to do this book. Also, thank you to Hayley's family, now my extended family, you've all been so incredibly warming towards me inviting me into your little circle in Cheshire.

A young Geordie Bhoy

When my game was beginning to take off…

Steve Watson and I with 'Young England'

Me and Nash as young footballers in relaxing times

My rock: Hayley and I

Mam and I

My 3 babies;
Zachary Dylan,
Scarlett Faye & Saffron Mai